Fair Value Accounting Fraud

Fair Value Accounting Fraud

New Global Risks and Detection Techniques

GERARD M. ZACK, CFE, CPA

John Wiley & Sons, Inc.

Published by John Wiley & Sons, Inc., Hoboken, New Jersey.
Published simultaneously in Canada.

For general information on our other products and services or for technical support,
please contact our Customer Care Department within the United States at (800)
762-2974, outside the United States at (317) 572-3993 or fax (317) 572-4002.

Wiley also publishes its books in a variety of electronic formats. Some content that
appears in print may not be available in electronic books. For more information about
Wiley products, visit our Web site at www.wiley.com.

Library of Congress Cataloging-in-Publication Data:

Zack, Gerard M.
    Fair value accounting fraud : new global risks and detection techniques/Gerard
M. Zack.
        p. cm.
    Includes bibliographical references and index.
    ISBN 978-0-470-47858-5 (cloth)
    1. Misleading financial statements. 2.   Accounting fraud. 3.   Fair value–Accounting.
I. Title.
HF5681.B2Z234 2009
657'.3–dc22

2009010848

10 9 8 7 6 5 4 3 2 1

This book is dedicated to my brothers, Bill and Ray. I am so lucky to have two brothers who have always been such great role models and who continue to be so deserving of my admiration and respect, yet who are also my best friends. I love you both dearly.

Contents

Preface

Depending on what you have read and who you have listened to, you may have formed the opinion that fair value accounting has had one or more of the following relationships with the global financial crisis that continues to worsen in 2009:

- It was one of the direct causes of the crisis.
- It exacerbated the crisis, which was initially caused by other factors.
- It hid or disguised the crisis for months, resulting in a delayed initial response to the crisis.
- It had nothing to do with the crisis—but it sure is fun to blame crises on accountants.

Fair value accounting is the accounting profession's equivalent of the automobile commercials you have seen on television, showing a vehicle racing around an obstacle course or bouncing over hills, along with a disclaimer saying something to the effect that "This is a professional stunt driver on a closed course. Do not try this at home!"

Fair value accounting is not for the timid. It is often not precise. It makes some people uncomfortable (they are called auditors). It involves a tremendous amount of judgment and estimation. It also frequently requires a highly specialized expertise. And whenever accounting involves a significant amount of judgment and estimation, it becomes infinitely more susceptible to manipulation and fraud.

The role that fair value accounting may have played in connection with the current economic mess is an interesting one to debate, but is not really the subject of this book. The issue that cannot be disputed, however, is that the accounting rules regarding the use of fair value accounting are extremely complicated. This complexity has most certainly led to inconsistencies in the application of these rules. While most of these inconsistencies are likely the result of honest mistakes and, in some cases, a poor understanding of the rules, some will inevitably be determined to be more deliberate. As a result, there are bound to be many cases of fair value accounting fraud in the coming years. Financial reporting fraud is nothing new. But the techniques used to perpetrate it change over time. And one of the trade-offs for the many benefits of fair value accounting is that it is likely to be the basis for some of the next major financial reporting frauds.

Regardless of whether you favor or dislike the use of fair value accounting, one thing most people agree on is that the rules are very complicated. In its December 2008 report on the use of fair value accounting in the United States, the Securities and Exchange Commission soundly endorsed the use of fair value accounting. It even encouraged the expansion of fair value applications in the financial statements. However, the SEC cautioned that better, more practical guidance is badly needed, and some of the fair value accounting standards are in of need clarification and simplification. Starting in January 2009 and continuing into April, the Financial Accounting Standards Board has taken steps to respond to the SEC's mandate for improved guidance. No doubt, additional guidance is on the way. The accounting standards are far from perfect, but as FASB and the International Accounting Standards Board continue to work together, greater consistency and clearer rules will hopefully result.

It is with the complexity of these rules in mind that I have chosen to tackle the subject of fair value accounting fraud with this book. The rules in the United States share many attributes with the rules used in countries that recognize the International Financial Reporting Standards. Yet there are many differences as well.

The purpose of this book is to raise awareness of the many risks of fraud based on how fair value accounting is utilized in the preparation of financial statements and how those applications differ under U.S. and international accounting standards. This book is not a guide on how to perform valuations. But it is designed to provide readers with an overview of the fair value applications and some of the most commonly used methods, especially as these subjects relate to the primary focus of this book—the risk of financial reporting fraud.

Gerard M. Zack
April 2009

How This Book Is Organized

This book is organized into five parts:

Part I   Introduction to Fair Value Accounting Fraud
Part II   Asset-Based Schemes
Part III   Liability-Based Schemes

Part IV   Other Fair Value Accounting Fraud Issues

Part V   Detection of Fair Value Accounting Fraud

Beginning in Chapter 2 and continuing through the end of Part IV, as fraud schemes are introduced, each will be highlighted in a special fraud risk text box. Each fraud scheme has been assigned a number, the first part of which corresponds to the chapter number. The fraud risks identified in Chapters 2 and 3 are broad risks that could apply to any application of fair value accounting. The risks identified in Chapters 4 through 21 are specialized risks associated with the specific accounting topic addressed in each chapter.

In the sections of the book surrounding each fraud risk text box, the details of the accounting rules and how those rules would be violated in connection with each fraud scheme are explained. All of the fraud schemes are listed in Appendix A for your reference.

Glossary of Abbreviations Used in This Book

Numerous acronyms and abbreviations are used throughout this book, starting in Chapter 2. Here are some of the most commonly used abbreviations. Each will be explained further as they are introduced in the book.

AICPA	American Institute of Certified Public Accountants
APB	Accounting Principles Board
ARB	Accounting Research Bulletin
EITF	Emerging Issues Task Force
FASB	Financial Accounting Standards Board
FIN	FASB Interpretation
FSP	FASB Staff Position
GAAP	Generally Accepted Accounting Principles
GAAS	Generally Accepted Auditing Standards
IAASB	International Auditing and Assurance Standards Board
IAS	International Accounting Standard
IASB	International Accounting Standards Board
IASCF	International Accounting Standards Committee Foundation
IFRIC	International Financial Reporting Interpretations Committee
IFRS	International Financial Reporting Standards (issued by IASB)
ISA	International Standard on Auditing (issued by IAASB)

PCAOB   Public Company Accounting Oversight Board
SAS   Statement on Auditing Standards (issued by AICPA)
SEC   Securities and Exchange Commission
SFAC   Statement of Financial Accounting Concepts (issued by FASB)
SFAS   Statement of Financial Accounting Standards (issued by FASB)
SIC   Standing Interpretations Committee
SOP   Statement of Position (issued by AICPA)

Acknowledgments

I want to thank April for many things, but especially for the love and support you have provided to me during a challenging period in my life. Words cannot adequately express my appreciation and love.

I also want to thank the great team at John Wiley & Sons, specifically:

Tim Burgard, Acquisitions Editor
Lisa Vuoncino, Production Editor
Helen Cho, Senior Editorial Assistant

You have made this process feel very much like a team effort.

Introduction to Fair Value Accounting Fraud

In this introductory section, the most important concepts of financial statement fraud and fair value accounting are introduced. To understand how to detect fair value accounting fraud, it is important to:

- Understand why and how financial statement fraud of any type is perpetrated
- Understand what is meant by fair value accounting and its broad applications in today's world
- Understand some of the core concepts associated with fair value accounting, including a basic understanding of the various methodologies used in determining fair value of an asset or liability

That is the purpose of Part I. It is only with this level of understanding that the fair value accounting issues and fraud risks explained in Parts II through IV will be fully understood.

CHAPTER 1

Overview of Financial Statement Fraud and Fair Value Accounting

Introduction to Financial Reporting Fraud

Anyone who has read a newspaper or watched the evening news in recent years is well aware that fraudulent financial reporting by big businesses has reached alarming levels. Equally startling is the frequency of fraudulent financial reporting by small businesses—as many bankers and government agencies will confirm—and even by non–business entities such as not-for-profit organizations.

In its *2008 Report to the Nation on Occupational Fraud and Abuse*, the Association of Certified Fraud Examiners (ACFE) identifies fraudulent reporting as one of the three categories of fraud (the other two being asset misappropriations and corruption) that collectively are estimated to cost almost $1 trillion per year in the United States. And financial statement fraud is certainly not limited to the United States.

Of the three categories of fraud tracked by the ACFE, fraudulent statements were the least common, occurring in just 10 percent of the cases studied. But when fraud occurs in that way, it packs quite a wallop. The median loss caused in the fraudulent statement schemes included in the 2008 study was $2 million. To put that in perspective, the median loss caused by asset misappropriation frauds included in the study was *only* $150,000, while the median loss caused by corruption schemes was $375,000.

Fraudulent financial reporting can be accomplished in many different ways. These methods can be classified into schemes that accomplish one or more of the following seven deceptions:

1. Inflating assets
2. Understating liabilities
3. Inflating revenues

4. Understating expenses
5. Creating timing differences (i.e., over multiple reporting periods, the total reported earnings are correct, but one period is overstated and another period is understated, such as by recognizing revenue prematurely—a form of borrowing from the future to make today look better)
6. Misclassifying balance sheet items (usually either noncurrent assets misclassified as current or current liabilities misclassified as long-term, in order to improve current ratios and other ratios)
7. Committing disclosure frauds (omitting key footnote disclosures in financial statements or misstating facts in disclosures)

In many cases, more than one of the preceding acts occurs. For example, overstatement of revenue often coincides with overstatement of assets, but it can also arise in connection with understating liabilities.

In addition, overstating or understating various elements of the financial statements can be done in several manners. In some cases, an asset or liability is properly identified and appears in the financial statements, but its amount is over- or understated. In other cases, an entire asset or source of revenue is fabricated. It is completely fictitious, not merely overstated. Other times, a liability that should be reported is omitted entirely.

This book is designed to address financial reporting frauds effectuated through the intentional misuse of fair value accounting standards. All seven of the categories of fraudulent financial reporting are affected by fair value accounting. The goal of this book is to explain how fair value accounting rules can be improperly applied to fraudulently present the financial condition or results of operations of an entity.

What Makes It Fraud?

The preparation of inaccurate or incomplete financial statements is nothing new. It has been going on for as long as there have been financial statements. But preparing misleading financial statements is not a fraud that is easily challenged. To have a strong legal case charging financial statement fraud, it must be demonstrated that the accounting standards with which those statements claim to conform are actually being violated and that such noncompliance is willful on the part of the preparers of the statements.

As a result, in order to determine whether fraud has occurred, it is essential to have a solid understanding of the accounting concepts involved in preparing financial statements.

Take a look at the report of the independent certified public accountant or auditor that accompanies any audited set of financial statements.

The auditor's opinion does not state that the financial statements are fairly stated. The auditor opines that the financial statements are fairly stated in all material respects in accordance with a particular set of formally established accounting principles. In the United States, those principles are referred to as generally accepted accounting principles, or GAAP. In many other countries, the standards cited by the independent auditor are the International Financial Reporting Standards (IFRS). Regardless of where the financial statements are issued, the auditor's opinion will state which set of accounting and reporting rules the financial statements have been prepared under.

Tricking the auditor, and therefore anyone else who reads and relies on the financial statements, into believing that the statements comply with a particular set of accounting principles when, in fact, the financial statements contain known deviations from those principles is what constitutes fraud.

Why Financial Reporting Fraud Is Perpetrated

Why do companies engage in fraudulent financial reporting? First of all, companies don't perpetrate these frauds; people do. So why would an individual, or a group of individuals, perpetrate financial statement fraud? The reasons are numerous and quite diverse. Some result in direct financial gain for the perpetrators, such as these three:

1. Salaries and bonuses for achieving stated financial goals
2. Increased values of company stock and stock options resulting from reporting strong financial results
3. Retaining one's job by falsifying the financial success of a particular department, location, product line, and so on that might otherwise be targeted for elimination by senior management due to poor performance

Other reasons for perpetrating financial statement fraud are less obvious. No direct financial gain may be involved. Examples of these motives include the following four:

1. Pressure from senior management, the board of directors, and outside parties, such as stock analysts, to achieve earnings expectations
2. Competitive pressures to outperform other businesses in the same industry
3. Pressure to comply with financial ratio debt covenants included in notes and bonds, in order to keep these debt instruments from going into default
4. Desire to convince lenders that the company is worthy of a new loan or an increased line of credit

5. Desire to persuade insurers that the company is a low-risk entity
6. Desire to convince investors that the business is a valuable investment for their funds

Some financial reporting frauds are committed at the highest levels of an organization. Senior management may be involved in an elaborate scheme to improve the apparent financial health and performance of the company. But in other cases, the financial reporting fraud may be perpetrated at lower levels of an organization. One particular division or location may be falsifying its financial results, without the knowledge or consent of senior management.

Some financial reporting frauds are surprisingly simple in their operation. Altering shipping records can make it look like next month's revenue was earned this month. Creating phony customer records and sales orders can make it look like more merchandise was sold. A salesperson can backdate a customer order to move sales into the earlier month. A warehouse manager can intentionally ship incorrect merchandise, knowing that the items ordered by a customer are currently out of stock, in order to accelerate the recognition of the revenue. A vendor invoice can be altered in a way that supports recording the payment to the vendor as an asset rather than as an expense.

Although some of these methods are more difficult than others to detect, they are all basically rather simple in how they are carried out.

Other fraud schemes are quite complicated. Altering physical documents may be followed by a series of complex journal entries to disguise the underlying fraud. Or numerous people are involved, perhaps including outsiders who are in collusion with company personnel to assist in the fraud.

Most instances that involve the use of fair value accounting techniques to perpetrate financial reporting fraud have two characteristics:

1. The methods are often extremely complicated (if for no other reason than the sheer complexity of the fair value accounting rules) and can be quite elaborate.
2. They are usually perpetrated by senior management rather than lower-level personnel.

In the ACFE's *2008 Report to the Nation on Occupational Fraud and Abuse,* only 22 percent of asset misappropriation schemes studied were perpetrated by owners or executives. Another 38 percent were perpetrated by managers, with 40 percent by employees.

The opposite can be said for fraudulent reporting: 53 percent of the fraudulent reporting schemes studied were perpetrated by owners or executives, 36 percent of the frauds were performed by managers, and only 11 percent were done by employees.

Although no formal study exists to support this conclusion, it is the author's belief that this statistic is likely to be even more heavily skewed toward owners and executives if the fraudulent reporting incidents studied were confined to those involving fair value accounting.

The ACFE also analyzed behavioral red flags that were present in connection with each of the three major categories of fraud. These behavioral red flags are useful in assessing an entity's risk of experiencing each type of fraud. In connection with financial statement fraud, five behavioral red flags were most frequently noted. The percentages of cases that included each red flag are as follows:

1. Living beyond means—41 percent
2. Wheeler-dealer attitude—30 percent
3. Financial difficulties—26 percent
4. Control issues, unwillingness to share duties—25 percent
5. Excessive pressure from within the organization—23 percent

Numerous other red flags also were noted in financial statement fraud schemes, but none more so than these five. (*Note:* The total adds up to more than 100 percent due to the fact that in many cases, multiple behavioral red flags were observed.)

The first four behavioral red flags were also common in connection with the other two categories of fraud (asset misappropriations and corruption). The fifth red flag, however, was observed much more frequently in financial statement frauds than in any other type of fraud. Excessive pressure from within the organization is the red flag most unique to financial statement fraud. These pressures usually are present with respect to earnings and/or revenue figures, but can also be applied with respect to other financial performance measures.

Using One Fraud to Hide Another

One important ingredient associated with occupational fraud is *concealment*. Unlike many violent crimes, perpetrators of most occupational frauds do not want the victim to know that the fraud even took place. And if the fraud is known to the victim, the perpetrator certainly does not want to be identified as the one who did it. Fraudsters will go to great lengths to conceal their crimes.

Recall the three categories of occupational fraud:

1. Asset misappropriations
2. Corruption
3. Fraudulent reporting

Sometimes, a financial reporting fraud can be utilized as a method of concealing an asset misappropriation. A fair value accounting fraud might just be the perfect choice for such concealment.

Let's look at an example to illustrate how this might work. Assume the chief financial officer (CFO) of a company has been misappropriating funds from the company through the use of a fictitious vendor. The CFO made up this fictitious vendor and has been submitting phony invoices on behalf of the nonexistent vendor. The vendor has supposedly been providing a service that only the CFO has full knowledge of, so the CFO approves the vendor invoices with little to no scrutiny from others.

The problem is that the CFO has drained the company's cash over time. And the payments have all been posted to a handful of expense accounts, whose balances are now beginning to get substantially larger than what others in management or the external auditor might expect.

One method of further concealing this fraud would be through a fair value accounting scheme. The CFO might inflate the fair value of the company's investment portfolio. Since many investments are grouped with cash and cash equivalents for purposes of calculating many financial ratios, such as the current ratio, the deteriorated financial condition caused by the fraudulent disbursements might be concealed, at least for a while, by engaging in the fair value fraud with the investments.

The CFO might even go one step further to conceal the fictitious vendor scheme. There is still the business of the larger-than-expected balances in certain expense accounts into which the fraudulent payments have been posted. Through a series of journal entries, the CFO might reclassify some or all of the fraudulent recognized unrealized gains on the investments into the expense accounts, or vice versa, so that the final balances in the expense accounts are more in line with expectations. Part of the logic the CFO uses in carrying out this reclassification part of the scheme is that many (perhaps most) members of management, the board, investors, and even auditors might be looking only at final balances in various line items of the financial statements. The details of the underlying transactions are often not looked at very closely.

Whether the CFO would succeed with this scheme depends on many factors, including the strategy employed by the internal and external auditors in performing their work. But the fact remains—perpetrators of frauds will do whatever is necessary to conceal their frauds. And sometimes, that involves perpetrating a second type of fraud to conceal the first.

CHAPTER 2

The Use of Fair Value in Financial Statements

Historical Cost versus Fair Value

To understand the evolution of accounting from a historical cost-based system to one that relies heavily on fair value accounting, it is first important to review how accrual accounting itself has evolved over the years.

In order to conform to the most widely accepted accounting standards developed throughout the world, financial statements generally must be prepared on the accrual method of accounting. But in many cases, especially with smaller businesses, cash-basis financial reporting may be perfectly acceptable, because the use of the financial statements is more limited—to simply monitor financial activities or to report revenues received to a bank in connection with a loan.

Under the cash basis of accounting, revenues are recorded when they are collected and expenses are recorded when they are paid. But with accrual accounting, the timing of revenue and expense recognition is different. Revenue is recorded when it is earned, which may come either before or after it is actually collected. Likewise, expenses and/or liabilities are recorded when the benefits have been received, such as when services have been provided by a vendor or goods are received. Accrual accounting is the foundation of all of the world's commonly used accounting standards, including both of the systems covered in this book.

But even accrual accounting has undergone much change—and that change is not limited to the increased use of fair value accounting. The very concept of when to recognize an asset or liability has evolved. One of the best examples of this is with asset retirement obligations, a topic explained in Chapter 13. Prior to the development of the current standards dealing with asset retirement obligations, the carrying amount of land or a building was the amount paid to acquire the asset, including any amounts borrowed. The thought of accruing an additional amount to the asset and an additional liability for a cost that might not be incurred for years was thought of as violating accrual accounting. Not anymore. Under the current rules, costs necessary to dismantle or retire such assets must be accrued today. So, the whole idea of when a cost has been incurred has changed as accrual accounting has evolved. Similar developments have occurred with respect to many other elements of the financial statements.

This brings us to the use of fair value accounting. For most of the history of accounting, financial reporting has been based on historical cost, under which purchased assets are reported at the amount paid for the asset, less accumulated depreciation where appropriate. Similar principles are utilized for other assets and liabilities, which have traditionally been reported at the face amount of what is owed.

Fair value accounting, by contrast, relies on the principle that an asset should be reported at an amount that reflects what the asset is worth, not what an entity paid for it. Likewise with liabilities—although for many liabilities, fair value is equal to the amount that is owed to a vendor or bank.

Upon initial observation, the effect of fair value appears to be potentially greater on assets than it is on liabilities. An investment in stock that was purchased many years ago for $1,000 that is now worth $100,000 looks much different when fair value accounting is utilized.

Arguments for and against fair value accounting have been ongoing for many years. The principal argument in favor of valuing all assets and liabilities at current fair values is that this provides information of greatest value to most investors and many other readers of audited financial statements. Fair value accounting can provide a more current picture of the financial condition of an enterprise than historical cost accounting.

The argument in favor of reporting assets at historical cost is that cost is rarely subjective. Unlike fair value accounting, which can require extensive use of judgment and often requires specialized expertise, historical cost accounting is usually objective. It is usually easy to prove.

Like it or not, the increased use of fair value accounting is likely here to stay. Both U.S. and international accounting standards now include extensive use of fair value accounting. A reversal of this concept would appear to be extremely unlikely.

In connection with the global economic downturn that became a crisis in 2008, many wondered whether fair value accounting was partly to blame and that its use should be suspended. The general consensus is that the use of fair value accounting should continue, albeit perhaps with some clarification and increased disclosures.

In its December 2008 *Report and Recommendations Pursuant to Section 133 of the Emergency Economic Stabilization Act of 2008: Study on Mark-to-Market Accounting*, the U.S. Securities and Exchange Commission

(SEC) not only encouraged the continued use of fair value accounting, it suggested an expansion of fair value accounting. This study was mandated by Congress in connection with an October 2008 law aimed at bringing stability to the financial institutions sector hit hard by the economic downturn. The law mandated that the SEC study the fair value accounting provisions described in SFAS 157 and other standards, examining six issues:

1. The effects of the fair value accounting standards on a financial institution's balance sheet
2. The impacts of these accounting standards on bank failures in 2008
3. The impact of these accounting standards on the quality of financial information available to investors
4. The process used by FASB in developing standards
5. The advisability and feasibility of modifications to such standards
6. Alternative accounting standards to those described in SFAS 157 and other fair value accounting standards

In its endorsement of fair value accounting, the SEC noted that the current accounting standards were each subject to a lengthy and thorough due diligence process. A quick suspension of fair value accounting (which was suggested by some members of Congress) would circumvent this due process and could actually result in greater uncertainty over financial reporting by investors and others.

Rather, in its report the SEC suggests that clarifications and modifications be made to SFAS 157 and some other standards with fair value accounting requirements. The Commission also stated that more practical, useful guidance on best practices and other fair value accounting applications is necessary.

Although its analysis of the use of fair value accounting was limited to a group of specific financial institutions, the SEC's conclusions clearly were intended for all entities subject to U.S. GAAP.

Sources of Accounting Principles

In the United States of America, accounting rules are collectively referred to as generally accepted accounting principles (GAAP). The primary source of U.S. GAAP is the Financial Accounting Standards Board (FASB). However, predecessors to the FASB (such as the Accounting Principles Board) issued many documents, some of which are still applicable. Documents issued by FASB include Statements of Financial Accounting Standards (SFASs), FASB Interpretations (FINs), and FASB Staff Positions (FSPs). In addition, within the FASB is the Emerging Issues Task Force (EITF), which issues further guidance.

The American Institute of Certified Public Accountants (AICPA) has also been responsible for certain elements of U.S. GAAP. In particular, Statements of Position (SOPs) issued by the AICPA are considered to be a component of U.S. GAAP if they have been approved by the FASB.

U.S. GAAP is undergoing a codification process that takes effect July 1, 2009. Under the new codified system, all sources of GAAP, whether they be SFASs, FINs, FSPs, or others, will be organized using a uniform referencing system that is organized by subject area. This is similar in structure to the U.S. auditing standards codification. The assignment of consecutive standard numbers will continue as new standards are promulgated (e.g., SFAS 162, 163, etc.). But each new source of GAAP will then be codified into the new system.

For purposes of this book, the original sources of GAAP have been cited for ease of reference. The FASB GAAP codification system will provide for easy cross-referencing between original standard numbers and the new referencing system.

International Financial Reporting Standards (IFRS) are the accounting rules used in preparing financial statements in many countries. These standards are promulgated by the International Accounting Standards Board (IASB). The primary documents included in the IFRS are separate standards (IFRS 1, IFRS 2, etc.), as well as International Accounting Standards (IAS), which are also numbered consecutively (IAS preceded IFRS and continue to be applicable, as well as amended by the IASB). Additional guidance is provided in the form of interpretations of these standards by the Standing Interpretations Committee (SIC), whose interpretations are numbered consecutively as SIC 1, SIC 2, and so forth.

The IFRS are either required or optional in approximately 113 countries, with several countries currently in the process of converting to a requirement to utilize IFRS. In some cases companies whose stock is publicly traded utilize IFRS, while nonpublic entities do not. The European Union (EU) has adopted virtually all IFRS with minor modifications. The list of non–EU countries that require or allow use of IFRS by some or all entities includes Australia, Egypt, Israel, Russia, and Switzerland.

Canada has adopted a plan requiring the use of IFRS by all publicly accountable entities starting with fiscal years beginning on or after January 1, 2011. Among the other countries that will soon begin utilizing IFRS are some other large nations, such as Brazil.

In the United States, the SEC has approved a plan requiring the use of IFRS by SEC-registered public companies by 2014, and permitting the use of IFRS by some companies beginning in 2010. In 2007, the SEC approved rules that permitted non-U.S. companies that are required to register with the SEC to submit financial statements prepared in accordance with IFRS, without a reconciliation of IFRS to U.S. GAAP.

According to estimates provided in a December 2008 report issued by the SEC, the market capitalization of exchange-listed companies in the European Union, Australia, and Israel account for approximately 26 percent of total global market capitalization. Once Canada and Brazil are added, that figure will grow to 31 percent.

So, the long and short of it is that the world is gradually converting over to one uniform set of accounting principles, improving anyone's ability to compare the financial statements of companies operating in different parts of the world. But until this is completed, users will continue to be perplexed by the many differences in accounting from one country to another.

U.S. GAAP versus IFRS

This book is designed to provide guidance on fair value accounting fraud risks under both U.S. GAAP and IFRS. Accordingly, throughout the book specific differences between U.S. GAAP and IFRS will be explained, as well as how some of these differences can lead to an increased risk of fraud. But for purposes of this introduction, there are three key differences between U.S. GAAP and IFRS that readers should be aware of:

1. IFRS has generally provided for greater use of fair value accounting than U.S. GAAP, which has relied more on historical cost. This difference has gotten less extreme in recent years, with U.S. GAAP introducing greater use of fair value accounting, but differences remain.
2. The IFRS approach to accounting standards tends to be much more principles-based, providing broad concepts that should be followed, but leaving the application of those concepts in the hands of management and auditors. This is true not only with respect to fair value accounting issues, but throughout IFRS. U.S. GAAP, by contrast, tends to be much more detailed in its guidance. Many standards start out with a broad concept, but the standard ultimately goes into great detail, including numerous examples of how the concept should be applied to specific types of transactions.
3. Even in areas in which U.S. GAAP and IFRS share the basic accounting principle in relation to a particular topic, the application of each can be very different. Subtle but important differences in definitions of terms, or in criteria used to evaluate an issue, can lead to dramatic differences in accounting treatment.

As U.S. GAAP and IFRS continue down the path toward convergence, it will be interesting to see how these differences are resolved.

Fair Value Option Added for U.S. GAAP

SFAS 159, *The Fair Value Option for Financial Assets and Financial Liabilities*, introduced an important new phase of fair value accounting to U.S. GAAP. Under SFAS 159, entities may elect the fair value option for many assets and liabilities. Electing the fair value option means that assets or liabilities that have previously been measured using one basis (e.g., cost) may now be carried at fair value on a recurring basis.

Most financial assets and financial liabilities are eligible for the fair value option under SFAS 159. Financial assets are explained further in Part II, but generally include cash, equity (ownership) interests in other entities, receivables, and certain other contracts. Only a handful of financial assets and financial liabilities are not eligible for the fair value option, such as equity interests in entities that the owner is required to consolidate, certain assets and liabilities resulting from employee benefit plans, lease-related assets and liabilities, and demand deposits of financial institutions.

For assets, electing fair value treatment under SFAS 159 means that assets that were previously carried at lower of cost or fair value (i.e., nonrecurring fair value adjustments could be made if fair value declines below carrying value, but no adjustments would be made if fair value exceeds carrying value) are carried at fair value on a recurring basis. What does this mean? It means that if the fair value of an asset increases above the cost of the asset, that gain is recognized in the financial statements and the asset is adjusted to the higher amount. Under historical cost accounting, declines in fair value below book value were recorded, but never gains above book value.

The fair value option established by SFAS 159 may be applied on an instrument-by-instrument basis, with only a few exceptions (e.g., investments otherwise accounted for by the equity method). As a result, in some instances, a single line item on the financial statements may comprise a combination of instruments, some of which are carried at fair value on a recurring basis as a result of making the SFAS 159 election and others that are carried at historical cost or another basis. Once made, SFAS 159 fair value elections are irrevocable unless a new election date occurs.

Fair Value Defined

SFAS 157, *Fair Value Measurements*, defines fair value as "the price that would be received to sell an asset or paid to transfer a liability in an orderly transaction between market participants at the measurement date." The term *market participant* excludes related parties.

IFRS defines fair value as "the amount for which an asset could be exchanged between knowledgeable, willing parties in an arm's length transaction." Unlike U.S. GAAP, the IFRS definition and explanation of fair value is spread out among several standards. However, as noted earlier, the IASB is working on an exposure draft on fair value measurement guidance that will serve as a counterpart to SFAS 157.

Fair value, as the term is used throughout this book, can be applied with respect to any of the following eight categories:

1. One specific asset
2. A group of assets
3. A specific liability
4. A group of liabilities
5. A net consideration of one or more assets less one or more related liabilities
6. A segment or division of an entity
7. A particular location or region of an entity
8. An entire entity

The guidance on fair value issues in SFAS 157 is rather extensive in comparison to IFRS. Four elements of the U.S. GAAP definition of fair value have special meaning:

1. *Orderly transaction*. It is assumed that fair value is based on an orderly transaction. This assumes exposure to the market for a period of time prior to the measurement date to allow for the usual and customary marketing activities for similar transactions. An orderly sale is not one that is forced due to liquidation or other distress. Signs of forced transactions may include:
   a. Insufficient time to properly market an asset to be sold, caused by an urgent necessity to dispose of the asset
   b. Existence of a single potential buyer or a very limited group of buyers
   c. A legal requirement to sell an asset, due to contractual provisions, laws, or regulations
      Determining whether a transaction is orderly (and therefore potentially a reliable source of information) or disorderly (and therefore not determinative of fair value) requires judgment. As a result, this could potentially be an area of intentional misrepresentation or concealment of information by management in connection with a fair value accounting fraud. FASB provided additional guidance on determining whether a sale is orderly in April 2009 in the form of FSP FAS 157-4, *Determining Fair Value When the Volume and Level of Activity for the Asset or Liability Have Significantly Decreased and Identifying Transactions That Are Not Orderly.*

Fraud Risk No. 2.1

Basing fair value determinations on other known transactions, when the transactions cited are not "orderly."

---

2. *Principal or most advantageous market.* The SFAS 157 concept of fair value assumes that the hypothetical transaction to sell an asset or transfer a liability would occur in the principal market for such transactions, meaning the market with the greatest volume of activity for the asset or liability under consideration. If no such principal market exists, then the most advantageous market should be considered. This would be the market that maximizes the amount that would be received to sell the asset or that minimizes the amount that would be paid to transfer the liability in question. Further discussion of active versus inactive markets is included in Chapter 3.

3. *Transaction costs versus transportation costs.* Fair value should be determined without regard to transaction costs, the incremental direct costs associated with selling an asset (e.g., commissions) or transferring a liability. However, if transporting an asset to the principal or most advantageous market would net the highest proceeds for an asset, the cost of transporting the asset should be considered in determining the asset's fair value (i.e., transportation costs should be subtracted from the gross selling price, whereas transaction costs should not).

4. *Highest and best use of assets.* As SFAS 157 applies to determining fair values of an asset, the highest and best use of the asset should be used in assessing fair value. This use may differ from the current use of the asset by the holder of the asset. Highest and best use means one that is physically possible, legally permissible, and financially feasible. It is based on the highest and best use of the asset by market participants (i.e., those who would potentially purchase the asset). Determining what the highest and best use of an asset is may also require judgment, meaning that it could be another factor subject to manipulation by management in a fair value accounting fraud scheme.

Fraud Risk No. 2.2

Misrepresenting the highest or best use of an asset in order to inflate its estimated fair value.

Although the basic terminology used in the U.S. GAAP and IFRS definitions of fair value are similar, they result in three subtle distinctions, summarized as follows:

1. The SFAS 157 definition is explicitly an exit price, whereas the IFRS definition does not explicitly state whether it is an exit price or an entry price.
2. SFAS 157 explicitly refers to and defines the term *market participants,* whereas IFRS uses the broader terminology *knowledgeable, willing participants in an arm's length transaction.*
3. With respect to fair values of liabilities, SFAS 157 is based on an assumed *transfer* of the liability (i.e., the liability continues, but is now the responsibility of a counterparty to a transaction in which it was transferred), whereas the IFRS definition is based on the amount at which a liability could be *settled,* which could include settling it with the current party (e.g., a vendor, lender, etc.), in addition to transferring the liability to a third party.

These are mostly minor differences. The primary concepts of fair value described by FASB and IASB are similar. And the revised definition of fair value that IASB is working on will likely move the IFRS definition even closer to the U.S. GAAP definition. The next section on international convergence will discuss this in further detail.

International Convergence

SFAS 159, the fair value option described earlier, is one example of a product resulting from a process that has been referred to as international convergence. As its name suggests, *international convergence* is a process aimed at smoothing out the many differences in accounting principles used throughout the world in order to facilitate the comparison of financial statements issued in different countries. FASB and IASB have been, and continue to be, working together to make the two sets of accounting standards as consistent as possible. After all, when the plug is finally pulled on U.S. GAAP for publicly traded companies in the United States, it is hoped that the transition will be smooth and that significant adjustments will not be necessary.

In September 2008, FASB and IASB announced an update to their 2006 memorandum of understanding regarding their international convergence project. Since 2006, FASB and IASB have worked closely in the development of standards. The 2008 update to their understanding states that the two organizations plan to complete all major joint projects by 2011. There are 11 such joint projects. Seven of them either have been completed or significant progress has been made. The other four are in various stages of discussion.

Another example of international convergence in progress relates to SFAS 157. As explained in the preceding section, SFAS 157 lays out a very detailed map of fair value concepts. The standard is also very specific in its disclosure requirements. The IFRS has no counterpart to SFAS 157 currently. Guidance on fair value accounting issues is dispersed among several standards, none of which is as detailed or requires the level of disclosures as SFAS 157.

That will soon change. By the time this book is published, IASB expects to have released an exposure draft of a new standard that will represent its version of SFAS 157. IASB has stated that it will look closely at SFAS 157 as it prepares its exposure draft. IASB plans to utilize a three-level hierarchy of inputs in its standard, mirroring SFAS 157. IASB hopes to finalize this standard in 2010.

In the United States, another question that frequently arises regarding international convergence is, what about all of the entities that are not publicly traded businesses? Right now, the only planned conversion from U.S. GAAP to IFRS is for public companies, as mandated by the SEC. That leaves a tremendous number of other entities wondering what their accounting principles will look like, such as privately held and small businesses, not-for-profit organizations, and units of government. At this point, it appears that there are four most likely routes that might be taken in the United States:

1. IFRS becomes GAAP in the United States, meaning that both public and other entities must use it, with perhaps some slight variations for nonpublic entities (i.e., the IFRS for Private Entities standard). U.S. GAAP as a separate set of principles would go away. Other comprehensive bases of accounting, such as cash and tax basis, would continue as the only alternatives to IFRS.
2. Some customization of either IFRS or IFRS for Private Entities is made to tailor it to U.S. reporting needs.
3. A separate U.S. GAAP remains, but in a modified form. U.S. GAAP would continue as a separate set of standards that would be used by private entities.
4. The current version of U.S. GAAP would be carried forward, subject to periodic change, as a separate set of standards for private entities.

The next few years should be interesting in the accounting world. There are a tremendous number of very different users of U.S. GAAP, each of whom will want to preserve or change certain elements of the current version of U.S. GAAP.

Some Principles of Financial Statement Presentation

Throughout this book, references will be made to certain sections of the financial statements that are impacted by fair value issues. Before doing so, and now that we've introduced some key concepts associated with fraudulent financial reporting in Chapter 1 and fair value in this chapter, let's take a look at what goes into a standard set of financial statements. Financial statements typically comprise the following six components:

1. *Balance sheet.* This statement lists an entity's assets, grouped by category, which equals (balances to) the sum of its liabilities and equity. In some cases, the balance sheet is referred to as a statement of financial position or other terms, based on the nature of the entity or the accounting standards being followed (e.g., international standards refer to it as a statement of financial position). This statement is used to assess an entity's financial condition as of a particular reporting date.

2. *Income statement.* This statement reports the revenues, expenses, gains, and losses of the entity, resulting in a bottom line called *net income.* This statement is also sometimes called a statement of earnings or other terms. When an accounting standard refers to an item being included in earnings or in profit or loss, it means that the item is reported in this statement. This statement reports the entity's results of operations for a particular period, resulting in a profit or loss for the period.

3. *Statement of other comprehensive income.* The term *other comprehensive income,* or simply *comprehensive income,* refers to all changes in equity resulting from all activities other than transactions with owners (e.g., primarily new investments of funds by owners and distributions to owners). Comprehensive income includes the net profit or loss reported in the income statement, as well as certain other activities, explained shortly.

4. *Cash flows statement.* The statement of cash flows presents an entity's activities for a period in terms of its sources and uses of cash. It serves a variety of purposes, one of which is to express the accrual basis income statement and other changes in the accrual basis balance sheet in terms of cash flows, or a cash basis version of activities resulting from operations, investing activities, and financing activities.

5. *Disclosure of changes in equity accounts.* Accounting standards require the reporting of certain changes in equity. In some cases, the only change in equity is the net profit or loss for the reporting period. In other cases, many items affect equity. Accordingly, depending on the nature of the entity, the standards being followed, and even the entity's preferences, changes in equity may appear as an additional basic financial

statement, may be included as an element of another statement, or may be reported in the notes to the financial statements.

6. *Notes to the financial statements.* Every complete set of financial statements includes a series of notes that explain key accounting policies used in the preparation of the basic financial statements and other required disclosures.

Opportunities for fraudulent financial reporting based on misapplication of fair value accounting concepts exist in each one of these financial statement components. Throughout this book, opportunities for overstating assets, understating liabilities, and fraudulent disclosures will be explained.

But there is another category of fraudulent reporting that needs to be explained here, since it too will be mentioned as a fraud risk in several chapters of this book. In connection with gains or losses associated with the use of fair value accounting, there are four categories into which these frauds could be classified:

1. Whether or not a gain or loss is recognized
2. The amount of a gain or loss (also referred to as its measurement in this book)
3. Where the gain or loss is to be recognized
4. Explanatory disclosures about fair value

The first two issues and the fourth issue have already been introduced. But the third issue—where a gain or loss is recognized—may be unfamiliar to many readers.

When a gain or loss resulting from the application of fair value accounting is recognized, it can be recognized in one of two areas in the financial statements:

1. Within profit or loss, meaning it is reported in the income statement (statement of earnings)
2. As a component of comprehensive income, meaning it is not considered to be a part of the net profit or loss for the period and, instead, is reported as another change in equity

This classification issue presents a risk for fraud—potentially reporting losses as comprehensive income that should be included in net profit or loss, or falsely including gains in net profit or loss that should be reported as comprehensive income. Why is this a risk? Because net profit or loss, not comprehensive income, is what is used to report earnings per share and as a basis for many other financial measures, such as certain key ratios. As a result, the intentional misclassification of certain gains and losses can impact some important financial measures, even though the assets or liabilities affected are stated at the proper fair value balances.

Referring to a gain or loss as being reported in comprehensive income means that it is not reported in profit or loss. Examples of items reported in comprehensive income include:

1. Changes in fair value of available-for-sale investments
2. The effective portion of the gain or loss on a cash flow hedge
3. Unrealized gains or losses resulting from a debt security transferred into the available-for-sale category from the held-to-maturity category
4. Foreign currency translation adjustments
5. Certain transactions associated with pension or other postretirement benefits

The first three items in particular have direct implications on several fair value accounting issues explained in this book. Each of these three issues will be explained in detail later (see Chapters 4, 5, and 16).

U.S. GAAP and IFRS are similar, but not identical, in terms of the requirements associated with the reporting of comprehensive income. U.S. GAAP is described in SFAS 130, *Reporting Comprehensive Income*. IFRS is addressed in the broader standard IAS 1, *Presentation of Financial Statements*, which explains presentation requirements for all of the financial statements (not just for comprehensive income), as well as the disclosures in the notes.

An amended version of IAS 1 takes effect for periods beginning on or after January 1, 2009, with earlier application permitted. This revised version of IAS 1 brings IFRS even closer to the requirements described in SFAS 130. For the purposes of this book, it is not necessary to go through a detailed analysis of the differences between U.S. GAAP and IFRS as they relate to financial statement presentation in general. This book will focus on the differences associated with the specific elements of the financial statements affected by fair value accounting. But for those readers who are interested, the "Basis for Conclusions" section of revised IAS 1 contains a discussion of some of these differences.

Effective Dates of Accounting Standards

The standards referred to in this book are generally effective for 2008 and later financial statements, except where noted (such as the revised IAS 1 described in the preceding section, compliance with which is not required until 2009). However, several of the standards described in this book have implementation dates that are very recent, or the standard itself became effective many years ago but was recently amended. So if you are considering whether a set of 2006 or 2007 financial statements you are reviewing may have been fraudulently prepared, keep in mind that some of the standards in this book didn't yet apply to those statements.

When considering the risk of fraud, it is important to identify the accounting and reporting standards that apply to the particular period being evaluated. Do not impose the requirements of a recent standard when evaluating whether fraud was involved in financial statements that were issued five years ago.

By the time fraud is suspected, it may have been years since the financial statements were issued. Always hold the financial statements to the standard of the rules that applied for the period under investigation—and those standards may be quite different from some of the standards described in this book. That is why when researching any of the standards referred to in this book, the first thing to look at is the standard's effective date.

Impact of Fraud on Financial Statements

Now that we've explained some of the key elements of the financial statements, let's see what those financial statements look like when fraud is introduced. In particular, let's focus on the balance sheet, income statement, and statement of comprehensive income.

The financial statements shown in Table 2.1 represent a typical example of a relatively simple entity, but one with several opportunities for fair value accounting fraud. In the "fairly stated" column are the entity's financial statements as they should be presented in accordance with applicable accounting principles (GAAP or IFRS). The JE column represents a journal entry made by management to perpetrate a fair value accounting fraud. In this case, the JE column represents the perpetration of a three-part fair value accounting fraud:

1. The first part records $350,000 of phony gains from false increases in fair value of marketable securities.
2. The second part of the fraud misclassifies $150,000 of unrealized losses from investment income to other comprehensive income.
3. The third component of the fraud reverses $100,000 of a previously recorded impairment loss associated with an intangible asset (for simplicity purposes, assume the loss had been classified in operating expenses).

Also for simplicity purposes, assume the income tax effect of the preceding entries is zero.

This fraud is rather simple. The purpose of providing this example is to illustrate the many effects that a fraud this simple can have on an entity's

TABLE 2.1 The Effect of Fraud

	Fairly Stated	JE	Fraudulently Stated
BALANCE SHEET			
Assets			
Current Assets			
Cash and cash equivalents	1,100,000		1,100,000
Investments—marketable securities	3,500,000	350,000	3,850,000
Accounts receivable	1,550,000		1,550,000
Inventories	2,150,000		2,150,000
Total Current Assets	8,300,000	350,000	8,650,000
Noncurrent Assets			
Investments	2,400,000		2,400,000
Properties, plant, and equipment, net	12,550,000		12,550,000
Intangible assets, net	4,850,000	100,000	4,950,000
Total Assets	28,100,000	450,000	28,550,000
Liabilities and Stockholders' Equity			
Current Liabilities			
Accounts payable	2,600,000		2,600,000
Accrued liabilities	2,300,000		2,300,000
Short-term debt	1,300,000		1,300,000
Total Current Liabilities	6,200,000		6,200,000
Noncurrent Liabilities			
Long-term debt	14,600,000		14,600,000
Total Liabilities	20,800,000		20,800,000
Stockholders' Equity			
Common stock	1,000,000		1,000,000
Capital in excess of par value	3,050,000		3,050,000
Retained earnings	4,350,000	600,000	4,950,000
Accumulated other comprehensive loss	(1,100,000)	(150,000)	(1,250,000)
Total Stockholders' Equity	7,300,000	450,000	7,750,000
Total Liabilities and Stockholders' Equity	28,100,000	450,000	28,550,000

(Continued)

TABLE 2.1 (Continued)

	Fairly Stated	JE	Fraudulently Stated
STATEMENT OF INCOME			
Revenues and Other Income			
Sales	18,500,000		18,500,000
Investment income	500,000	500,000	1,000,000
Total Revenues and Other Income	19,000,000	500,000	19,500,000
Costs and Other Deductions			
Operating expenses	11,300,000	(100,000)	11,200,000
Administrative expenses	5,400,000		5,400,000
Interest expense	1,200,000		1,200,000
Total Costs and Other Deductions	17,900,000	(100,000)	17,800,000
Income before income taxes	1,100,000	600,000	1,700,000
Income tax expense	300,000		300,000
Net Income	800,000	600,000	1,400,000
STATEMENT OF COMPREHENSIVE INCOME			
Net Income	800,000	600,000	1,400,000
Unrealized Holding Gain (Loss) on Securities			
Net gain (loss) for the period	(300,000)	(150,000)	(450,000)
Reclassification to net income of net realized loss	100,000		100,000
Total	(200,000)	150,000	(350,000)
Comprehensive Income	600,000	450,000	1,050,000

financial statements. First, let's examine the effect that each fraud has on some of the accounts involved:

1. The inflated fair value of marketable securities represents 10 percent of the original balance.
2. The reclassification of unrealized losses has no effect on assets or liabilities.
3. The reversal of impairment loss is less than 1 percent of operating expenses and only 2 percent of intangible assets.

However, the effect on certain key financial performance measures is much more dramatic. The company's net profit increased by a whopping 75 percent. This translates into a 75 percent jump in earnings per share, one of the key measures used in evaluating a company's stock.

Many other financial ratios were also enhanced by this scheme. For example, the current ratio jumped from 1.338 to 1.395. That doesn't sound like much, does it? Would your opinion change if you knew that the company's debt obligation included a requirement to maintain a current ratio of at least 1.35? Anything less puts the debt into default.

A simple example, to be sure. But it serves the purpose of illustrating potential motives for perpetrating a fraud like this, as well as the effects of financial statement fraud.

Throughout the remainder of this book, much more complex fair value accounting frauds will be explained. Each has the potential for dramatic effects on the many financial ratios and performance measures that are used to evaluate entities, as well as the managers who run the entities.

CHAPTER 3

Methods of Determining Fair Value

Introduction

This book is not intended to be a comprehensive guide to determining fair values. Rather, it is designed to be a guide to the numerous complex accounting rules that rely on fair valuations for the measurement of various assets, liabilities, revenues, and expenses. It is these rules that are often violated in connection with fraudulent financial reporting.

Yet, a discussion of the fair value accounting rules would be incomplete without at least providing an overview of some of the key principles involved in determining the fair value of an asset or a liability. After all, fraudulent financial reporting can involve misapplication of an accounting rule, misapplication of a valuation methodology, or a combination of both.

Most fair value measurements utilize one of three approaches to determining fair value:

1. Market approach
2. Income approach
3. Cost approach

Each approach is explained in SFAS 157, and these explanations are provided in the following box. It is not the purpose of this book to provide a detailed guide on how to value assets, liabilities, or businesses. Rather, it is to provide an overview of the models as a basis for understanding where the opportunities for fair value accounting fraud exist and to introduce certain key theories that will be useful in understanding later discussions of specific applications of fair value accounting.

SFAS 157 Approaches to Determining Fair Value

Paragraph 18 of SFAS 157 provides the following descriptions of the three categories of fair value models:

a. *Market approach.* The market approach uses prices and other relevant information generated by market transactions involving identical or comparable assets or liabilities (including a business). For example, valuation techniques consistent with the market approach often use market multiples derived from a set of comparables. Multiples might lie in ranges with a different multiple for each comparable. The selection of where within the range the appropriate multiple falls requires judgment, considering factors specific to the measurement (qualitative and quantitative). Valuation techniques consistent with the market approach include matrix pricing. Matrix pricing is a mathematical technique used principally to value debt securities without relying exclusively on quoted prices for the specific securities, but rather, relying on the securities' relationship to other benchmark quoted securities.

b. *Income approach.* The income approach uses valuation techniques to convert future amounts (e.g., cash flows or earnings) to a single present amount (discounted). The measurement is based on the value indicated by current market expectations about those future amounts. Those valuation techniques include present value techniques; option-pricing models, such as the Black-Scholes-Merton formula (a closed-form model) and a binomial model (a lattice model), which incorporate present value techniques; and the multiperiod excess earnings method, which is used to measure the fair value of certain intangible assets.

c. *Cost approach.* The cost approach is based on the amount that currently would be required to replace the service capacity of an asset (often referred to as current replacement cost). From the perspective of a market participant (seller), the price that would be received for the asset is determined based on the cost to a market participant (buyer) to acquire or construct a substitute asset of comparable utility, adjusted for obsolescence. Obsolescence encompasses physical deterioration, functional (technological) obsolescence, and economic (external) obsolescence and is broader than depreciation for financial reporting purposes (an allocation of historical cost) or tax purposes (based on specified service lives).

> SFAS 157 states that its guidance does not apply to the fair-value-based measurements using option-pricing models under SFAS 123 (see Chapter 18 for an explanation of SFAS 123).

Market Approach

The market approach uses prices and other information generated by market transactions involving identical or comparable assets or liabilities. As noted in SFAS 157, use of the market approach sometimes involves estimating where within a range of multiples or other inputs an appropriate multiple or input should be. This requires the use of judgment, and all factors that are specific to the asset or liability being measured should be considered. Some of these factors may be quantitative, but they are often qualitative.

One of the most significant benefits of using the market approach is that it is based primarily on actual data. The data are often in the form of well-documented, publicly available prices recorded in active markets, such as with stock trades. Other data used in the market approach may not be as readily available as prices from stock markets, but are nonetheless objective and useful, such as the prices at which specific entities, lines of business, operating divisions, or locations are sold.

Fraud Risk No. 3.1

Drawing inappropriate conclusions about an asset's fair value based on consideration of a range of prices or other inputs available from transactions in a market.

Of course, an important potential downside to the market approach is often that either active markets do not exist for a particular item or the comparison of the item in question with the known transactions in the market is complicated. The issue of formerly active markets becoming inactive will be explored further in Chapter 4.

Often, there are known transactions in a market, but none are for assets or liabilities that are identical to the one for which a value is needed. The process of drawing this comparison can be extremely complex.

Income Approach

The income approach uses valuation techniques to convert future amounts (e.g., cash flows or earnings) to a single present amount (discounted). The most commonly used future amounts in the formula are cash flows, earnings, or some component of earnings (e.g., earnings before taxes and interest, etc.). Consideration of future amounts can extend for many periods into the future or only a few. This requires much judgment. In some industries or for certain assets, specific time periods have become standard. But in most cases, the number of future periods to consider is a matter of judgment.

Fair value determined using the income approach varies based on three primary factors:

1. **The amount of cash flow**—the higher the cash flow, the higher the value.
2. **The timing of the cash flows**—the sooner the cash flow, the higher the value.
3. **The risks associated with the cash flows**—the lower the risk, the higher the value.

Each of these three factors can be a target for misrepresentation in a fraudulent determination of fair value under the income approach.

Within the income approach, valuation experts frequently utilize three distinct methods to value businesses or individual assets:

1. Discounted cash flow
2. Capitalized cash flow
3. Excess cash flow

Each of these three methods is explained in this section.

Fraud Risk No. 3.2

Misapplication of the income approach by using improper amounts for cash flows, manipulating the timing of future cash flows, or using an inappropriate discount rate, resulting in an inaccurate present value.

Discounted Cash Flow Method

The discounted cash flow method is the most commonly used application of the income approach. It is applied by calculating the present value of estimated future cash flows. This method can be applied to a single asset, a group of assets, a division, region, or an entire company. Cash flows may be estimated for a very short period of time or very long periods, up to infinity if an income stream is expected to continue forever.

The discount rate used in the income approach represents the rate of return that an investor would require. This rate considers three elements:

1. A basic rate of return without any consideration of risk, or how much of a return an investor desires in exchange for the use of the investor's money
2. Anticipated rates of inflation, which corresponds to the expected depreciation in purchasing power while funds are invested
3. Risk associated with the uncertainty regarding the amount or timing of the estimated future cash flows

Each of these three elements requires the use of judgment and estimation, making them prone to potential manipulation in the perpetration of a fair value accounting fraud.

Capitalized Cash Flow Method

The capitalized cash flow method is a shortcut version of the discounted cash flow method. Unlike the discounted cash flow method, under the capitalized cash flow model, both the discount rate and the rate of growth in cash flow are assumed to remain constant in perpetuity.

Under the discounted cash flow model, separate cash flow projections can be developed for each future period, rather than assuming a particular growth rate over time. Then, if appropriate, different discount rates can be applied to each future period's cash flow. For example, different discount rates may be utilized to factor in the greater uncertainty in cash flows that are further into the future than those that are in the very near future.

Excess Cash Flow Method

The excess cash flow method, also known as the excess earnings method, is sometimes used to value the intangible assets of a business rather than an entire business. It is referred to in the Internal Revenue Service's Revenue Ruling 68-609 as having application to intangible asset valuation. The basic steps involved in the excess cash flow approach are as follows:

1. Determine the fair value of net tangible assets of an entity.
2. Determine normalized future cash flows in total (the concept of normalization is explained shortly), and break those cash flows down as follows:
   a. Cash flows attributable to net tangible assets
   b. Cash flows attributable to intangible assets, which is simply the difference between total cash flows and cash flows attributable to net

tangible assets (i.e., separate determination of cash flows from intangible assets is not done)

3. Determine what an appropriate rate of return on net tangible assets would be (also referred to as the weighted average cost of capital).

4. Determine an appropriate rate of return on the intangible assets.

5. Determine the fair value of intangible assets based on the capitalization rate determined in step 4.

6. Determine a total fair value by adding the fair value of the net tangible assets to the fair value of the intangible assets.

7. Determine the fair value of the entity's equity by subtracting any interest-bearing debt obligations from the amount determined in step 6.

To properly apply the income approach, future cash flows must be normalized. Normalization represents the process of making projections of future cash flows most representative of what can be expected of the future. In other words, certain items that have historically impacted cash flows and that may be considered in estimates of future cash flows may need to be eliminated in order to get a true picture of what future cash flows will be like. For example, one of the more common adjustments necessary to normalize cash flows is for nonrecurring items, such as one-time expenditures.

Generally, there are many more considerations in normalizing the cash flows when valuing an entire business than there would be for valuing a single asset. In valuing an entire business, adjustments may be necessary for a variety of ownership, capitalization, debt, income tax, and other factors that may not be necessary when valuing a single asset.

Expected Cash Flow

A fourth possible approach to determining present values of future cash flows takes a different approach to measuring risk. This method, referred to as the expected cash flow approach, is described in SFAC 7, *Using Cash Flow Information and Present Value in Accounting Measurements*.

In the three methods of applying the income approach explained so far, the various risks associated with future cash flows are considered in developing a single discount rate that is applied to those future cash flows. Under the expected cash flow approach, risk is handled in a different manner. Instead of incorporating it into the discount rate, it is handled by determining multiple expectations of future cash flows and assigning probabilities to each. The element of risk is removed from the discount rate, leaving a much more reliable discount rate based primarily on an expected rate of return.

Under the expected cash flow approach, a weighted average of the various present values is calculated, based on the probabilities assigned to each calculation.

Cost Approach

The cost approach to determining fair value is based on assessing what the cost would be to replace an asset, or the service capacity of an asset, and then making adjustments to that cost figure. The primary adjustment to the cost figure is for obsolescence.

Fraud Risk No. 3.3

Using inappropriate replacement cost estimates or making inaccurate adjustments for obsolescence in determining fair value under the cost approach.

The obvious risks associated with the cost approach concern the replacement cost estimate and adjustments for obsolescence and any other relevant factor. Replacement cost estimates may in some cases be fairly easy, such as in cases in which an asset was purchased fairly recently and the same model of that asset is still being sold. Estimating replacement cost of unusual or custom-designed, custom-built assets becomes much more complicated and may require external assistance.

Adjustments for obsolescence can also be very easy or very difficult. But these adjustments, as well as other adjustments to the initial replacement cost, are an easy target for manipulation.

Internal versus Externally Developed Valuations

Fair values can be determined internally or externally. When they are determined internally, management should make sure that the personnel involved in the process have the proper expertise for the specific valuation issues involved.

Externally developed valuations should be prepared by independent valuation experts with experience in valuing the specific types of assets, liabilities, or businesses in question. Management should determine that external valuation specialists are properly credentialed and experienced in the specific types of valuations needed. References should be checked and licenses and certifications verified.

Fraud Risk No. 3.4

Obtaining a tainted valuation report in support of a fraudulent fair value measurement used in the financial statements, using any of five techniques.

But in other cases, including some involving fair value accounting fraud, management doesn't want the best valuation specialist. Instead, management wants to find a valuation specialist willing to provide a report that supports what management wants to use as a fair value in the financial statements.

Unscrupulous members of management may go to great lengths to obtain a report in support of a preferred fair value, all to dupe auditors and others who may question a particular value in the financial statements. Improper valuations used in support of a fair value accounting fraud can be generated internally or may come from third-party experts. When third-party valuation experts are involved, there are five situations in which a fraudulent valuation can result:

1. *Bribed appraiser.* In a worst-case scenario, an outside party may be bribed in order to issue a valuation report that supports a fair value accounting position of management. This is the most egregious offense in this area and also one of the most difficult to detect.

2. *Conflict of interest.* If there is a concealed financial or other relationship between either the entity or a member of management and the outside valuation specialist, the specialist is not independent and the report may support a fraudulent valuation preferred by management.

3. *Unwitting accomplice.* In the first two cases, the appraiser is an accomplice to the fraud and he/she knows it. In other cases, a third-party valuation specialist may unwittingly prepare a valuation report in support of a fraud, as a result of pressures applied by management, suppression of information by management, reliance on phony data provided by management, or other tactics. This is most likely to occur when the outside party is either inexperienced or careless in his/her work.

4. *Sham valuation specialist.* Another method that could be used to perpetrate fraud is the preparation of a completely fictitious valuation report from a nonexistent valuation specialist. This approach is similar to any other phony/sham vendor scheme in that the perpetrator prepares false documentation that makes it appear that an actual vendor exists.

5. *Altered report.* Management may have arranged for and received a valuation report from a respected professional valuation expert. But the report does not support the position preferred by management. Could it be possible for management to make alterations to the report prepared by the valuation expert in order to make it appear that the expert supported the fraudulent valuation reflected in the financial statements of the entity? Reports should be reviewed carefully for signs of altered text, missing pages, additions inserted into the report, or other signs of alteration.

Other than the obvious signs of alteration described in the last situation, there are other signs that a valuation report may be flawed. Those flaws may be a sign of fraud, not merely carelessness by an appraiser. Here are 10 signs to watch out for in valuation reports:

1. Mathematical and clerical errors, including cross-references that don't agree, grammatical mistakes, and similar careless errors
2. Apparent exaggeration and excessive reliance on positive factors, or downplaying negative factors
3. A report that lacks a sufficient level of detail, especially details involving the data used in support of the valuation (interest rates, cash flow assumptions, etc.) and descriptions of valuation methodologies utilized
4. Misrepresentation of the specialist's licenses, education and training, or credentials—don't be fooled by a specialist with a lot of certifications after his/her name—verify those licenses and other credentials
5. The use of unusual valuation methods or methods that are not known as being commonly accepted for a particular type of valuation (or making unexplained modifications to a commonly accepted method)
6. A report that does not contain a statement certifying the valuation specialist's independence from the entity
7. Use of data that would not be known to prospective buyers of an asset—remember that the SFAS 157 definition of fair value is based on what market participants would pay for the asset
8. Evidence that there was an extremely short turn-around time on the report—this could be a sign that not much effort was put into the valuation, that the report was prepared quickly to satisfy an urgent need of management
9. Evidence that the report was cut and pasted from other reports—we've seen reports that had the name of the wrong client, clearly a sign that the report was prepared using a "cookie cutter" mentality
10. Excessive reliance on mathematics and formulas, without adequate narrative explanation

Valuation reports should be reviewed carefully for these warning signs. Just because a fair value is supported by a professional-looking report is not a justification for blindly accepting it as accurate.

Inputs to Valuation Methods

SFAS 157 establishes a hierarchy of inputs that may be used in determining fair values. Inputs are the various pieces of data that are utilized in arriving at a fair value. In some cases, only a single input is necessary. In other cases, many different inputs are used in arriving at a value.

Inputs can be classified as either observable or unobservable. *Observable* inputs are inputs that reflect the assumptions that market participants would use in pricing the asset or liability developed based on market data obtained from sources independent of the reporting entity. Examples of observable inputs include the following seven:

1. Market prices from active markets for identical securities (e.g., publicly traded stocks and mutual funds)
2. Market prices for similar assets or liabilities
3. Historical rates of interest
4. Historical rates of inflation
5. Default rates
6. Business valuation multiples used in recorded sales of other businesses
7. Real estate market prices based on square feet and location

Unobservable inputs are inputs that reflect the reporting entity's own internal assumptions about the assumptions that market participants would use in pricing the asset or liability based on the best information available in the circumstances. Examples of unobservable inputs include the following three:

1. Projections of future cash flows, revenues, expenses, earnings, volume of production, and so on
2. Self-assessed risk factors (e.g., default risk, etc.) that are applied in connection with valuing certain items (e.g., valuing one's own debt)
3. Other extrapolations of historical or verifiable information, such as growth rates

Some inputs may fall into either the observable or unobservable category, depending on whether market participants would likely have access to the information. For example, terms of licenses, contracts, and other agreements may or may not be publicly available for market participants. Availability to market participants affects the classification of the input.

SFAS 157 requires the classification of all inputs used in determining fair values into one of three levels. Which level(s) of inputs were used in arriving at fair values are required financial statement disclosures under SFAS 157. Those levels are explained in the following box.

The SFAS 157 Hierarchy of Inputs

Paragraphs 24, 28, and 30 of SFAS 157 provide the following explanations of the three-level hierarchy of inputs used in determining fair value of assets and liabilities:

Level 1 inputs are quoted prices (unadjusted) in active markets for identical assets or liabilities that the reporting entity has the ability to access at the measurement date. An active market for the asset or liability is a market in which transactions for the asset or liability occur with sufficient frequency and volume to provide pricing information on an ongoing basis. A quoted price in an active market provides the most reliable evidence of fair value and shall be used to measure fair value whenever available.

SFAS 157 notes that Level 1 inputs should not be used when quoted prices are not representative of fair value.

Level 2 inputs are inputs other than quoted prices included within Level 1 that are observable for the asset or liability, either directly or indirectly. If the asset or liability has a specified (contractual) term, a Level 2 input must be observable for substantially the full term of the asset or liability. Level 2 inputs include the following:

a. Quoted prices for similar assets or liabilities in active markets
b. Quoted prices for identical or similar assets or liabilities in markets that are not active—that is, markets in which there are few transactions for the asset or liability, the prices are not current, or price quotations vary substantially, either over time or among market makers (e.g., some brokered markets), or in which little information is released publicly (e.g., a principal-to-principal market)

(continued)

(Continued)

  c. Inputs other than quoted prices that are observable for the asset or liability (e.g., interest rates and yield curves observable at commonly quoted intervals, volatilities, prepayment speeds, loss severities, credit risks, and default rates)

  d. Inputs that are derived principally from or corroborated by observable market data by correlation or other means (market-corroborated inputs)

Level 3 inputs are unobservable inputs for the asset or liability. Unobservable inputs shall be used to measure fair value to the extent that observable inputs are not available, thereby allowing for situations in which there is little, if any, market activity for the asset or liability at the measurement date. However, the fair value measurement objective remains the same—that is, an exit price from the perspective of a market participant that holds the asset or owes the liability. Therefore, unobservable inputs shall reflect the reporting entity's own assumptions about the assumptions that market participants would use in pricing the asset or liability (including assumptions about risk). Unobservable inputs shall be developed based on the best information available in the circumstances, which might include the reporting entity's own data. In developing unobservable inputs, the reporting entity need not undertake all possible efforts to obtain information about market participant assumptions. However, the reporting entity shall not ignore information about market participant assumptions that is reasonably available without undue cost and effort. Therefore, the reporting entity's own data used to develop unobservable inputs shall be adjusted if information is reasonably available without undue cost and effort that indicates that market participants would use different assumptions.

Adjustments to Level 2 quoted prices and other inputs should be tailored to the specific asset or liability. These adjustments should customize any Level 2 quoted prices or other inputs to arrive at an appropriate fair value for the asset or liability. Examples of adjustments to Level 2 prices or other inputs that may be necessary include these six:

1. The condition of the asset or liability
2. The degree to which the inputs are comparable to the asset or liability
3. The volume and level of activity in the market(s) within which the inputs were observed
4. The amount of time that has lapsed since the observed transaction or other input

5. The terms of the instruments subject to the transaction

6. The existence and nature of any transactions that are related to transaction(s) being evaluated or used as inputs (i.e., is the transaction one of several related transactions, which could impact the input)

An adjustment to a Level 2 input that is significant to the final fair value measurement in its entirety can result in the conclusion that the measurement should be classified as Level 3, depending on the level in the fair value hierarchy within which the inputs used to determine the adjustment fall. For example, if significant internally developed adjustments were used to adjust a Level 2 market quote, the end result is likely a Level 3 input.

Fair Value Guidance under IFRS

As noted earlier, IFRS is not as detailed in its discussion of the methods used to determine fair value (although more detailed guidance is due out in final form in 2010). IAS 39, *Financial Instruments: Recognition and Measurement*, provides some general guidance about fair valuation techniques. The IFRS guidance is generally consistent with U.S. GAAP in that it expects fair values to be determined using the following four principles:

1. The objective is to establish what the transaction price would have been on the measurement date in an arm's length exchange motivated by normal business considerations (i.e., not a distressed transaction).

2. Valuation techniques should incorporate all factors that market participants would consider in setting a price and be consistent with accepted economic methodologies for pricing similar financial instruments.

3. In applying valuation techniques, an entity should use estimates and assumptions that are consistent with available information about the estimates and assumptions that market participants would use in determining a price.

4. The best estimate of fair value at initial recognition of a financial instrument that is not quoted in an active market is the transaction price, unless the fair value is evidenced by other observable market transactions or is based on a valuation technique whose variables include only data from observable markets.

Availability of Market Evidence

A quoted market price in an active market for an identical asset is the most representative indicator of an asset's fair value. In most instances, no further adjustment to this market price is necessary to arrive at a reliable estimate of fair value.

However, as events of 2008 illustrated, markets change, and once active markets can become less active or inactive markets. These changes impact how an entity may arrive at fair value estimates.

In September 2008 the SEC issued guidance (2008-234—see Appendix B) on determining fair values in light of the difficulties that arose in connection with the economic downturn and market volatility. In this guidance, SEC stated that when an active market for a security does not exist, the use of internal management estimates to determine fair value is appropriate. These estimates should incorporate current expectations of market participants regarding future cash flows and appropriate risk premiums.

In other words, if the market approach, using Level 1 or Level 2 inputs, once was practical but now is not, due to the market(s) becoming inactive, it is acceptable to switch to the income approach with the use of Level 2 and 3 inputs.

When management estimates of cash flows are utilized in place of quotes from active (or, more appropriately, formerly active) markets, different SFAS 157 inputs are being relied on to determine fair value (Level 3 inputs rather than Level 1 or 2). But, as the SEC points out in its guidance, unobservable Level 3 inputs can be more appropriate than observable Level 2 inputs, especially if significant adjustments would be required to the observable Level 2 inputs. In some cases, reliance on multiple inputs from a variety of sources may provide the most reliable estimate of fair value.

In October 2008, FASB issued FASB Staff Position (FSP) No. 157-3, *Determining the Fair Value of a Financial Asset When the Market for That Asset Is Not Active*. FSP 157-3 reaches the same conclusion as the SEC guidance issued a month earlier. Only FSP 157-3 applies to all entities following U.S. GAAP, unlike the SEC guidance, which is issued with respect to publicly traded companies only.

Asset-Based Schemes

Asset-based fraudulent financial reporting schemes typically involve one or more of the following seven approaches:

1. Creating phony assets, accomplished by capitalizing expenditures that should be reported as expenses or through the use of journal entries (sometimes a complex series of entries) to create an asset on the books
2. Failing to record impairment losses on legitimate assets, resulting from declines in fair values of assets below their recorded book values
3. Misclassifying unrealized losses in other comprehensive income that should be included in profit or loss
4. Using inappropriately long useful lives in connection with recording depreciation or amortization expense on long-lived assets requiring such expense, resulting in assets remaining on the books at higher book values and for longer periods than what would be appropriate
5. Misclassifying noncurrent assets as current in order to inflate an entity's current ratio
6. Misclassifying long-lived assets as nondepreciable or nonamortizable when the assets should be subject to depreciation or amortization, resulting in the recorded book value remaining on the books for longer than it would have if it were subject to depreciation or amortization
7. Fraudulently recording gains on assets that are carried at fair value.

The incentives behind each of these categories of fraud are similar—to make an entity appear to be more financially attractive than it really is. And fair value accounting plays a role in virtually every one of these schemes to varying degrees.

Before explaining specific accounting rules and the frauds that can be perpetrated based on those rules, a few general concepts and definitions are important for readers to understand.

Assets can be classified as either financial or nonfinancial assets. Generally, *financial assets* include all of the following:

- Cash
- Evidence of an ownership interest (an equity instrument) in another entity
- A contract that conveys to one entity a right to either (1) receive cash or another financial instrument from a second entity (e.g., trade accounts and notes receivable) or (2) exchange other financial assets or financial liabilities on potentially favorable terms with the second entity

The IFRS definition of financial assets includes a fourth category—certain contracts that will or may be settled in the entity's own equity instruments.

Nonfinancial assets are simply all assets that are not financial assets. Common nonfinancial assets that will be the subject of possible fair value accounting fraud issues in this section of the book include intangible assets, as well as property and equipment.

Some nonfinancial assets are classified as current assets, such as inventory. Current assets are those that are expected to be realized (i.e., converted to cash) with one year or one reporting cycle of the entity or are held primarily for the purpose of being traded (e.g., certain securities). Other assets, such as land and intangible assets, are classified as noncurrent assets.

A *financial liability* is a contract that imposes on one entity an obligation to either (1) deliver cash or another financial instrument to a second entity (e.g., accounts and notes payable) or (2) exchange other financial assets or financial liabilities on potentially unfavorable terms with the second entity. Similar to its definition of financial assets, the IFRS definition also includes certain contracts that will or may be settled in the entity's own equity instruments. Examples of financial liabilities include accounts payable, debt, and accrued liabilities.

Nonfinancial liabilities are satisfied using methods other than delivering or exchanging financial assets or financial liabilities. The most common nonfinancial liability is deferred revenue—income received in advance for which an entity has an obligation to provide services.

The term *financial instrument* is used (under both U.S. GAAP and IFRS) with respect to any contract that results in one entity gaining a financial asset while another entity gains either a financial liability or an equity instrument. The terms *financial instrument* and *financial asset* are used throughout this section of the book.

In addition, certain assets are described as long-lived assets. This description merely means that the asset is expected to last more than one year or operating cycle. Some long-lived assets are subject to depreciation or amortization, which results in the reporting of expense over the estimated useful life of the asset. For example, an asset with an estimated useful life of ten years would be capitalized and then written off to expense over the next ten years.

Other long-lived assets are not subject to depreciation or amortization. Examples of nondepreciable assets include land and certain intangible assets. Both depreciable and nondepreciable assets are potential targets for fair value accounting fraud.

Part II of this book is devoted to explaining the primary opportunities for fair value accounting fraud involving assets.

CHAPTER 4

Investments in Debt and Publicly Traded Equity Securities

The typical entity has many different investments to select from. Fair value accounting is either directly used to account for, or has an indirect effect on, the vast majority of these investments. This chapter explores the fair value implications on two of the most common investments—debt and equity securities for which there is a readily determinable market value. These are equities that are actively traded on a public market.

Scope of Investments Covered

Debt securities often provide for a fixed rate of return that is guaranteed not to fluctuate during the term of the debt. Included among the many examples of debt securities are those issued by governments and government agencies (such as the U.S. Treasury, U.S. federal agencies, states and municipalities, and non-U.S. governments and government agencies), bonds issued by corporations, mortgage-backed securities, and many others. Excluded from this definition of debt securities are trade accounts receivable resulting from sales, consumer and real estate loans of financial institutions, and other receivables not associated with a "security" (i.e., it is either traded on a market or is represented by a registered instrument and considered to be an investment).

Equity investments can include a wide range of assets, including the following five types:

1. Wholly or majority-owned subsidiary companies
2. Investments in individual equity securities that are actively traded in public markets
3. Investments in mutual funds that are publicly traded
4. Equity holdings in nonpublic companies

5. Ownership interests in noncorporate entities, such as partnerships and other forms of joint ventures

The equity securities addressed in this chapter are those that are publicly traded in active markets, such as those traded on stock exchanges. Other equity securities, which are excluded from the scope of this chapter, include these three:

1. Equity interests that are accounted for by consolidation
2. Ownership interests that are accounted for using the equity method of accounting
3. Equity interests in non–publicly traded companies that are neither consolidated nor accounted for using the equity method of accounting

Each of these categories of equity interests have their own fair value accounting issues and are addressed in Chapter 5.

Sources of U.S. GAAP and IFRS

U.S. GAAP for debt and equity investments is found in several documents. SFAS 115, *Accounting for Certain Investments in Debt and Equity Securities,* provides guidance on all debt securities, but only on equity securities that have readily determinable fair values (readily determinable is defined below). Those investments will be the sole focus of this chapter.

In addition, certain specialized industries that have their own rules on accounting for investments, such as brokers and dealers in securities and defined benefit pension plans, are excluded from the scope of SFAS 115. Not-for-profit organizations have their own counterpart to SFAS 115 in the form of SFAS 124. Accounting standards addressing other equity instruments will be introduced in Chapter 5.

IFRS for debt and unconsolidated equity securities is addressed in IAS 39, *Financial Instruments: Recognition and Measurement,* which provides a framework for the accounting for all types of financial instruments, including but not limited to investments in debt and equity securities. As a result, IAS 39 applies to all investments in this chapter, as well as those covered in Chapter 5, whereas SFAS 115 applies solely to the investments addressed in this chapter.

Under U.S. GAAP, the fair value of an equity security is considered to be "readily determinable" (and therefore included within the scope of SFAS 115) if sales prices or bid-and-asked quotations are currently available on a securities exchange registered with the SEC or in the over-the-counter market, as long as those prices or quotations for the over-the-counter market are reported publicly. Likewise, fair values of mutual funds are readily determinable if per-share amounts are published and used as a basis for trading.

The fair value of an equity security traded only in a foreign market is readily determinable if that foreign market is of a breadth and scope comparable to one of the U.S. markets.

Classification and Treatment—U.S. GAAP

Investments covered by SFAS 115 are to be classified into one of three categories:

1. *Held-to-maturity securities.* Debt securities that the holder has the intent and ability to hold to maturity. These securities are to be carried at amortized cost.
2. *Trading securities.* Debt and equity securities that are bought and held primarily for the purpose of selling them in the near term. These securities are to be reported at fair value on a recurring basis, with unrealized gains and losses included in earnings (i.e., included in profit or loss of the entity).
3. *Available-for-sale securities.* Debt and equity securities not classified as either held-to-maturity securities or trading securities. These securities are carried at fair value, with unrealized gains and losses excluded from earnings and reported in other comprehensive income rather than in profit or loss.

Each of these categories is explained further later.

Fraud Risk No. 4.1

Improper classification (or reclassification) of a security among the various categories; for example:

- A trading security misclassified as available for sale, in order to shift the reporting of unrealized losses out of profit and loss and into other comprehensive income
- An available for sale security misclassified as trading, in order to report unrealized gains in profit and loss rather than in other comprehensive income
- A debt security being misclassified as held-to-maturity when in fact management no longer intends to hold the security to maturity or considers it to be available for sale in response to changes in market conditions

Classification and Treatment—IFRS

IAS 39 requires that financial instruments, with certain exceptions, be measured at fair value on a recurring basis. Two types of investments are exempt from the requirement to record financial instruments at fair value:

1. Any held-to-maturity investment, which should be measured at amortized cost (which includes a deduction for impairment), similar to U.S. GAAP explained in the preceding section.
2. An equity security that does not have a quoted market price in an active market and whose fair value cannot be reliably measured, which should be measured at cost, subject to possible impairment if fair value is less than cost. Again, this is similar to U.S. GAAP.

In addition to held-to-maturity investments, IAS 39 identifies three other types of financial assets that will be included within the scope of this book's discussion:

1. Those designated as "*at fair value through profit or loss*" upon initial recognition
2. Those designated as available-for-sale
3. Those that are classified as loans and receivables (explained further in Chapter 6)

Each of these terms is defined in IAS 39, as summarized in the following box.

Definitions—IFRS

Paragraph 9 of IAS 39, *Financial Instruments: Recognition and Measurement,* includes the following definitions of key terms used in this chapter:

   Held-to-maturity investments—Nonderivative financial assets with fixed or determinable payments and fixed maturity that an entity has the positive intention and ability to hold to maturity other than:

a. those that the entity upon initial recognition designates as at fair value through profit or loss;
b. those that the entity designates as available for sale; and
c. those that meet the definition of loans and receivables.

An entity shall not classify any financial assets as held to maturity if the entity has, during the current financial year or during the two preceding financial years, sold or reclassified more than an insignificant amount of held-to-maturity investments before maturity (more than insignificant in relation to the total amount of held-to-maturity investments) other than sales or reclassifications that:

   i. are so close to maturity or the financial asset's call date (for example, less than three months before maturity) that changes in the market rate of interest would not have a significant effect on the financial asset's fair value;

   ii. occur after the entity has collected substantially all of the financial asset's original principal through scheduled payments or prepayments; or

   iii. are attributable to an isolated event that is beyond the entity's control, is non-recurring and could not have been reasonably anticipated by the entity.

    Financial asset or financial liability at fair value through profit or loss—A financial asset or financial liability that meets either of the following conditions:

   a. It is classified as held for trading. A financial asset or financial liability is classified as held for trading if it is:

      i. acquired or incurred principally for the purpose of selling or repurchasing it in the near term;

      ii. part of a portfolio of identified financial instruments that are managed together and for which there is evidence of a recent actual pattern of short-term profit-taking; or

      iii. a derivative (except for a derivative that is a financial guarantee contract or a designated and effective hedging instrument). *Note:* Derivatives are explained further in Chapter 15.

   b. Upon initial recognition it is designated by the entity as at fair value through profit or loss. An entity may use this designation only when permitted by paragraph 11A [which deals with embedded derivatives] or when doing so results in more relevant information, because either

      i. it eliminates or significantly reduces a measurement or recognition inconsistency (sometimes referred to as 'an accounting mismatch') that would otherwise arise from measuring assets or liabilities or recognizing the gains and losses on them on different bases; or

(continued)

ii. a group of financial assets, financial liabilities or both is managed and its performance is evaluated on a fair value basis, in accordance with a documented risk management or investment strategy, and information about the group is provided internally on that basis to the entity's key management personnel (as defined in IAS 24 *Related Party Disclosures*, revised in 2003)—for example, the entity's board of directors and chief executive officer.

In IFRS 7, paragraphs 9 to 11 and B4 require the entity to provide disclosures about financial assets and financial liabilities it has designated as at fair value through profit or loss, including how it has satisfied these conditions. For instruments qualifying in accordance with (ii) above, that disclosure includes a narrative description of how designation as at fair value through profit or loss is consistent with the entity's documented risk management or investment strategy.

Investments in equity instruments that do not have a quoted market price in an active market, and whose fair value cannot be reliably measured (see paragraph 46(c) and Appendix A paragraphs AG80 and AG81), shall not be designated as at fair value through profit or loss.

Available-for-sale financial assets—Non-derivative financial assets that are designated as available for sale or are not classified as

a. loans and receivables,
b. held-to-maturity investments or
c. financial assets at fair value through profit or loss.

An investment that has the characteristics of a held-to-maturity investment is not required to be classified as such (i.e., it can be treated as at fair value through profit or loss). This classification is an election made by management.

The "at fair value through profit or loss" classification is a designation that management may assign to any financial asset, provided the described criteria are met. Included in this category are *trading securities,* which are securities acquired for the principal purpose of selling them in the near future, defined similarly as under U.S. GAAP.

As the term suggests, "at fair value through profit or loss" means that an investment is carried at its fair value, which may be greater than or less

TABLE 4.1 Carrying Amounts of Investments

Category of Investment	U.S. GAAP	IFRS
Held-to-maturity debt securities	C/F	C/F
Trading securities	F	F
Available for sale	F [1]	F [1]

C = Amortized cost
F = Fair value
C/F = Cost, but with the option for carrying at fair value
[1]Unlike other investments carried at fair value, unrealized gains and losses on available-for-sale investments are not reported in profit and loss, but, instead are reported in other comprehensive income.

than its original purchase price or other basis. Any unrealized gains or losses due to appreciation or depreciation in fair value are reported in the income statement of the owner.

Unrealized gains and losses on available-for-sale instruments, however, are not reported in profit and loss (consistent with U.S. GAAP). Instead, they are classified in other comprehensive income.

Held-to-maturity financial assets are to be measured at amortized cost using the effective interest method.

See Table 4.1 for a summary how each category of investment is measured under U.S. GAAP and IFRS.

The Effective Interest Method

Paragraph 9 of IAS 39 defines the ***effective interest method*** as a method of calculating the amortized cost of a financial asset or a financial liability (or group of financial assets or financial liabilities) and of allocating the interest income or interest expense over the relevant period. The *effective interest rate* is the rate that exactly discounts estimated future cash payments or receipts through the expected life of the financial instrument or, when appropriate, a shorter period to the net carrying amount of the financial asset or financial liability. When calculating the effective interest rate, an entity shall estimate cash flows considering all contractual terms of the financial instrument (for example, prepayment, call and similar options) but shall not consider future credit losses. The calculation includes all fees and points paid or received between parties to the contract that are an integral part of the effective interest rate (see IAS 18 *Revenue*), transaction costs, and

(continued)

all other premiums or discounts. There is a presumption that the cash flows and the expected life of a group of similar financial instruments can be estimated reliably. However, in those rare cases when it is not possible to estimate reliably the cash flows or the expected life of a financial instrument (or group of financial instruments), the entity shall use the contractual cash flows over the full contractual term of the financial instrument (or group of financial instruments).

Reclassifications in General

As the preceding discussion indicates, which category an investment is classified in can have a significant impact on an entity's reported financial position and earnings. Accordingly, reclassifications between categories can have a major impact on financial statements.

Under U.S. GAAP, reclassifications of investments from one category to another are permissible, although SFAS 115 points out that transfers from the held-to-maturity category should be rare (see the earlier discussion of factors to consider in reclassifying securities from the held-to-maturity category).

The transfer of a security between categories must be accounted for at fair value on the date of reclassification. Recognition of unrealized gains and losses must conform to the new category when such transfers are done. For example, for a security transferred into the trading category, the portion of the unrealized holding gain or loss at the date of the transfer that has not been previously recognized in earnings shall be recognized in earnings immediately.

Recall from Chapter 2 that SFAS 159 also introduced a fair value option that permits most financial assets, including all of those covered in this chapter, to be carried at fair value on a recurring basis. The SFAS 159 election can be made on an instrument-by-instrument basis. However, once made, the fair value option is irrevocable (i.e., an investment, or any other financial asset, cannot be reclassified out of the fair value category).

IAS 39 was amended in October 2008 (retroactive to July 1, 2008) to align its reclassification provisions with those of SFAS 115, despite the fact that the general consensus has been that the reclassification provisions of U.S. GAAP were inferior to the stricter provisions that IAS 39 contained prior to these amendments.

Under the revised standard, a financial instrument cannot be reclassified out of the fair value through profit or loss category if it was classified there when it was first recognized under the fair value option. This is similar to the SFAS 159 provision stating that once a fair value option is elected, it is permanent for that instrument.

However, recall from the earlier discussion that a financial instrument can be classified as at fair value through profit or loss, either upon initial recognition or if it is classified as "held for trading." This is where the amendments to IAS 39 mirror the provisions of U.S. GAAP, but also caused a bit of a controversy.

If an asset is no longer being held for the purpose of selling it in the near term (i.e., a "trading" security), it can be reclassified out of the fair value through profit or loss category (potentially reclassifying its unrealized losses from profit or loss to other comprehensive income) if the entity is experiencing "rare circumstances." The global financial crisis could be considered one of these rare circumstances.

Derivatives may never be reclassified out of the fair value through profit or loss category.

The October 2008 revisions to IAS 39 have drawn much criticism. In its December 2008 issue of *Moody's Global Credit Research*, Moody's Investors Service, Inc. criticized the IASB for not subjecting the amendments to its normal due process, claiming that "in perception (if not reality), the IASB caved to the will of EU leaders and finance ministers in quickly pushing through the amendments." Indeed, members of the European Union pressured the IASB to make these changes, feeling that the weaker U.S. GAAP provisions placed European companies at a competitive disadvantage against U.S. companies during the global economic crisis.

Prior to the October 2008 amendment, IAS 39 prohibited the reclassification of a financial instrument into or out of the fair value through profit or loss category while it is held or issued (with the exception of reclassifications out of the held-to-maturity category into available for sale).

The fraud risk here is clear. If a decline in fair value is recognized, it can be classified in one of two places in the financial statements: as a component of profit or loss or in other comprehensive income. Mischaracterizing a security can result in misclassification of the unrealized loss (or unrealized gains for that matter, but the greater risk is with respect to the risk of attempts to hide declines in value of assets held).

Reclassifications from the Held-to-Maturity Category

Under both U.S. GAAP and IFRS, investments in debt securities should be classified as held-to-maturity (and therefore measured at amortized cost unless the fair value option has been elected) only if the reporting entity has the positive intent and ability to hold those securities to maturity. Equity securities generally cannot be classified as held-to-maturity because they do not have a fixed maturity date.

Despite initial intentions, an entity's plans to hold a debt security to maturity may change over time. And, as explained in the preceding section, this change can result in a reclassification of the investment to another category, such as the trading category, which would require a change in carrying amount and possibly a change in how unrealized gains and losses are reported.

The following box provides examples of conditions that could affect an entity's intent regarding holding a debt security until its maturity.

Factors Impacting Whether an Entity Will Hold a Security to Maturity

Paragraph 8 of SFAS 115 provides the following list of conditions that could cause an entity to change its intent regarding holding a particular security to maturity without necessarily raising similar questions for other debt securities:

a. Evidence of a significant deterioration in the issuer's credit-worthiness

b. A change in tax law that eliminates or reduces the tax-exempt status of interest on the debt security (but not a change in tax law that revises the marginal tax rates applicable to interest income)

c. A major business combination or major disposition (such as sale of a component of an entity) that necessitates the sale or transfer of held-to-maturity securities to maintain the enterprise's existing interest rate risk position or credit risk policy

d. A change in statutory or regulatory requirements significantly modifying either what constitutes a permissible investment or the maximum level of investments in certain kinds of securities, thereby causing an enterprise to dispose of a held-to-maturity security

e. A significant increase by the regulator in the industry's capital requirements that causes the enterprise to downsize by selling held-to-maturity securities

f. A significant increase in the risk weights of debt securities used for regulatory risk-based capital purposes

Of course, this list is not meant to be all-inclusive. Other unanticipated events may also cause an entity to sell or transfer one particular held-to-maturity security without necessarily raising doubts about its intent to hold other debt securities to maturity.

Reclassifying a security, or electing not to reclassify a security, in a changing economic climate requires much judgment. But it also is an area that is ripe for fraud in the form of misrepresenting an entity's intent to hold or not hold a particular debt security until it matures.

In some cases, the best evidence of whether positions taken in financial statements are proper is past history. In past financial statements, when management has asserted that certain securities would or would not be held to maturity, did this subsequently prove to be true? But the global economic crisis of 2009 is a completely different set of circumstances, and one that makes such judgments even more difficult.

Sales of Held-to-Maturity Securities

Paragraph 9 of SFAS 115 states that a particular debt security should not be categorized as held-to-maturity if it would be available to be sold in response to any of the following:

a. Changes in market interest rates and related changes in the security's prepayment risk
b. Needs for liquidity (e.g., due to the withdrawal of deposits, increased demand for loans, surrender of insurance policies, or payment of insurance claims)
c. Changes in the availability of and the yield on alternative investments
d. Changes in funding sources and terms
e. Changes in foreign currency risk

Finally, if an entity frequently sells debt securities prior to maturity, or has recently sold a significant number of held-to-maturity securities prior to their maturities, this can cast doubt on the entity's ability or intent to hold its remaining securities until maturity. Frequent sales prior to maturity should be followed up with a careful review of the classification of all other debt securities.

Fraud Risk No. 4.2

Failing to reclassify a debt security out of the held-to-maturity category despite selling certain other debt securities prior to maturity.

Determination of Fair Value

For equity securities covered by SFAS 115, fair value should be easy to determine. Since the only equities covered are those with readily determinable fair values, it is simply a matter of researching the trading price of a security on a particular date.

For debt securities, some may be publicly traded, while many will not. For those that are publicly traded, researching their trading price as of the desired date is conducted, just like with publicly traded equities.

For debt securities that are not publicly traded, there are a variety of pricing techniques used to determine fair value. In many cases a reasonable estimate of fair value can be determined using discounted cash flow analysis, matrix pricing, option-adjusted spread models, and fundamental analysis. The selection of a specific technique and the application of that technique require judgment. The techniques used to value a debt security carried as an asset are basically the same as those used to determine fair value of a debt obligation carried as a liability (see Chapter 11).

Fraud Risk No. 4.3

Manipulating the determination of fair value of a debt security by utilizing inappropriate discount rates in the calculation of present value.

Debt securities will have a coupon interest rate. Interest payments will be based on the coupon rate multiplied by the face value of the security. For example, a $100,000 security with a 5 percent coupon rate paid annually would result in a $5,000 payment each year.

But fair value is not necessarily equal to the face value of $100,000. Depending on market conditions at the time the security was purchased, the buyer may have paid more or less than $100,000. As a result, the debt security's yield to maturity may differ from its coupon rate of interest.

There are a variety of factors that have an impact on a debt security's yield to maturity, expressed as various categories of risk. Three of the most important are the following:

1. *Default risk.* This is the risk that the issuer/borrower will fail to pay some or all of a debt obligation. The primary factor impacting default risk is the financial condition of the issuer/borrower. Default risk falls under the category of nonperformance risk, one of the risk factors required to be considered under SFAS 157. Default risk may be mitigated based on the existence, nature, and liquidation value of collateral. Uncollateralized debt will usually carry a greater risk than collateralized debt. With collateralized debt, its fair value is usually at least equal to the liquidation value of the underlying assets that have been pledged as collateral. Of course, determining the liquidation value of the underlying assets may not always be a simple task.
2. *Interest rate risk.* This is the risk associated with changes in interest rates over time. If market rates of interest increase to levels in excess of a debt security's coupon rate of interest, the trading price of a bond decreases, and vice versa. When determining market rates of interest, rates should be located for debt securities that are as similar as possible to the debt security being evaluated in terms of amount and maturity dates, as well as other relevant factors.
3. *Call risk.* A call feature enables the issuer to repay an obligation prior to its due date. Call risk represents the likelihood of such a call feature being exercised, which would impact the value of the debt to market participants.

After considering these factors, it may be concluded that the yield to maturity is greater than or less than a debt security's coupon rate, resulting in a different fair value, generally as follows:

If Coupon rate > Yield to maturity, then Fair value > Face value
If Yield to maturity > Coupon rate, then Face value > Fair value

In assessing the fair value of debt securities, interest rate risk is perhaps the easiest to measure, since there is often a plethora of pertinent data available from active markets from which to draw a comparison. It is the other risk factors that make fair value determinations of non–publicly traded debt securities interesting.

From an investment management perspective, a version of this fair value, or yield-to-maturity, calculation is done in connection with initially purchasing a debt security to determine what a fair purchase price would be. Subsequent to the acquisition of the security, however, determination of fair value can be trickier.

Effective Interest Method Illustrated

Consider the following example of the effective interest method:

Assume a debt security with a face value of $100,000 bearing a coupon rate of interest of 5 percent paid annually is purchased for $103,248. This results in a yield to maturity rate of 4.265 percent. The entity records this asset at its cost of $103,248, which equals its fair value at the date of acquisition. Under the effective interest method, amortization and interest income recognition would be as follows:

Beginning Balance	Interest Income	Interest Receipt	Ending Balance
103,248	4,404	5,000	102,652
102,652	4,378	5,000	102,030
102,030	4,351	5,000	101,381
101,381	4,324	5,000	100,705
100,705	4,295	5,000	100,000

The entity would recognize interest income each year at 4.265 percent (e.g., $4,404 in the first year), not at the 5 percent coupon rate. The $5,000 per year interest received would offset the interest accruals, resulting in an amortized balance of $100,000 on the day that the debt security matures. On this date, the entity should receive the face amount of $100,000.

But as interest rates change during the five-year period, or other risk factors change, what does this do to the fair value of the security? If the fair value option of SFAS 159 is elected, these changes would have to be considered in determining fair value.

As with other fair value determinations, information used to calculate the fair value of debt securities may be internally generated or come from outside sources (i.e., observable versus unobservable inputs, using the SFAS 157 terminology). In some cases, a similar debt security that is publicly traded may be identified that can be useful in estimating fair value of a non–publicly traded security. In other cases, the discounted cash flow methodology summarized in the preceding paragraphs would be a more appropriate and reliable estimate of fair value.

Active versus Inactive Markets

The global economic crisis of 2009 has raised an issue that hasn't been seen on a wide scale for many years. Recall that SFAS 157 makes a distinction between various inputs used in determining fair value. The most reliable inputs are usually those that are the result of active markets, such as stock prices quoted in public markets. These inputs are most reliable because of two simple factors:

1. They come from external sources rather than being developed internally by management.
2. They involve numerous market participants (this is what makes the market "active").

But what happens when a once-active market turns inactive? How, then, should management develop estimates of fair value? With a less active market, the few known transactions in the market may not be representative of the true fair value of a particular asset or liability.

In late 2008, FASB addressed this issue with the release of FSP FAS 157-3. As one would expect, the guidance suggests that when a market becomes inactive, two changes may need to be made to the process of estimating fair value:

1. Switching from the market approach to another approach, likely the income approach (because the market approach may result in a greater need to make significant adjustments due to the reduced volume of activity)
2. Using entirely different inputs, likely changing from level 1 or 2 inputs to level 2 or 3 inputs

This change introduces another opportunity for fraud. Recall that level 3 inputs are "unobservable," meaning they are developed internally by management.

Fraud Risk No. 4.4

False representations about whether a market is active or inactive, or about whether known market transactions used for comparison purposes were "orderly" or not orderly, resulting in use of inappropriate values, valuation methods, or inputs to manipulate a fair value measurement.

Accountants, auditors, and investigators should be on the lookout for indications that a once-active market has become less active or inactive. The most obvious sign of this is a significant decrease in trading volume on the markets. Another sign may be a widening in the difference between bid and ask prices.

FSP 157-3 provides an illustration of changing from the market approach to the income approach, using a collateralized debt obligation security as its example. But the process would be similar regardless of the nature of the security:

1. If in the past market prices were available for identical assets, determine whether there is evidence of quoted market prices for similar assets.
2. Determine the availability of reliable inputs that could be used to make an adjustment from the quoted prices for similar assets (or dated prices for identical assets).
3. Identify changes in market factors and inputs since the date of the most recent active market quotations, such as market rates of interest, implied rates of return, and so on.
4. Identify and review any relevant reports from analysts or ratings agencies, such as Moody's.
5. For collateralized securities, review the performance of the underlying collateral (e.g., mortgage loans, etc.).

Maximizing the use of inputs that come from external sources generally results in a more reliable estimate. And remember—the goal in determining fair values under SFAS 157 is to estimate the assumptions that market participants would use to estimate fair value as of the measurement date.

In April 2009, additional guidance on the issue of declining activity in a market was provided in the form of FSP FAS 157-4, *Determining Fair Value When the Volume and Level of Activity for the Asset or Liability Have Significantly Decreased and Identifying Transactions That Are Not Orderly*. This FSP reinforces the basic objective of fair value determinations—that the fair value of an asset when a market is no longer active remains the price that the asset would be sold for in an orderly transaction. This can be tricky when there are fewer and fewer market transactions to use as a basis for valuing an asset—were the few transactions available for comparison done in an orderly or a not orderly manner? The fact that a market is not active does not by itself result in an assumption of a distressed or forced liquidation (i.e., not orderly) sale. The FSP states that the determination of whether other, known, transactions in a market were orderly or not orderly, for purposes of comparisons with assets held by an entity, should be based on the weight of all available evidence. The FSP also provides guidance on determining whether a market has become inactive, as well as on whether a transaction is orderly or not orderly.

Temporary versus Other-than-Temporary Impairments—U.S. GAAP

Realized gains and losses, which occur once a security is sold, are always included in the profits or losses of a company. Unrealized gains and losses, however, can be treated either as part of profit and loss or may be excluded from profit and loss and shown as other comprehensive income. One of the determinants of where unrealized losses are reported is the category of investment, as explained earlier (e.g., available-for-sale, trading, etc.). But another factor is whether a loss is considered to be temporary or other-than-temporary.

SFAS 115 requires that declines in fair value below carrying value be classified as temporary or other-than-temporary. The term *other-than-temporary* is not meant to be synonymous with permanent—it is designed to distinguish certain declines from those that are temporary. An impairment in value need not be considered permanent in order to be classified as other-than-temporary. Several factors should be considered in determining whether a decline in fair value is temporary or other-than-temporary. This is a complicated issue, and one that has been addressed in several documents:

> FSP FAS 115-1 and 124-1, *The Meaning of Other-Than-Temporary Impairment and Its Application to Certain Investments*
> FSP FAS 115-2 and FAS 124-2, *Recognition and Presentation of Other-Than-Temporary Impairments* (issued in April 2009)
> EITF 03-1, *The Meaning of Other-Than-Temporary Impairment and Its Application to Certain Investments*
> EITF 99-20, *Recognition of Interest Income and Impairment on Purchased Beneficial Interests and Beneficial Interests That Continue to Be Held by a Transferor in Securitized Financial Assets*
> FSP EITF 99-20-1, *Amendments to the Impairment Guidance of EITF Issue No. 99-20* (issued in January 2009)
> SEC Staff Accounting Bulletin 59, *Accounting for Noncurrent Marketable Equity Securities*
> SAS 92, *Auditing Derivative Instruments, Hedging Activities, and Investments in Securities*

Fraud Risk No. 4.5

Improperly treating a decline in fair value as a temporary impairment when it should be treated as other-than-temporary.

Why is this distinction important? Because if a decline in fair value is considered to be other-than-temporary, the cost basis of the security must be written down to its reduced fair value (it is the income statement equivalent of recognizing a loss on a security that has been sold, only the entity still holds this security). The write-down must be reported in earnings for the period in which the impairment is deemed to be other-than-temporary. And the write-down in basis is permanent—meaning that subsequent recoveries in fair value would not be recognized unless the security is sold (unless fair value treatment has been elected).

Making the determination of whether a decline is temporary or not requires much judgment and the careful consideration of many factors. This, of course, means that it can be susceptible to fraud.

Ten factors must be considered in making the determination of whether an impairment loss is other-than-temporary:

1. The length of time (duration) and extent to which the security's fair value has been less than its cost (i.e., the severity and magnitude of the impairment)
2. The financial condition and near-term prospects of the issuer, including any known events that have occurred
3. The intent and ability of the holder to retain its investment for a period of time that is long enough to allow for an expected recovery in fair value (i.e., even if a security can be expected to subsequently increase in value, can the entity afford to hold onto it for that long?)
4. The implied and historical volatility of the security
5. Whether the decline in fair value was affected by macroeconomic conditions or by specific information pertaining to an individual security (declines attributable to adverse conditions that are related to a specific issuer, industry, or geographic area are considered to be stronger indicators that an impairment is other-than-temporary than conditions such as uncertainty regarding a category of investment or other marketwide factors)
6. Downgrades by rating agencies or negative reports by analysts
7. Reductions or elimination of expected dividend payments
8. Missing interest payments or scheduled repayments of principal
9. Write-downs in fair value of the liability by the issuer of debt securities (see Chapter 11 for an explanation of fair value accounting for debt obligations of issuers)
10. Modifications in the report issued by the independent auditors of the issuer (e.g., going concern issues, departures from GAAP or IFRS)

See also the next section on impairment losses under IFRS, since factors described in IAS 39 relative to impairment losses may also apply to the U.S.

GAAP distinction between temporary and other-than-temporary declines in fair value.

The Effect of FSP FAS 115-2 and FAS 124-2

In April 2009, FASB issued FSP FAS 115-2 and FAS 124-2, *Recognition and Presentation of Other-Than-Temporary Impairments*. This document modifies the criteria for determining whether an impairment loss is other-than-temporary. The modification applies solely to the consideration of debt securities. The FSP eliminates the prior requirement that to avoid recognizing an other-than-temporary impairment loss an entity must demonstrate both the intent and ability to hold the debt security for a sufficient period of time for the loss to be recovered with subsequent increases in fair value. Instead, a loss must be treated as other-than-temporary only if one of the following two conditions is present:

1. The entity has the intent to sell the debt security.
2. More likely than not, the entity will be required to sell the security prior to a recovery in its fair value.

This modification of the criteria means that instead of having to prove that a debt security will be held long enough for a loss to reverse itself, it is assumed that the security can be held long enough for the reversal to occur unless evidence exists that the security will be sold prior to the reversal. This loosening of the rules likely will result in fewer unrealized losses being recognized as other-than-temporary.

The primary fraud risk in this area is that financial statements could be issued that classify impairment losses as temporary, when in fact they should be classified as other-than-temporary. The objective of such a fraud is obvious—moving unrealized losses off the income statement so that earnings ratios are not adversely impacted by the losses.

In connection with this classification issue, the opportunity for fraud may be elevated when more subjective, less objective, data are being used as the basis for the classification. For example, from the preceding list of factors to consider, the duration and severity of an impairment can usually be clearly and objectively determined, as would rating agency downgrades, missing dividend or interest payments, and modifications to auditor's reports.

Many of the other factors, however, require quite a bit of judgment. And that is where the potential for fraud becomes greater. The third factor in particular, evaluating an entity's intent and ability to hold on to an investment until the impairment in value reverses itself, can be especially difficult to do.

Impairment Losses—IFRS

Whereas U.S. GAAP makes a distinction between temporary and other-than-temporary declines in fair value, IFRS makes a similar distinction between impairment losses and other unrealized losses due to temporary fluctuations in fair value. And the consequences are similar. Gains and losses on available-for-sale assets are generally recognized on other comprehensive income, not in profit or loss. However, if the loss is considered to be an impairment, the loss is to be recognized in profit or loss.

Impairment Loss Indicators

Under paragraph 59 of IAS 39, a financial asset or a group of financial assets is impaired, and impairment losses are incurred if, and only if, there is objective evidence of impairment as a result of one or more events that occurred after the initial recognition of the asset (a *loss event*) and that loss event (or events) has an impact on the estimated future cash flows of the financial asset or group of financial assets that can be reliably estimated. It may not be possible to identify a single, discrete event that caused the impairment. Rather, the combined effect of several events may have caused the impairment. Losses expected as a result of future events, no matter how likely, are not recognized. Objective evidence that a financial asset or group of assets is impaired includes observable data that comes to the attention of the holder of the asset about the following loss events:

a. significant financial difficulty of the issuer or obligor;
b. a breach of contract, such as a default or delinquency in interest or principal payments;
c. the lender, for economic or legal reasons relating to the borrower's financial difficulty, granting to the borrower a concession that the lender would not otherwise consider;

d. it becoming probable that the borrower will enter bankruptcy or other financial reorganization;

e. the disappearance of an active market for that financial asset because of financial difficulties; or

f. observable data indicating that there is a measurable decrease in the estimated future cash flows from a group of financial assets since the initial recognition of those assets, although the decrease cannot yet be identified with the individual financial assets in the group, including:

  i. adverse changes in the payment status of borrowers in the group (e.g., an increased number of delayed payments or an increased number of credit card borrowers who have reached their credit limit and are paying the minimum monthly amount); or

  ii. national or local economic conditions that correlate with defaults on the assets in the group (e.g., an increase in the unemployment rate in the geographical area of the borrowers, a decrease in property prices for mortgages in the relevant area, a decrease in oil prices for loan assets to oil producers, or adverse changes in industry conditions that affect the borrowers in the group).

The fact that a once-active market is no longer active is not, by itself, evidence that an impairment has been incurred.

Once an impairment loss on an equity security classified as available for sale has been recognized in profit or loss, it cannot be reversed through profit or loss.

Debt securities classified as available for sale, however, are treated differently. If subsequent increases in fair value can be objectively related to an event that occurred after the impairment loss was recognized, the loss can be reversed through profit or loss.

Summary of Fraud Risks

This chapter has dealt with some of the most complicated rules involving fair value accounting. In summary, another way of looking at the many methods of perpetrating fair value accounting fraud in the complicated area of debt and equity securities is to categorize the approaches as follows:

- Overstating gains resulting from increases in fair values of securities
- Recognizing but understating losses resulting from declines in fair values of securities
- Failing to recognize any loss on a security that has declined in value
- Misclassifying gains or losses from changes in fair value, based on misclassifying the underlying security, changing the security's classification, or improperly characterizing the nature of a decline in fair value as temporary

CHAPTER 5

Ownership Interests
in Nonpublic Entities

In addition to debt securities and publicly traded equities, an entity may hold other types of investments, including these three:

1. Equity interests in non–publicly traded corporations
2. Ownership interests in noncorporate entities, such as partnerships and joint ventures
3. Nonfinancial assets, such as land, buildings, property, and so on held as investment property

The focus of this chapter is on the first two categories—ownership interests that fall outside the scope of the publicly traded companies covered in Chapter 4. See Chapter 10 for a discussion of the accounting for land and buildings held as investment property.

Sources of U.S. GAAP and IFRS

U.S. GAAP covering the accounting for ownership interests is found in quite a few standards and other documents. Those with the most frequent application include the following:

ARB 51, *Consolidated Financial Statements*
FIN 46R, *Consolidation: Variable Interest Entities*
APB No. 18, *The Equity Method of Accounting for Investments in Common Stock*
SOP 78-9, *Accounting for Investments in Real Estate Ventures*
EITF 00-1, *Investor Balance Sheet and Income Statement Display Under the Equity Method for Investments in Certain Partnerships and Other Ventures*

EITF 02-14, *Whether an Investor Should Apply the Equity Method of Accounting to Investments Other than Common Stock*
EITF 03-16, *Accounting for Investments in Limited Liability Companies*
EITF 04-5, *Determining Whether a General Partner, or General Partners as a Group, Controls a Limited Partnership or Similar Entity When the Limited Partners Have Certain Rights*

The primary source of IFRS for the ownership interests addressed in this chapter is identical to the standard that applied in Chapter 4—IAS 39, *Financial Instruments: Recognition and Measurement*—which provides a framework for the accounting for all types of financial instruments. Two other standards under IFRS also have application to this chapter's discussion:

IAS 28, *Investments in Associates*
IAS 31, *Interests in Joint Ventures*

Introduction

In terms of ownership interests in non–publicly traded corporations and in noncorporate entities, there are many similarities between U.S. GAAP and IFRS and a few differences. Both U.S. GAAP and IFRS have rules dealing with consolidations of certain corporate and noncorporate entities that are controlled by another entity. In addition, use of the equity method of accounting is required for certain nonconsolidated entities over which an entity exercises substantial influence.

Table 5.1 summarizes the basic accounting treatments associated with various levels of ownership and control under both U.S. GAAP and IFRS.

Neither consolidated investments nor equity method investments are carried at fair value under U.S. GAAP or IFRS—at least not directly. However, there are certainly indirect fair value accounting implications and fraud risks (not to mention that equity method investment holdings are also eligible for the fair value accounting option). The fair value accounting fraud issues lie

TABLE 5.1 Accounting for Various Levels of Ownership Interests

Nature of Equity Interest	Treatment
Controlling financial interest	Consolidation
Significant influence over the entity	Equity method w/fair value option
Nonpublic entities w/o significant influence	Cost w/fair value option
Publicly traded companies	Fair value (see Chapter 4)

not in whether consolidation or the equity method of accounting was or was not applied. It is easy to determine from a set of financial statements whether holdings in other entities have been consolidated or whether the equity method of accounting has been used. Rather, it is in the accounts of the underlying entity over which the reporting has control or influence where the risk of fraud exists.

Accordingly, rather than explain the circumstances under which consolidation or the equity method should be utilized, let's focus on how a fair value accounting fraud would be perpetrated under each of these methods of accounting.

Consolidated Financial Statements

In a consolidation, the assets, liabilities, revenues, expenses, gains, and losses of the controlled entity (often called the subsidiary) are included in the financial statements of the parent company. Intercompany transactions and balances are eliminated.

In a consolidation, the risk of fair value accounting fraud is obvious—the assets, liabilities, revenues, expenses, gains, and losses of the subsidiary entity are subject to all of the exact same types of fair value accounting frauds that are explained throughout this book.

Jointly Controlled Entities versus Jointly Controlled Assets

IAS 31 *Interests in Joint Ventures* defines a jointly controlled entity as a joint venture that involves the establishment of a corporation, partnership or other entity in which each venturer has an interest. The entity operates in the same way as other entities, except that a contractual arrangement between the venturers establishes joint control over the economic activity of the entity. Under IFRS, a venturer may recognize its interest in a jointly controlled entity using either of two methods:

1. Proportionate consolidation
2. The equity method of accounting

Proportionate consolidation, explained later, represents a difference between IFRS and U.S. GAAP. Unlike IFRS, which permits proportionate consolidation for all joint ventures, U.S. GAAP shies away from proportionate consolidation, permitting it only in very limited instances and for certain industries. Equity method accounting is the norm for most joint ventures under U.S. GAAP.

Fraud Risk No. 5.1

Overstating the value of assets, or understating liabilities, of a joint venture accounted for using proportionate consolidation or proportionate recognition of individual assets that are jointly held by venturers, resulting in proportionately overstated assets on the financial statements of each partner in the venture.

However, a jointly controlled entity differs from an arrangement in which multiple entities jointly own and control assets contributed to, or acquired for the purpose of, the joint venture. With jointly controlled assets, a separate entity does not exist. Rather, two or more venturers jointly control a group of assets that are used for their benefit. In most of these arrangements, each venturer often takes a proportionate share of the output from the assets, and each bears an agreed share of the expenses incurred (as distinguished from each having a share of the net profit or loss, which is how most joint ventures are structured).

These types of joint ventures do not involve the establishment of a separate corporation, partnership, or other entity, or a financial structure that is separate from the venturers themselves. Each venturer has control over its share of future economic benefits through its share of the jointly controlled assets.

In the case of interests in jointly controlled assets, IFRS requires that each venturer recognize five items in its financial statements:

1. Its share of the jointly controlled assets, classified according to the nature of the assets
2. Any liabilities that it has incurred
3. Its share of any liabilities incurred jointly with the other venturers in relation to the joint venture
4. Any income from the sale or use of its share of the output of the joint venture, together with its share of any expenses incurred by the joint venture
5. Any expenses that it has incurred in respect of its interest in the joint venture

The fraud risk here is, once again, obvious. If the individual assets that are jointly controlled are overstated through the misapplication of fair value accounting, then the proportionate share of those assets on the financial statements of each venture will, in turn, also be overstated. The same is true with the understatement of liabilities.

Equity Method Investments

The fair value accounting fraud potential of the equity method may not be quite so obvious. Under the equity method of accounting, the holder maintains an asset account to reflect its investment in the other entity. Generally, that asset is measured based on the percentage of the equity it holds in the other entity, plus or minus certain adjustments. An income statement account is reported that generally reflects the holder's percentage interest in the profits or losses of the other entity. The entity in which the holder has an interest may be a corporation, partnership, or other form of entity.

Take the following simple example. Assume that Company A has $10 million of assets and $6 million of liabilities. One of Company A's owners is Company B. Company B owns 30 percent of the outstanding stock of Company A and utilizes the equity method of accounting to account for its investment in Company A.

As a result, Company B would report a $1.2 million asset for its investment in A (net assets of $4 million times 30 percent). If during the next year Company A made a $1 million profit, and ended the year with total assets of $10.5 million and total liabilities of $5.5 million at year-end, Company B would report a $300,000 income item in its income statement ($1 million times 30 percent) and a $1.5 million investment balance at year-end (net assets of $5 million times 30 percent).

The fair value fraud potential again lies at the investee level (Company A in the preceding example). If the assets, revenues, or gains of the business are overstated, or its liabilities, expenses, or losses are understated, as a result of a fair value accounting fraud, then the owner's financial statements will, in turn, reflect an inflated asset account and an inflated income statement effect. Intentional manipulation of the fair value accounting rules at Company A will result in misstatements in the financial statements of Company B.

Fraud Risk No. 5.2

Inflating the value of assets, or understating liabilities, of a joint venture accounted for by the equity method of accounting, resulting in an overstated asset on the financial statements of the partner in the venture.

The next question becomes, at whose direction were the fair value accounting frauds at Company A perpetrated? Remember, Company B has a

30 percent interest in A and, therefore, substantial influence over it. Could it be that Company B directed the fair value accounting fraud at Company A so that its own financial statements would appear stronger, and with a less obvious manipulation?

When the equity method of accounting is utilized with respect to joint ventures, the financial statements of those businesses should be reviewed carefully for the same signs of fair value accounting frauds as those that could be perpetrated at the owner/parent level.

For more on the equity method of accounting, see APB No. 18 and IAS 31.

Proportionate Consolidation

Somewhere between consolidation and the equity method of accounting is one additional method of accounting. Though its application is limited, in certain instances the proportionate consolidation method is used.

Under the proportionate consolidation method, the holder of an interest in another business reports its proportionate share of the assets, liabilities, revenues, expenses, gains, and losses of the other entity. In the example used in the preceding section, Company B, the 30 percent owner of Company A, would not reflect a single asset equal to 30 percent of the net assets/equity of Company A as it did under the equity method. Under the proportionate consolidation method, Company B would report separate assets each equal to 30 percent of each of the assets of A, and liabilities equal to 30 percent of each of B's liabilities, and so on (likewise with revenues and expenses).

Under the proportionate consolidation method, the fair value accounting fraud risk is similar to those explained earlier. If Company A's assets are overstated due to fair value accounting fraud, Company B's proportionately consolidated assets (30 percent) would also be overstated.

Fair Value Option

As indicated earlier, under both U.S. GAAP (SFAS 159) and IFRS (IAS 39), an ownership interest in another entity may be carried at fair value on a recurring basis. Thus, an ownership interest that would otherwise be carried at cost or using the equity method of accounting may be carried at fair value if sufficient information is available to make such a fair value measurement.

Fraud Risk No. 5.3

Electing fair value accounting treatment for a noncontrolling ownership interest that might otherwise be accounted for at cost or by using the equity method, and then misapplying a valuation method to inflate the carrying amount of the investment.

In most instances, if fair value treatment is elected for non–publicly traded ownership interests, such as those discussed in this chapter, the income approach, or some variation thereof, will be used to measure fair value. As explained in Chapter 3, a fraudulent application of the income approach could involve manipulation of several factors, most commonly the estimates of future cash inflows or the discount rate used.

CHAPTER 6

Loans and Receivables

The final category of financial asset that will be covered in this book involves loans and accounts receivable. These assets represent claims that an entity has against customers and others resulting from selling goods, providing services, or lending money to them. Also included within the scope of the term *receivables* are amounts that may be accrued in connection with interest, royalties, dividends, and claims against third parties. (However, see Chapter 17 for a discussion of contingencies for additional explanation of recognizing assets in connection with recoveries of losses.)

Receivables may originate in the form of legally binding contracts or notes. Or they may result from a purchase order followed up by delivery of goods or services. Still others, such as pledges of contributions received by a charitable nonprofit organization, may originate as verbal promises. Most receivables are legally enforceable, but many are not.

Loans and receivables may be collateralized by nonfinancial assets, such as real estate pledged as collateral on a mortgage loan. Others, like many lines of credit, may be collateralized by financial assets, such as accounts receivable.

Finally, most loans, and many other receivables, are interest-bearing. Some even include provisions for a higher default rate of interest if a customer becomes delinquent with repayments.

Regardless of what an accounting standard requires, most receivables are initially recorded at fair value, which equals cost (e.g., when one party lends cash to another) or the fair value of goods or services (when a company records accounts receivable from customers). After that, the accounting can become more complicated.

Sources of U.S. GAAP and IFRS

U.S. GAAP does not have one single accounting standard dealing with all forms of loans and receivables. Some of the sources of GAAP that are most frequently applied include the following:

SFAS 114, *Accounting by Creditors for Impairment of a Loan, an Amendment of FASB Statements No. 5 and 15*

SFAS 118, *Accounting by Creditors for Impairment of a Loan—Income Recognition and Disclosures—An Amendment of Statement No. 114*

SOP 01-6, *Accounting by Certain Entities (Including Entities with Trade Receivables) That Lend to or Finance the Activities of Others*

SOP 03-3, *Accounting for Certain Loans or Debt Securities Acquired in a Transfer*

AICPA Practice Bulletin 6, *Amortization of Discounts on Certain Acquired Loans*

For purposes of making a distinction between a loan and accounts receivable, SFAS 114 includes accounts receivable with terms in excess of one year within the scope of the term loans.

Loans and receivables also fall within the scope of SFAS 159. Introduced in Chapter 2, SFAS 159 provides for an election to utilize fair value accounting on a recurring basis for many assets, including loans and receivables.

In addition, some loans, most commonly mortgage loans, can be securitized, meaning, they are bundled together and converted into a security. Once mortgage loans have been securitized, they become subject to the provisions of SFAS 115, *Accounting for Certain Investments in Debt and Equity Securities*. As such, they may be classified as trading securities or one of the other categories defined in SFAS 115. See Chapter 4 for further details on SFAS 115.

IFRS for loans and receivables is addressed in IAS 39, *Financial Instruments: Recognition and Measurement*, the same standard that was explained in Chapters 4 and 5 in reference to investments in debt and equity securities.

Loans and Receivables—IFRS

IAS 39, paragraph 9, defines loans and receivables as nonderivative financial assets with fixed or determinable payments that are not quoted in an active market other than:

a. Those that the entity intends to sell immediately or in the near term (i.e., those quoted in an active market), which should be classified as held for trading, and those that the entity upon initial recognition designates as at fair value through profit or loss;

b. Those that the entity upon initial recognition designates as available for sale; or

c. Those for which the holder may not recover substantially all of its initial investment, other than because of credit deterioration, which shall be classified as available for sale.

Recognition and Measurement—U.S. GAAP

Under U.S. GAAP, loans and receivables (including trade receivables) may be carried at their outstanding principal balance, which generally equals the amortized cost for a loan, or at fair value, if the SFAS 159 election is made (see Chapter 2) to carry these assets at fair value on a recurring basis. Nonmortgage loans that are held for sale, and for which the SFAS 159 fair value option has not been elected, should be carried at lower of cost or fair value.

Once the initial carrying amount of a loan or receivable has been established, the next step is to monitor collections and assess whether the recorded amounts appear to be collectible. In the case of accounts receivable, management should either write off or write down specific accounts that are deemed uncollectible or carry an allowance for uncollectible accounts. Allowances represent estimates of uncollectible balances, not initially attributable to specific accounts, usually based on past experience.

Fraud Risk No. 6.1

Overestimating expected future cash flows for loans and receivables, in order to avoid or minimize the recognition of bad debts or impairments.

The accounting for loans is a bit more structured. SFAS 114, *Accounting by Creditors for Impairment of a Loan, an Amendment of FASB Statements No. 5 and 15,* requires the recognition of an impairment when it becomes probable that an entity will not be able to collect all amounts due under the contractual terms of a loan (i.e., all accrued interest as well as the outstanding principal balance). GAAP does not require the use of a particular method for assessing collectability. When an impairment is recognized, generally a valuation allowance is established, with a corresponding charge to bad debt expense.

When a loan becomes impaired, the creditor should measure the impairment based on the present value of expected future cash inflows, using a discount rate equal to the loan's effective interest rate. The effective interest rate of a loan is the contractual interest rate adjusted for any net deferred loan fees or costs, premium, or discount. Alternatively, impairment can be measured based on an observable market price, if one exists, or based on the fair value of any collateral.

Fraud Risk No. 6.2

Using inflated estimates of the fair value of collateral in order to minimize the recognition of an impairment of a loan.

The difficulty in estimating future cash flows makes the discounted cash flow model particularly prone to fraud. When evaluating estimates, the accuracy of past estimates should be considered by auditors or others. These estimates are usually generated internally and are therefore difficult to evaluate. In some respects, evaluating the fair value of collateral may sometimes be easier to audit or verify, since more reliable external evidence may exist to substantiate a valuation.

Creditors are permitted to select a measurement method on a loan-by-loan basis. As a result, this can become quite difficult to analyze, when some loans are measured based on discounted cash flow estimates, some based on observable market prices, and others on the fair value of collateral.

Special rules apply for loans with credit deterioration that were acquired in a transfer. Two models apply to the accounting for these loans, depending on when the loan was acquired. SOP 03-3, *Accounting for Certain Loans or Debt Securities Acquired in a Transfer*, applies to loans acquired in fiscal years beginning after December 15, 2004. AICPA Practice Bulletin 6, *Amortization of Discounts on Certain Acquired Loans*, applies to loans acquired before that date.

A detailed explanation of the two models is beyond the scope of this book—and not really necessary for our purposes. Each model requires estimation of future cash flows expected to be collected over the life of a loan. When those estimates indicate that the purchaser of the loans will not be able to collect the cash flows previously expected, then the loan is to be considered impaired, and the asset's carrying value should be reduced.

Recognition and Measurement—IFRS

Under IAS 39, when any financial asset or financial liability is recognized initially, it should be measured at its fair value (which for loans and receivables will generally be equal to cost at inception). In the case of a loan or receivable that is not carried at fair value through profit or loss, transaction costs that are directly attributable to the acquisition or issue of the asset should also be included in this fair value measurement.

Subsequent to initial recognition, however, loans and receivables are to be measured at amortized cost using the effective interest method.

Effective Interest Method—IFRS

As described in paragraph 9 of IAS 39, the *effective interest method* is a method of calculating the amortized cost of a financial asset or a financial liability (or group of financial assets or financial liabilities) and of allocating the interest income or interest expense over the relevant period. The *effective interest rate* is the rate that exactly discounts estimated future cash payments or receipts through the expected life of the financial instrument or, when appropriate, a shorter period to the net carrying amount of the financial asset or financial liability. When calculating the effective interest rate, an entity shall estimate cash flows considering all contractual terms of the financial instrument (for example, prepayment, call and similar options) but shall not consider future credit losses. The calculation includes all fees and points paid or received between parties to the contract that are an integral part of the effective interest rate (see IAS 18 *Revenue*), transaction costs, and all other premiums or discounts. There is a presumption that the cash flows and the expected life of a group of similar financial instruments can be estimated reliably. However, in those rare cases when it is not possible to estimate reliably the cash flows or the expected life of a financial instrument (or group of financial instruments), the entity shall use the contractual cash flows over the full contractual term of the financial instrument (or group of financial instruments).

Similar to the U.S. GAAP provisions explained in the preceding section, if objective evidence exists that there is an impairment loss on loans and receivables, the amount of the loss is measured as the difference between the asset's carrying amount and the present value of estimated future cash flows (excluding future credit losses that have not been incurred) discounted at the financial asset's original effective interest rate (i.e., the effective interest rate computed at initial recognition). The carrying amount of the loan or receivable is then reduced either directly or through use of an allowance account. The amount of the loss must be recognized in profit or loss (not in other comprehensive income).

CHAPTER 7

Intangible Assets and Goodwill

Intangible assets are assets lacking a physical substance, but that provide future economic benefits, generally in the form of the ability to produce income. Examples include copyrights, trademarks and service marks, patents, customer lists, contract or sales backlogs, and various contractually based assets. Intangible assets can result from any of the following activities:

- They may be created by the owner of the asset, either through a specific project designed to create an intangible asset or through their emergence as an asset over time (e.g., the gradual development of a customer list).
- They may be separately acquired in a transaction with another party (e.g., the purchase of a contract from another entity).
- They may be acquired in connection with a merger with or acquisition of another entity.

Intangible assets acquired in connection with the first two activities are covered in this chapter. Chapter 8 is devoted to mergers and acquisitions, including the acquisition of intangible assets included in such business combinations.

Goodwill is often discussed in the same documents as intangible assets since it has many similarities to certain intangibles. But goodwill is considered a separate category of asset, defined as the excess of the cost of an acquired entity over the net of the amounts assigned to assets acquired and liabilities assumed. Internally developed goodwill is not recognized as an asset. Since goodwill results from business combinations, its initial recognition will be explained in Chapter 8 on business combinations. But the treatment of goodwill after its initial recognition will be covered in this chapter, along with all other intangible assets.

Sources of U.S. GAAP and IFRS

Intangible asset accounting under U.S. GAAP is explained in SFAS 142, *Goodwill and Other Intangible Assets*. The international accounting standard covering intangible assets is IAS 38, *Intangible Assets*. There are four key accounting issues subject to possible manipulation:

1. Capitalization versus expensing of costs associated with intangible assets
2. Carrying amounts (book values) of intangible assets
3. Classifying intangible assets as indefinite life assets (not subject to amortization) versus finite life assets (subject to amortization)
4. Determining appropriate useful lives for purposes of calculating amortization expense

Each of these issues will be explained in this chapter. Some of these issues, such as whether or not to capitalize costs incurred in developing an intangible asset, are not fair value accounting issues per se. But since later sections that directly relate to fair value accounting build from these earlier issues, all of them will be explained in this chapter.

Asset versus Expense

Research costs associated with intangible assets are to be expensed as incurred under both IFRS and U.S. GAAP. Research generally includes gathering knowledge, evaluating information, developing or researching alternatives, and designing potential new or improved products, systems, or services. After the research phase, costs of developing intangible assets may be capitalized, but only if certain criteria are met. And the criteria applicable under U.S. GAAP differ from those included under IFRS, generally resulting in development costs being more likely to be capitalized under IFRS than under U.S. GAAP.

Under SFAS 142, costs of internally developing an intangible asset may be capitalized only if all three of the following characteristics are present:

1. The intangible asset is specifically identifiable.
2. The asset has a determinate life (it has a limited and determinable life).
3. The asset is not inherent in a continuing business and related to an entity as a whole.

Failing to meet any of these three criteria results in the requirement to expense rather than capitalize the costs associated with internally developing an intangible asset. Fraud in the form of inappropriately capitalizing costs that should be reported as expenses could result if management misrepresents any of the preceding factors described in SFAS 142. The effect of this type of fraud is to overstate assets, understate expenses, and overstate profits.

Fraud Risk No. 7.1

Capitalizing costs incurred in developing an intangible asset internally, when the criteria for recognition of an asset have not been met.

Under IAS 38, costs of developing an intangible asset may be capitalized only if six criteria are met. But these criteria deal primarily with the feasibility of the entity completing the development of the asset and the probability of the entity generating future economic benefits from the asset.

In addition, IAS 38 states that an intangible asset must be identifiable, similar to the first and third criteria under SFAS 142. In order to be identifiable, the asset must meet one of the following two criteria:

1. It must either be separate or capable of being separated from the entity and sold, transferred, licensed or rented.
2. It must arise from contractual or other legal rights, regardless of whether those rights are transferable or separable from the entity or from other rights and obligations.

Where the IFRS criteria are less stringent than U.S. GAAP is with respect to the second criterion described under SFAS 142. IFRS has no such requirement for an internally developed intangible asset to have a limited and determinable life (meaning it must be amortizable, as will be explained later).

Under both IAS 38 and SFAS 142, separately acquired intangible assets (outside of those acquired in a business combination, explained in Chapter 8), such as those purchased from another entity or from an individual, would ordinarily be capitalized, assuming they meet the criteria of being identifiable and having future economic benefit.

Note

The capitalization criteria of SFAS 142 pose an accounting dilemma for entities that internally develop an intangible asset. The SFAS 157 concept of fair value is based on what an unrelated outside party would

(continued)

pay for an asset. As a result, many internally developed intangible assets clearly have a fair value in that sense, since outside parties would willingly pay to obtain them. However, in order to utilize fair value accounting, the item must first meet the definition of an asset. And the SFAS 142 criteria for recognizing an asset focus on issues unrelated to fair value, and can be difficult to meet.

Web Site Costs

In today's economy, businesses pour significant resources into their presence on the Internet. The question of whether the costs associated with an entity's Web site should be capitalized or expensed as incurred is another accounting issue that can lead to fraud when the rules are misapplied. Both U.S. GAAP and IFRS address this issue.

Under the IFRS, SIC 32, *Intangible Assets—Web Site Costs*, issued in March 2002, states that an entity's Web site represents an internally developed intangible asset. Accordingly, the criteria of IAS 38, explained in the preceding section, should be applied in determining whether costs should be accounted for as an asset or as operating expenses. SIC 32 points out that demonstrating how a Web site will generate probable future economic benefits may require that it can be shown that the Web site is capable of generating future revenues, including direct revenues from enabling orders to be placed via the site.

U.S. GAAP addresses Web site costs in EITF 00-2. Unlike SIC 32, EITF 00-2 does not classify Web sites as intangible assets. Instead, EITF 00-2 provides guidance as to which costs associated with a Web site should be capitalized as assets and which should be expensed as incurred. It utilizes guidance similar to that provided in SOP 98-1, which addresses the costs of internal-use software. EITF 00-2 states that all Web site costs incurred during the planning stage should be expensed as incurred. But, certain costs incurred during the application and infrastructure development phase and the graphics and content development stages should be capitalized, generally referencing the guidance of SOP 98-1. All operating stage costs should then be expensed as incurred.

Measurement

Under U.S. GAAP, intangible assets should be initially recorded at fair value. Given the nature of intangible assets that are capitalized, fair value usually equates to the purchase price of the asset, when purchased from a third party, or an accumulation of development costs, as explained earlier.

However, if a group of intangible assets are purchased for a single amount from the holder of these intangible assets, the amount paid should be allocated among the various assets acquired based on their relative fair values. This type of transaction could be prone to fair value accounting fraud in the form of overallocating the purchase price to assets not subject to amortization or to assets with longer useful lives, underallocating to assets with short useful lives. This type of fraud would result in the basis of the intangible assets remaining on the books for longer than appropriate periods of time. Amortization of intangible assets will be explained further in the next section.

Unlike IFRS, after the initial recording of an intangible asset, SFAS 142 does not provide for the recognition of gains if the fair value of the asset subsequently increases. Only impairment losses from subsequent declines should be recorded, as explained later, as well as accumulated amortization.

The possibility of recording subsequent increases in fair value as gains creates an additional fraud risk under the IFRS that does not exist under U.S. GAAP.

Fraud Risk No. 7.2

Recording false gains from purported increases in fair values of intangible assets (IFRS risk only).

IAS 38 states that an intangible asset should be measured initially at cost. After initial recognition, IAS 38 permits an entity to carry its intangible assets at either cost (less any accumulated amortization and impairment losses) or fair value. IAS 38 permits entities to elect a revaluation model, under which the carrying amount of an intangible asset may be increased if there is evidence of an increase in its fair value. However, this revaluation model may only be elected if there is an active market for the intangible asset. And IAS 38 indicates that active markets do not exist if an intangible asset is unique, such as with brands, music, patents, and trademarks.

When an increase in fair value of an intangible asset is recorded under IAS 38, the gain is reported in other comprehensive income and accumulated in equity under the heading of revaluation surplus (i.e., these gains are segregated from other gains and the cumulative amount of such gains is segregated in the equity section from other retained earnings). Therefore, it should generally be easy to determine if an entity following IFRS has recorded gains due to revaluations of intangible assets.

Finite Life Intangible Assets

Both U.S. GAAP and IFRS classify intangible assets into two categories: (1) those with finite lives and (2) those with indefinite lives. Intangible assets with finite lives should be amortized (expensed on a pro rata basis) over their estimated useful lives. Useful lives are normally expressed in months or years, but may also be in terms of units of production or other measures of usefulness. Some of the most important determinants of the useful life of an intangible asset are the following nine:

1. Product life cycles of similar assets
2. Pace of technological change
3. Historical experience in estimating useful lives of other intangible assets
4. The expected use of the asset by the entity
5. Whether the expected use is dependent on other assets or other entities
6. The level and cost of maintenance that would be necessary to prolong or maintain a useful life
7. Expected or known actions of industry competitors
8. Management's plans for the asset (e.g., is a replacement technology already in the research phase, and management hopes to have it on the market soon?)
9. The level of obsolescence that is evident

Once a useful life is determined, the asset's carrying amount, less any expected residual value, is amortized to expense over that period.

Intangible assets with finite lives may have a fixed and easily determined life, such as with certain contracts, leases, and many other assets that have a set expiration date. However, it should be noted that if a fixed expiration can easily be renewed or extended indefinitely (e.g., by simply reregistering or relicensing for a nominal fee or effort), the asset can be considered to have an infinite life. Misrepresenting the ease with which a renewal or extension can be accomplished would allow an otherwise amortizable asset to escape amortization.

Other finite life intangible assets do not have legally fixed lives and instead are subject to an estimate of their useful lives. These estimates should be based on management's expected use of the asset, possible effects of obsolescence, level of maintenance required, expected actions of competitors, life cycles of similar assets, and any other relevant factor. Obviously, these estimates should be examined carefully.

Fraud Risk No. 7.3

Using unrealistically long useful lives to amortize intangible assets with finite lives (including failing to shorten useful lives as new information indicates the estimate should be modified).

In addition, if it becomes apparent that a previous estimate of a useful life is no longer accurate, the estimate should be adjusted, which adjusts amortization expense recognition going forward. Changes in estimates are different from corrections of errors in prior financial statements. When an accounting estimate of this nature is changed, there is no effect on opening balances. Rather, amortization expense is adjusted going forward.

For example, if an intangible asset with an initial basis of $1 million has been estimated to have a useful life of 10 years, annual amortization expense would be $100,000. But what would happen if in year 3, it comes to management's attention that the asset will likely only be of use for a total of six years? At the beginning of year 3, the asset's book value is $800,000 (its $1 million initial basis less two years' worth of amortization at $100,000 per year). But that $800,000 asset now has a remaining useful life of only four years. Therefore, amortization expense in years 3 through 6 should be at the rate of $200,000 per year, not $100,000. When changes in estimates like this are considered to be material, special footnote disclosure requirements apply. But, this is yet another potentially fraudulent method of extending (or failing to shorten) the useful life of an asset in order to overstate the financial condition of an entity.

Establishing unrealistically long useful lives for amortization purposes upon the initial recognition of an asset is a fraud risk that is fairly obvious. Failing to shorten a useful life is a fraud risk that is often not even considered, but one that is every bit of a risk.

Residual Value

Another potential use of fair value accounting to perpetrate financial statement fraud lies in the determination of residual value, if any, of an intangible asset. Under both U.S. GAAP and IFRS, the amount of a finite life intangible asset subject to amortization should be its total basis less any residual value.

Fraud Risk No. 7.4

Inflating the estimated residual value of an intangible asset with a finite life, thereby reducing the amount charged to amortization expense each period.

Although slightly different language is used, the two standards define residual value very similarly. Residual value is assumed to be zero unless one of two factors is present:

1. There is a commitment from a third party to purchase the intangible asset at the end of its useful life.
2. Residual value can be estimated by reference to an existing market, and that market is likely to exist on the expiration of the asset's useful life.

Either of these two factors could be subject to fraud. But the second factor, in particular, is subject to significant judgment regarding fair value and existence of a market for the asset. Therefore, the second factor is more vulnerable to fraud due to the level of judgment that may be involved in making a determination of residual value.

Indefinite Life Intangible Assets

Intangible assets with indefinite lives are not subject to amortization. Instead, indefinite life intangibles should be tested for impairment in fair value periodically. If fair value has declined below book value, an impairment loss should be recorded. See the next section for more on impairment testing of intangible assets.

Fraud Risk No. 7.5

Improperly claiming that an intangible asset has an indefinite life, in order to carry the asset at its basis without reduction for amortization, as would be required if the asset were classified as having a finite life.

In addition, intangibles originally thought to have an indefinite life may need to be converted to finite life assets, subject to amortization, as new information comes to an entity's attention (e.g., technological advances that make an asset previously thought to have an indefinite life likely to become obsolete in a few years). This is another tricky area—assessing whether an asset previously thought to have an indefinite life has reached a point where the end of its usefulness can be estimated. Once the end of an asset's usefulness can be reasonably estimated, it is time to begin amortizing the asset over that period.

Impairment Losses

Testing for impairment of intangible assets is addressed in two different accounting standards under U.S. GAAP. For intangible assets subject to amortization, with finite lives (or those converted to finite life assets), impairment testing is covered under SFAS 144, explained in Chapter 9. For intangible assets with indefinite lives (i.e., not subject to amortization) and goodwill, impairment testing is addressed in SFAS 142.

Under IFRS, impairment of all intangible assets is covered under IAS 36, the same standard that applies to impairments of other nonfinancial assets (see Chapter 9).

Fraud Risk No. 7.6

Failing to properly test for or recognize an impairment in connection with goodwill or other intangible assets with indefinite lives.

For intangible assets with indefinite lives, SFAS 142 states that testing for impairment should be done no less frequently than annually. If an impairment is determined to have occurred, the asset's basis is permanently decreased to the lower amount (fair value). The loss is recognized in earnings, not other comprehensive income. And there can be no subsequent recoveries of the loss.

Goodwill is a special category of intangible asset. It is treated as an asset with an indefinite life, meaning it is not to be amortized. However, it is subject to a requirement to be tested for impairment on an annual basis, unless certain conditions are present, one of which is that the most recent valuation exceeded the book value of the goodwill by a substantial margin.

Since goodwill results from the acquisition of a business, it is assigned to specific reporting units of that business, if there is more than a single unit. Since goodwill represents a premium paid by a buyer (the excess of the purchase price over the net fair value of assets minus liabilities), it means the buyer saw some inherent value in the reporting unit. Therefore, it is important to be on the lookout for signs that this value has declined in subsequent periods. Some examples of indicators that goodwill may have become impaired include the following:

- Downturns in the industry in which the business unit operates
- Downturns in the local economy in which the business operates
- Introduction of new competitors, or advances made by existing competitors
- Changes in key personnel at the entity or at its competitors
- Changes in laws and regulations impacting the entity's business
- Adverse results of audits, inspections, or actions by regulators
- Adverse publicity resulting from accidents, legal claims, or other damaging incidents
- Changes in technology

There are many different methods of calculating the fair value of goodwill for purposes of impairment testing. Quoted market prices for goodwill are rare, but can sometimes be located. More common methods are using a multiple of earnings or revenue that is commonly used for a particular industry. Perhaps the most common method, however, is calculation of the present value of estimated future cash flows attributable to a business unit.

Finally, if a segment of a business is to be sold or otherwise disposed, goodwill attributable to that unit should be identified for impairment and eventual write-off.

Concluding Remarks

Opportunities for fraud are abundant in the area of intangible assets. Overstating assets can be accomplished by simply classifying an intangible asset as one that has an indefinite life when, in fact, it has a finite life that can be reasonably estimated. Doing so enables the entity to carry the asset on its books without reducing it for amortization expense each period. Other, less obvious techniques for inflating assets and understating expenses are to use unrealistically long useful lives (which spreads amortization expense over too long of a period), overstating any estimated residual value of the asset (which lowers the amortizable basis, which also understates amortization expense each period), or improperly calculating fair value of goodwill or other intangible assets.

Evaluating whether any of these methods are being used to inflate assets can be very difficult. It requires that extensive knowledge of the specific intangible asset be obtained.

CHAPTER 8

Business Combinations

When one business merges with or acquires another business, the resulting accounting treatment is ripe for financial statement fraud. All of the acquired assets and assumed liabilities must be recorded on the books of the acquirer. This poses a number of accounting challenges and requires significant use of judgment and estimation. Anytime this much judgment and estimation is involved, the risk of fraud escalates.

Sources of U.S. GAAP and IFRS

U.S. GAAP for business combinations is covered under SFAS 141 (as revised in December 2007). All references to SFAS 141 in this chapter are references to the revised version of the standard. SFAS 141 also refers to two other documents that may need to be considered when accounting for business combinations:

ARB No. 51, *Consolidated Financial Statements*
FIN 46, *Consolidation of Variable Interest Entities*

The international standard that addresses business combinations is IFRS 3 (as revised in January 2008), *Business Combinations*.

Business Combination versus Asset Acquisition

Business combinations involve gaining control over one or more businesses, resulting in the acquisition of assets and liabilities. If assets acquired do not constitute a business, their acquisition should be accounted for as an asset acquisition, not a business combination. This concept alone can be a basis for financial reporting fraud, as will be explained later.

A business is an integrated set of activities and assets capable of being conducted and managed for the purpose of providing return. The potential return is not limited to profits or dividends. Return can also be a reduction in costs or other economic benefits and still qualify as a business. A business consists of inputs and processes applied to those inputs, resulting in outputs.

Under U.S. GAAP, a business combination is a transaction or other event in which an acquirer obtains control of one or more businesses. The methods used to acquire a business can vary, from the typical transfer of cash, to transferring other types of assets, issuing stock, assuming or incurring liabilities, or some combination of multiple types of consideration.

From a legal and tax standpoint, there are also many different ways to handle an acquisition. Here are three examples:

1. One business becomes a wholly owned subsidiary of another.
2. The assets of one business are transferred to, and become assets of, another business.
3. A new entity is created, into which the assets of both businesses are transferred (this technique is also sometimes called a *roll-up transaction*).

Normally, determining which entity is the acquirer and which is acquired is a simple step. But, it can sometimes not be entirely clear, especially when several entities are involved. ARB No. 51, *Consolidated Financial Statements*, as amended, provides guidance on identifying which entity is the acquirer. Additional guidance is found in the appendix of SFAS 141. FIN 46, *Consolidation of Variable Interest Entities*, should be consulted if the acquisition involves a variable interest entity.

Fraud Risk No. 8.1

Improperly accounting for an acquisition of assets as a business combination, resulting in a fraudulent allocation of the purchase price.

The fraud risk associated with distinguishing a business combination from an acquisition of assets is that in an asset acquisition, the purchase price is allocated among the assets acquired. A similar principle applies to a business combination, in that a purchase price is allocated among the acquired assets and liabilities. However, in a business combination, goodwill can result, something that would not result from an asset acquisition. In addition, in a business combination it is sometimes easier to justify segregating portions of the purchase price for acquired intangible assets that are not even on the financial statements of the acquired entity.

The effect of mischaracterizing an asset acquisition as a business combination is that if portions of the purchase price are allocated to goodwill (and perhaps to other intangible assets), assets can be inflated in the long term. Recall from Chapter 7 that goodwill is not subject to amortization. Instead, it is subjected to the much more subjective impairment testing. This can result in retaining an asset on the books for longer periods of time than if the purchase price was allocated to depreciable/amortizable or consumable assets.

Accounting for Business Combinations

Both U.S. GAAP and IFRS prohibit the pooling-of-interests method of accounting for business combinations. Under the pooling-of-interests method, assets acquired in a combination would generally be recorded on the books of the acquirer at the same book value that they had on the acquired entity's books.

Instead, U.S. GAAP and IFRS both require that an entity that acquires the assets and liabilities of another entity in a business combination allocate the purchase price to the identifiable assets acquired and liabilities assumed based on the fair value of each underlying asset and liability. IFRS 3 refers to this as the acquisition method, while SFAS 141 calls it the purchase method of accounting—but the basics are the same. The differences between the two standards are relatively minor for our purposes.

The acquirer in a business combination should take the following steps to properly account for the transaction:

1. Identify all assets acquired in the transaction, recognizing that some acquired assets, especially intangible assets, may not be represented as assets on the books of the acquired business. (Recall from Chapter 7 that often the developer of an intangible asset is not permitted to capitalize the costs associated with developing an intangible asset, even though the asset may have value to outside parties and, indeed, helps the developer of the asset to generate revenue.) See the next section for additional guidance on identifying intangible assets.
2. Identify all liabilities assumed in the transaction.
3. Determine the acquisition date, which is the date that the acquiring entity obtains control over the acquiree. This is an important date, since the next step, involving fair value accounting, is to be performed as of the acquisition date.
4. Determine the fair value of each identified asset acquired and liability assumed on the acquisition date.

5. Determine the purchase price associated with the transaction, which may involve items other than cash.
6. Determine the extent of any goodwill resulting from the transaction, which is simply the excess of the purchase price over the net fair value of assets acquired minus the liabilities assumed in the transaction.
7. Measure and recognize any noncontrolling interest in the acquiree. This step applies in cases in which an acquirer acquires a less than 100 percent interest in another entity. Further guidance on accounting for noncontrolling interests is found in SFAS 160.

IFRS 3 identifies and describes virtually the same steps.

Occasionally, step 6 results in the identification of a bargain purchase—one in which the purchase price is less than the net fair value of the assets acquired and liabilities assumed. Generally, when this happens, the acquirer should recognize a gain on the acquisition date. This gain is recognized in earnings (profit or loss).

Before recognizing a gain, however, SFAS 141 basically says, "Check your numbers." The standard says that the acquirer should "reassess whether it has correctly identified all of the assets acquired and all of the liabilities assumed." It also states that the acquirer should reconsider the methods and procedures used to assign fair values to the assets and liabilities.

Fraud Risk No. 8.2

Improper allocation of the purchase price in a business combination, usually in the form of overallocation to assets not subject to depreciation or amortization, or to assets with longer useful lives.

The primary fraud risks in the allocation of the purchase price in a business combination are as follows:

1. Allocating part of the purchase price to intangible assets that do not qualify for recognition. This is explained further in the next section.
2. Assigning too much of the purchase price to assets that are not subject to depreciation or amortization. Examples include the following:
   a. Land
   b. Intangible assets with indefinite lives (see Chapter 7)
3. Overallocating the purchase price to assets with longer useful lives than those with shorter useful lives or that will be consumed in the near term. This enables the entity to retain a greater percentage of the purchase

price as assets on the financial statements for longer periods of time. For example, overallocation of the purchase price to a building, with a useful life of 40 years and underallocating to equipment with useful lives of 7 years results in stretching out the book value of assets for longer periods of time.

4. Failing to recognize liabilities that were assumed in connection with a business combination.

Testing the allocation of the purchase price in a combination is a complex procedure that may require the use of outside experts with a variety of valuation specialties, from real estate appraisers to industry experts and intellectual property specialists.

Identification of Intangible Assets

In a business combination, the acquirer should recognize separately from goodwill any identifiable intangible assets that have been acquired. The key word in the preceding sentence is *identifiable*. An intangible asset is identifiable if it has either of the following two characteristics:

1. It is separable, meaning that it is capable of being separated from the entity and sold, transferred, licensed, rented, or exchanged (regardless of whether the acquiring entity actually intends to do so).
2. It arises from contractual or other legal rights, regardless of whether those rights are transferable or separable from the entity or from other rights and obligations.

In many cases, the identification of intangible assets is obvious, since they were an integral part of the negotiations leading up to the agreement on a purchase price. But in other cases, intangible assets aren't separately considered in the negotiation phase, with the focus instead being on the acquired entity taken as a whole. In these cases, identification of intangible assets can become much more complicated.

Fraud Risk No. 8.3

Improper allocation of a portion of the purchase price in a business combination to intangible assets that do not qualify for separate recognition.

Paragraphs A31, A36, A44, A46, and A51 in an appendix to SFAS 141 (summarized in the following box) provide a comprehensive listing of examples of intangible assets, classified into five categories, that may be acquired in a business combination and that could meet the criteria for recognition as assets.

Intangible Assets

Intangible assets that are followed by the symbol (L) arise from contractual or other legal rights. Those followed by the symbol (S) do not arise from contractual or other legal rights but are separable. Note that intangible assets identified with the symbol (L) might also be separable, but separability is not a requirement for an asset to meet the contractual-legal criterion.

Marketing-Related Intangible Assets

- Trademarks, trade names, service marks, collective marks, certification marks (L)
- Trade dress (unique color, shape, package design) (L)
- Newspaper mastheads (L)
- Internet domain names (L)
- Noncompetition agreements (L)

Customer-Related Intangible Assets

- Customer lists (S)
- Order or production backlog (L)
- Customer contracts and related customer relationships (L)
- Noncontractual customer relationships (S)

Artistic-Related Intangible Assets

- Plays, operas, ballets (L)
- Books, magazines, newspapers, other literary works (L)
- Musical works such as compositions, song lyrics, advertising jingles (L)
- Pictures, photographs (L)
- Video and audiovisual material, including motion pictures or films, music videos, television programs (L)

Contract-Based Intangible Assets

- Licensing, royalty, standstill agreements (L)
- Advertising, construction, management, service or supply contracts (L)
- Lease agreements (whether the acquiree is the lessee or the lessor) (L)
- Construction permits (L)
- Franchise agreements (L)
- Operating and broadcast rights (L)
- Servicing contracts such as mortgage servicing contracts (L)
- Employment contracts (L)
- Use rights such as drilling, water, air, timber cutting, and route authorities (L)

Technology-Based Intangible Assets

- Patented technology (L)
- Computer software and mask works (L)
- Unpatented technology (S)
- Databases, including title plants (S)
- Trade secrets, such as secret formulas, processes, recipes (S)

Business Combinations Achieved in Stages

In some transactions, the acquirer obtains control of an entity in which it already held an equity interest, albeit not a controlling interest, prior to the business combination. For example, as of December 31, 2008, one entity held a 25 percent interest in another. But in January 2009, it purchased another 50 percent interest, bringing its total interest to 75 percent. At that point, the entity controls the other entity and a business combination has taken place.

This type of multistep process is sometimes called a *step acquisition*. SFAS 141 refers to it as a business combination achieved in stages.

When this happens, the acquirer must first remeasure its equity interest held immediately prior to the business combination (i.e., when it held the 25 percent interest in the preceding example). This remeasurement must be done at fair value. The difference between the fair value and the book value should be recognized as a gain or loss, and this gain or loss is to be included in earnings (not in comprehensive income).

Fraud Risk No. 8.4

Improper calculation of the fair value of the prebusiness combination, noncontrolling interest in an entity that is then acquired in a step acquisition, in order to manipulate the timing or amount of gain or loss recognized in earnings.

If the acquirer had previously recognized changes in the value of its equity interest as a component of other comprehensive income (which would be the case if it had been treated as an investment classified as held for sale—see Chapter 4), then the amount previously recognized in other comprehensive income would have to be reclassified and included in the gain or loss recognized in earnings.

CHAPTER 9

Asset Impairments

An asset impairment occurs when the fair value of an asset declines below the amount at which it is recorded on the books (its carrying amount). Impairment losses may occur with respect to depreciable/amortizable assets as well as assets not subject to depreciation or amortization. In addition, an impairment loss may be identified with respect to either an individual asset or for a group of assets considered together.

One aspect of accounting for impairments that can be confusing is that there are different criteria for determining impairment losses, depending on the nature of the asset being tested, particularly under U.S. GAAP. For example, investments in equity and debt securities are subject to their own impairment testing, as explained in Chapter 4. Goodwill and intangible assets with indefinite lives have their own specific criteria, explained in Chapter 7.

In this chapter, the focus is on impairments of long-lived assets, with the exception of assets like goodwill that have their own rules elsewhere.

One category of long-lived asset most commonly associated with impairment losses is intangible assets. As explained earlier, some intangible assets are amortized over an estimated useful life, while others are not subject to amortization. Intangible assets not subject to amortization should be evaluated for impairment losses periodically. But even those intangible assets that are being amortized or depreciated may incur an impairment loss. Accounting standards specify how and when impairment assessments should take place.

In periods of economic downturns, impairment losses become even more common, including those incurred with respect to depreciable property. For example, an entity that purchased a new building shortly before the current economic downturn may find it necessary to adjust the basis of the asset downward as a result of declining market prices for real estate.

Sources of U.S. GAAP and IFRS

U.S. GAAP for impairments of long-lived assets is SFAS 144, *Accounting for the Impairment or Disposal of Long-Lived Assets*.

IFRS for asset impairments in connection with long-lived assets is found in two sources. IAS 36, *Impairment of Assets*, covers assets that are in use by an entity. However, if a noncurrent asset is classified as held for sale, it is covered under IFRS 5, *Non-current Assets Held for Sale and Discontinued Operations*, rather than IAS 36. Under IFRS, once a noncurrent asset is held for sale, it is covered under IFRS 5 instead of IAS 36. An asset is held for sale when its carrying amount will be recovered primarily through its sale, rather than through ongoing use of the asset. Accordingly, most long-lived noncurrent assets are covered under IAS 36 when they are first acquired, but at some point later may be held for sale and are then covered under IFRS 5. IFRS 5 requires that noncurrent assets held for sale be carried at the lower of cost or fair value, less selling costs.

There are important differences in the scopes of the SFAS 144 and IAS 36. Where they are similar is that each standard excludes from its scope several categories of assets, including the following:

- Inventories
- Financial assets, which have separate guidelines for impairment losses (see SFAS 115 for U.S. GAAP as it relates to certain investments and IAS 39 for IFRS on financial instruments, both explained in Chapter 4, and IAS 40 for IFRS on investment property, explained in Chapter 10)
- Deferred tax assets

But where U.S. GAAP and IFRS differ is that IAS 36 applies to all intangible assets (other than those arising from certain insurance contracts), including goodwill. SFAS 144 specifically excludes from its scope each of the following:

- Goodwill
- Intangible assets that are not being amortized (i.e., those with indefinite lives in accordance with the preceding section) that are to be held and used

In developing SFAS 144, FASB concluded that the separate impairment criteria for goodwill included in SFAS 142, explained in Chapter 7, should be retained, resulting in a different approach to testing for impairment for goodwill than for other intangible assets.

Therefore, the only intangible assets that are covered under the impairment criteria of SFAS 144 are those with finite lives, subject to amortization.

There are other differences in scope between SFAS 144 and IAS 36, but for purposes of our discussion in this chapter, they are not material.

Definition of an Impairment Loss

Under SFAS 144, an impairment loss is to be recognized if the carrying amount of a long-lived asset is not recoverable (e.g., via sale) *and* exceeds its fair value.

IAS 36 utilizes slightly different language to arrive at a similar concept, but one that can potentially lead to a different conclusion for some assets. IAS 36 states that an impairment loss occurs when the carrying amount of an asset exceeds its recoverable amount. The recoverable amount is defined as the higher of an asset's fair value, less costs to sell, or its value in use. *Value in use* is defined as the present value of future cash flows expected to be derived.

In other words, an impairment loss exists under IAS 36 if the carrying amount of an asset exceeds its recoverable amount, which is the greater of:

- Fair value, less costs to sell, or
- Present value of future cash flows

Recall that IAS 36 applies only to assets in use by an entity—not to assets held for sale. Therefore, fair value is measured based on the greater of fair value or that asset's *value in use.*

Value in Use

Paragraph 30 of IAS 36 states that the following elements shall be reflected in the calculation of an asset's value in use:

a. an estimate of the future cash flows the entity expects to derive from the asset;
b. expectations about possible variations in the amount or timing of those future cash flows;
c. the time value of money, represented by the current market risk-free rate of interest;
d. the price for bearing the uncertainty inherent in the asset; and
e. other factors, such as illiquidity, that market participants would reflect in pricing the future cash flows the entity expects to derive from the asset.

(continued)

Paragraph 39 states that estimates of future cash flows shall include:

a. projections of cash inflows from the continuing use of the asset;

b. projections of cash outflows that are necessarily incurred to generate the cash inflows from continuing use of the asset (including cash outflows to prepare the asset for use) and can be directly attributed, or allocated on a reasonable and consistent basis, to the asset; and

c. net cash flows, if any, to be received (or paid) for the disposal of the asset at the end of its useful life.

The differences in definitions used under U.S. GAAP and IFRS can result in different conclusions regarding impairment losses. Most often, where differences exist they may result in earlier recognition of impairments under IFRS than under U.S. GAAP. This is due primarily to two factors:

1. The SFAS 144 test for recoverability is based on undiscounted cash flows (i.e., is the asset's carrying amount recoverable, regardless of how far into the future?), whereas IAS 36 uses the present value of future cash flows.

2. SFAS 144 bases impairment on whether the carrying amount exceeds fair value, whereas IAS 36 uses fair value, less costs to sell. Recall from Chapter 2 that the SFAS 157 definition of fair value ignores transaction costs in determining fair value of an asset.

These differences, particularly the first one, can result in significant differences in both the identification and measurement of an impairment.

When to Test for Impairment

U.S. GAAP and IFRS are also similar in how they address the issue of when it is necessary to test for impairment in value of a long-lived asset.

SFAS 144 states that an asset should be tested for impairment whenever events or changes in circumstances indicate that its carrying amount may not be recoverable. SFAS 142 states that goodwill and intangible assets that are not subject to amortization (i.e., those with indefinite lives) should be tested for impairment at least annually.

IAS 36, like SFAS 142, includes a requirement to test intangible assets with indefinite useful lives, as well as goodwill, for possible impairment on an annual basis, even if there are no obvious indicators of impairment. This testing for impairment need not be performed at year-end. It can be done at any time during the year. But it should be done at the same time every year.

With respect to assets other than intangible assets, IAS 36 states that testing for impairment losses should be performed only if there are indications that an asset may be impaired, similar to SFAS 144.

Indicators of Impairment of Assets

One of the keys to properly recording impairment losses is proper recognition of the signs that an impairment loss may have occurred. These same signs are what a fraud examiner or auditor should be aware of in evaluating whether an impairment loss may have been omitted from a set of financial statements. Both U.S. GAAP and IFRS identify some of the most important warning signs that an impairment exists.

Indicators of Impairment Losses under U.S. GAAP

Paragraph 8 of SFAS 144 identifies the following examples of events or changes in circumstances that could indicate that the carrying amount of a long-lived asset may not be recoverable:

a. A significant decrease in the market price of a long-lived asset (asset group)
b. A significant adverse change in the extent or manner in which a long-lived asset (asset group) is being used or in its physical condition
c. A significant adverse change in legal factors or in the business climate that could affect the value of a long-lived asset (asset group), including an adverse action or assessment by a regulator
d. An accumulation of costs significantly in excess of the amount originally expected for the acquisition or construction of a long-lived asset (asset group)
e. A current-period operating or cash flow loss, combined with a history of operating or cash flow losses or a projection or forecast that demonstrates continuing losses associated with the use of a long-lived asset (asset group)

(continued)

> **f.** A current expectation that, "more likely than not," a long-lived
> asset (asset group) will be sold or otherwise disposed of signifi-
> cantly before the end of its previously estimated useful life (The
> term *more likely than not* refers to a level of likelihood that is more
> than 50 percent.)

Under both U.S. GAAP and IFRS, failure to recognize an impairment in
connection with a long-lived asset is a fraud risk that is particularly challenging. In many cases, assessment of an asset's fair value is easy when
the asset is new. As it ages and is used, there are fewer market comparisons and the market prices that are available required significant adjustment
to account for age, use, degree of obsolescence, and so on. This is often the
case with specialized equipment, unique buildings, and certain other assets.

Other assets may actually become easier to value over time. This is
sometimes the case with certain intangible assets. Assessing future cash flows
can be very difficult when an intangible asset is first acquired. But, after a
baseline and short history of cash flows has been established, forecasts of
the next several years' cash flows may actually become more reliable.

One thing is certain. Given the global reach and severity of the economic
crisis of 2009, it is inevitable that the assets of many entities have become
impaired.

Fraud Risk No. 9.1

Failing to recognize that an asset has experienced an impairment.

The strategy employed when an entity intentionally fails to recognize an
impairment loss is to conceal the fact that a loss has been incurred, either by
concealing pertinent facts that would indicate a loss or by mischaracterizing
or improperly describing the nature of the asset. The perpetrator is hoping
that the reader of the financial statements fails to see the warning signs that
an impairment loss has occurred.

Indicators of Impairment Losses under IFRS

IAS 36, *Impairment of Assets*, provides guidance on determining
whether an asset impairment has been incurred. Paragraph 12 states

that in assessing whether there is any indication that an asset may be impaired, an entity shall consider, as a minimum, the following indications:

External sources of information:

a. During the period, an asset's market value has declined significantly more than would be expected as a result of the passage of time or normal use.

b. Significant changes with an adverse effect on the entity have taken place during the period, or will take place in the near future, in the technological, market, economic or legal environment in which the entity operates or in the market to which an asset is dedicated.

c. Market interest rates or other market rates of return on investments have increased during the period, and those increases are likely to affect the discount rate used in calculating an asset's value in use and decrease the asset's recoverable amount materially.

d. The carrying amount of the net assets of the entity is more than its market capitalization.

Internal sources of information:

e. Evidence is available of obsolescence or physical damage of an asset.

f. Significant changes with an adverse effect on the entity have taken place during the period, or are expected to take place in the near future, in the extent to which, or manner in which, an asset is used or is expected to be used. These changes include the asset becoming idle, plans to discontinue or restructure the operation to which an asset belongs, plans to dispose of an asset before the previously expected date, and reassessing the useful life of an asset as finite rather than indefinite.

g. Evidence is available from internal reporting that indicates that the economic performance of an asset is, or will be, worse than expected.

Paragraph 14 of IAS 36 expands on item (g), indicating that evidence from internal reporting that indicates that an asset may be impaired includes the existence of:

a. Cash flows for acquiring the asset, or subsequent cash needs for operating or maintaining it, that are significantly higher than those originally budgeted;

b. Actual net cash flows or operating profit or loss flowing from the asset that are significantly worse than those budgeted;

(continued)

> **c.** A significant decline in budgeted net cash flows or operating profit, or a significant increase in budgeted loss, flowing from the asset; or
>
> **d.** Operating losses or net cash outflows for the asset, when current period amounts are aggregated with budgeted amounts for the future.
>

The third external factor from the preceding list of external factors (market interest rates) is one of the potentially significant differences between IFRS and U.S. GAAP. Recall from the earlier explanation of the definitions of impairment losses that U.S. GAAP compares undiscounted cash flows with carrying amount, whereas IFRS compares the present value of future cash flows with the carrying amount in determining whether a loss has been incurred. As a result, changes in market interest rates become an impairment indicator under IFRS, but are not necessarily a factor under U.S. GAAP.

Fraud Risk No. 9.2

Recognizing an impairment loss, but understating its extent through the use of improper measurement techniques.

Extent of Impairment Loss

The amount of an impairment loss is equal to the amount by which its carrying value exceeds its recoverable amount, based on fair value or expected cash flow methodologies, as explained earlier. However, acknowledging that an impairment has occurred by recognizing it in the financial statements may actually be a method of disguising a much bigger loss.

Under this method, a completely different strategy is utilized. By acknowledging that a loss has been incurred, the perpetrator is hoping that the reader assumes that the financial statements have been prepared honestly. The reader may not scrutinize the calculation of the loss very closely, since the preparer of the financial statements has voluntarily disclosed the existence of a loss, creating an air of honesty.

Accordingly, recognized impairments should be analyzed every bit as carefully as the conclusion that an impairment has not been incurred.

Reversal of Previous Impairment Losses

The issue of reversals of previously recognized impairment losses is another area where IFRS and U.S. GAAP have significant differences. Neither SFAS 144 nor SFAS 142 permit the recovery of a previous impairment loss. Under U.S. GAAP, the recognition of an impairment loss is permanent.

Fraud Risk No. 9.3

Improper reversal of a previously recognized impairment loss (IFRS only).

IAS 36 allows for the reversal of previously recorded impairment losses with respect to all intangible assets except for goodwill. Likewise, IFRS 5 allows for reversals of impairment losses as well. Under both IAS 36 and IFRS 5, the reversal of impairment losses can never exceed the cumulative amounts of losses previously recognized.

Reversals of Impairment Losses under IFRS

Paragraph 111 of IAS 36 states that in assessing whether there is any indication that an impairment loss recognized in prior periods for an asset other than goodwill may no longer exist or may have decreased, an entity shall consider, as a minimum, the following indications:

External sources of information:

a. The asset's market value has increased significantly during the period.
b. Significant changes with a favorable effect on the entity have taken place during the period, or will take place in the near future, in the technological, market, economic or legal environment in which the entity operates or in the market to which the asset is dedicated.

(continued)

c. Market interest rates or other market rates of return on investments have decreased during the period, and those decreases are likely to affect the discount rate used in calculating the asset's value in use and increase the asset's recoverable amount materially.

Internal sources of information:

d. Significant changes with a favorable effect on the entity have taken place during the period, or are expected to take place in the near future, in the extent to which, or manner in which, the asset is used or is expected to be used. These changes include costs incurred during the period to improve or enhance the asset's performance or restructure the operation to which the asset belongs.

e. Evidence is available from internal reporting that indicates that the economic performance of the asset is, or will be, better than expected.

A careful review of the preceding excerpt from IAS 36 shows that reversals of impairment losses can only be recorded when one or more of the underlying estimates about an asset's recoverable amount have changed. For example, a change in the basis for determining the recoverable amount from fair value less selling costs to value in use, or vice versa, would be a potentially legitimate basis for reversing an impairment loss. Likewise, changing estimated amounts or timing of future cash flows, or changes in the components of fair value or selling costs, would be potentially acceptable bases for reversing an impairment loss.

An important principal under IAS 36 is that a reversal of an impairment loss reflects an increase in the estimated service potential of an asset, either from use or from sale. IAS 36 requires an entity to identify the change in estimates that causes the increase in estimated service potential.

An asset's value in use may become greater than the asset's carrying amount simply because the present value of future cash inflows increases as they become closer. However, in this case, the service potential of the asset has not actually increased. Therefore, IAS 36 prohibits the reversal of an impairment loss just because of the passage of time (sometimes called the *unwinding* of the discount), even if the recoverable amount of the asset becomes higher than its carrying amount.

This last provision, which prohibits reversals of certain impairments, is an important consideration for auditors and investigators. Reversals of impairments originally based on discounted cash flows are prohibited if they are based solely on the passage of time, resulting in an increased present value. Only other changes in estimates can result in a reversal. To the untrained auditor or investigator, reversals based on the passage of time can appear to be reasonable. Yet recognizing such gains is not permitted and could actually be a method of perpetrating fraud.

Under IFRS, reversals of impairment losses can only be recorded up to the amount of the loss (i.e., the original carrying amount is the maximum carrying amount, unless the asset is of the type for which such gains can be recorded, such as with property and equipment). For amortizable intangible assets, increased carrying amount resulting from a reversal cannot exceed the carrying amount that would have resulted using the original basis, less accumulated amortization to date.

One area in which IFRS and U.S. GAAP agree in terms of reversals of impairment losses pertains to goodwill. Reversals of losses reported regarding goodwill are prohibited under IFRS, as well as U.S. GAAP.

When a recovery of an impairment loss is recognized under IFRS, it is reported in profit and loss, similar to how the loss itself was classified.

CHAPTER 10

Property and Equipment (Including Investment Properties)

P roperty and equipment (also referred to as fixed assets and as property, plant, and equipment) is a category of assets that includes tangible and long-lived assets, usually with useful lives of more than one year or accounting period. These assets are generally held for the production of goods or services, for rental to others, or for administrative purposes.

Sources of U.S. GAAP and IFRS

The international standard covering property and equipment is IAS 16, *Property, Plant and Equipment*, unless the property represents an investment, in which case its accounting treatment is addressed in IAS 40, *Investment Property*. Property is an investment property if it is held for rental or appreciation in value rather than for the entity's own use in producing goods or services or for administrative uses. Properties held for sale in the ordinary course of business (e.g., properties bought and sold, not held) are also excluded from the scope of IAS 40. IAS 40 provides numerous examples of properties that do or do not qualify for treatment as investment property.

There is no single U.S. accounting standard that is a direct counterpart to either IAS 16 or IAS 40. Rather, U.S. GAAP for property and equipment is found in a variety of sources, from statements addressing the definition of an asset to statements dealing with capitalization of interest (SFAS 34) and depreciation (ARB No. 43 and APB Opinion No. 12). Impairments of property and equipment are covered under SFAS 144, the standard addressed in Chapter 9.

Initial Recognition

Both U.S. GAAP and IFRS require that property and equipment be initially recognized at cost. Both sources of accounting provide an explanation of which costs should be included in determining the initial measurement of property and equipment, with a few potential differences. For instance, both IFRS and U.S. GAAP require the capitalization of construction-period interest costs. But IFRS also permits capitalization of other ancillary construction-period costs, whereas U.S. GAAP does not.

If an asset is received in exchange for a nonmonetary asset, the newly acquired asset should be recorded at its fair value on the date of the transaction.

Though not a fair value accounting issue per se, the accounting for subsequent costs associated with property and equipment can have indirect implications on fair value issues. In most areas, IFRS and U.S. GAAP are consistent in their treatment of subsequent costs. For example, subsequent costs of servicing an asset should be reported as expenses, not capitalized. In addition, the cost of replacing components of assets (e.g., the furnace in a building) should be capitalized as assets, with the carrying amount of the replaced items being written off. However, there are also differences that go beyond the scope of this book.

Measurement after Initial Recognition

After the initial recognition of property and equipment, IFRS offers an accounting option not available under U.S. GAAP. IAS 16 permits an entity to choose between the cost model (i.e., continue to carry the assets at cost, less depreciation) or a revaluation model. Under the revaluation model, the carrying value of property and equipment can be increased over its initial carrying amount if fair value has increased. The selection of the revaluation model cannot be done on an asset-by-asset basis. Rather, one option or the other must be selected for an entire class of property and equipment. Examples of classes of assets identified in IAS 16 include land, land and buildings, machinery, motor vehicles, furniture and fixtures, and office equipment.

Frequency of revaluation is not dictated under IFRS. It need not be done on an annual basis. Instead, IAS 16 states that revaluations should be done with sufficient regularity to ensure that carrying value does not differ materially from fair value. In addition, among the many required financial statement disclosure requirements of IAS 16 is the requirement to disclose whether an independent valuation specialist was involved in revaluing property and equipment if the revaluation option is elected.

Fraud Risk No. 10.1

Recording phony increases in fair value of property and equipment under the revaluation option (IFRS only).

The revaluation model obviously creates one additional fraud risk that does not exist under U.S. GAAP. In some cases, fair value determinations may be quite simple, such as with certain assets for which market-based evidence is plentiful (e.g., markets for identical or similar assets exist and a comparison is rather simple). But in other cases, a readily determinable market value may be difficult to find. In those cases, IAS 16 suggests use of an income or depreciated replacement cost approach (see Part I for discussion of these valuation techniques).

Falsely inflating values of property and equipment under the revaluation model could be accomplished in many ways, such as these three:

1. Misstating the condition of an asset for purposes of comparing the asset to a market for similar assets in varying conditions
2. Misclassifying an asset based on misleading information about its capabilities, resulting in comparing it to superior assets in a market
3. For assets without an active market, using inaccurate data in determining a value under the income or depreciated replacement cost approach

One other possibility for fraudulent presentation of the revaluation method concerns the classification of the gain itself. IAS 16 states that any gains recognized above the original basis must be recognized in other comprehensive income (not in operating profit or loss) and accumulated in a separate category within the equity section of the balance sheet. If an entity falsely classifies such gains in with other operating profits or losses, by grouping the gains with other items rather than separately identifying them, a reader could be misled with respect to the composition of the entity's increase in equity for the year.

Fraud Risk No. 10.2

Misclassifying increases in value of property and equipment under the revaluation model by incorrectly including them in profit or loss (IFRS only).

Investment Property

IAS 40 permits the use of a fair value model of accounting for properties that are designated as investment property. However, unlike the IAS 16 fair value model, the IAS 40 model results in the appreciation or depreciation in fair value being reported as part of profit or loss (much like the IAS 39 classification of other investments as fair value through profit or loss).

Generally, if the fair value model is elected, it must be used for all investment property. However an entity may elect either the fair value model or the cost model for all investment property backing liabilities that pay a return linked directly to the fair value of, or returns from, specified assets including that investment property and choose either the fair value or cost model for all other investment property.

Changing from one model to the other (e.g., fair value to cost) is permitted only if the change results in a more appropriate presentation. IAS 40 states that this is highly unlikely to be the case for a change from the fair value model to the cost model.

IAS 40 provides a significant amount of guidance on fair value determinations for investment properties. Some of this guidance is similar to the guidance from SFAS 157 explained in Part I, such as the greater reliability of using prices obtained from an active market over the use of internal estimates, and the need for making appropriate adjustments to market prices for assets that are similar but not identical to the asset in question. IAS 40 also suggests, but does not require, the use of independent appraisers.

Fair value determinations also should not consider the effects of internal synergies between the property and other assets, tax benefits, or other factors unique to the owner. Nor should it factor in any elements of the owner's financing arrangement or other factors that would not have a bearing on what knowledgeable and willing buyers and sellers would consider in negotiating a value.

Fair value determinations of investment property that generates rent income should be customized to the terms of the lease. For example, if the property is furnished, fair value should factor in not only the building, but the furnishings as well. When this is done, the furnishings should not also be recognized as a separate asset in the financial statements. This concept of not double-counting assets is an important element of the accounting for investment property and the subsequent fair value determination.

As noted earlier, there is no U.S. GAAP counterpart to IAS 40. Therefore, no specific literature exists in U.S. GAAP that specifically addresses investment property. Accordingly, most investment property, including that held by most real estate companies, is accounted for using the cost model, like other property and equipment, for U.S. GAAP purposes. There are, however, certain types of specialized entities—such as many investment companies, employee benefit plans that invest in real estate, and bank-sponsored real estate trusts—that carry investments at fair value.

Impairment Losses

Impairment losses occur when the asset property and equipment declines in fair value to an amount that is less than its carrying value, net of accumulated depreciation. IAS 16 states that for property and equipment, the guidance of IAS 36 on impairment losses should be applied in determining whether a loss has occurred. IAS 36 was explained in Chapter 9.

Likewise, under U.S. GAAP, the guidance of SFAS 144 should be followed to determine whether an impairment loss should be reported.

Fraud Risk No. 10.3

Failure to recognize an impairment loss on property and equipment.

Under both IFRS and U.S. GAAP, impairment losses to reflect declines in fair value to an amount that is less than the initially recognized carrying value should be included in profit or loss. However, under IAS 16, when the impairment loss merely reduces gains previously recognized from the revaluation option explained earlier, the loss should be recognized in comprehensive income to the extent of any previously recognized gains. After that, any further losses below the original basis should be reported in profit and loss.

Ultimately, property and equipment may become so impaired that the asset has no further future economic benefit. If that point is reached, the asset should be written off completely.

PART III

Liability-Based Schemes

Liability-based fraudulent financial reporting schemes typically involve one or more of the following:

- Omitting liabilities from the financial statements
- Undervaluing recognized liabilities, using inappropriate valuation techniques or revenue recognition practices
- Misclassifying current liabilities as noncurrent in order to inflate an entity's current ratio
- Electing to use fair value accounting for eligible liabilities and then recording fraudulent valuations on the underlying liabilities, sometimes resulting in the fraudulent reporting of gains in connection with reduced values of liabilities

The incentives behind each of these categories are similar to those explained in Part II—to present an entity as being more financially attractive than it really is. Fair value accounting plays a role in virtually every one of these schemes to varying degrees.

The U.S. GAAP definition of a liability is found in FASB Concepts Statement No. 6, *Elements of Financial Statements*. SFAC 6 defines liabilities as "probable future sacrifices of economic benefits arising from present obligations of a particular entity to transfer assets or provide services to other entities in the future as a result of past transactions or events."

Under IFRS, a liability is defined as a present obligation of the enterprise arising from past events, the settlement of which is expected to result in an outflow from the enterprise of resources embodying future benefits.

Nowhere has fair value accounting garnered more criticism than in the area of liabilities. Unlike many assets, which have active markets that can be relied on for reliable estimates of fair value, there are far fewer markets to utilize in measuring the fair value of a liability. This usually results in management needing to develop a hypothetical model, which may or may not be an accurate measure of what it would cost to settle a liability today.

Most models for fair valuing liabilities rely on interest rates and the term of the liability as two primary inputs to determining fair value.

But, *credit risk,* the risk that the debt will not be paid, is another factor that impacts fair value. And this is where the biggest problems (and potential for fraud) can come into play in valuing liabilities.

The most vocal critics of fair value accounting for liabilities claim that liabilities, such as debt, are generally already stated at the amount that the liability will be settled for. So why go through an elaborate theoretical calculation to value a liability when the current plans and expectations are to settle the obligation for the amount explained in the terms of the debt?

Indeed, one of the most interesting elements of fair value accounting is that as the chances of a company honoring and repaying its liabilities decrease, so does the fair value, and therefore the recorded amount, of those liabilities. In other words, a company's own credit worthiness, or credit riskiness, impacts the fair value of the liability in such a way that can be very misleading to readers of a set of financial statements. Decreasing balances in debt and other liability accounts (and, therefore, improvements reported in current ratios and certain other financial performance measures) may be a product of a well-run company repaying those obligations due to its financial success. Or, it may be the sign of a company that has written its liabilities down because it considers itself such a credit risk that the likelihood of repayment is less than 100 percent.

CHAPTER 11

Debt Obligations

D ebt obligations are liabilities associated with money that has been borrowed by an entity. Examples of debt obligations include:

- Loans from financial institutions (e.g., mortgages, lines of credit, and commercial loans from banks, finance companies, etc.)
- Unsecured promissory notes
- Bonds
- Mortgage-backed securities
- Asset-backed securities

In addition to a stated rate of interest (referred to as the *coupon rate* for most bonds) debt instruments can have three other important features that can impact their accounting treatment:

1. *Call provisions.* These provisions permit the issuer of the debt to repay the obligation prior to the stated maturity date, usually at some premium (to compensate the holder of the debt instrument for the reduction in interest income that the holder will receive).
2. *Put provisions.* These provisions enable the lender (the holder of the debt instrument) to require the borrower to repay the debt obligation prior to the scheduled maturity date, usually on specified dates and also often at par (face) value (thus enabling the lender to reinvest in other, more attractive, investment options it has available).
3. *Conversion options.* These provisions provide a bondholder with the ability to convert a bond into a specified quantity of shares of the issuing company's common stock.

Sources of U.S. GAAP and IFRS

IFRS for debt is IAS 39, *Financial Instruments: Recognition and Measurement*, the same standard referred to in several chapters of Part II. Under U.S.

GAAP, there is not a single standard that covers all aspects of debt. However, SFAS 159, *The Fair Value Option for Financial Assets and Financial Liabilities*, can be applied to debt, as explained later.

Measurement

Under both U.S. GAAP and IFRS, debt is generally initially recognized at an amount equal to the proceeds received or, if proceeds are not provided in cash, the fair value of the consideration received. Examples in which noncash consideration is provided are in transactions in which a financial institution makes payments directly to a third party that has provided assets to the borrower, such as with many equipment, automobile, and real estate loans.

After the initial issuance of debt, the subsequent measurement of debt under both U.S. GAAP and IFRS is to be measured at amortized cost using the effective interest method (unless a fair value option is elected, as explained later). However, U.S. GAAP and IFRS have differences in how the effective interest method is applied. Both also have a fair value option, which will be explained later.

Under U.S. GAAP, amortization is based on contractual cash flows over the contractual life of the instrument, with only two possible exceptions:

1. Puttable debt is to be amortized over the period from the date of issuance to the first put date.
2. Callable debt is to be amortized over *either* the contractual life or the estimated life of the instrument (once either of these options is selected, it must be applied consistently).

Fraud Risk No. 11.1

Improper amortization of a debt obligation based on false representations of contract terms.

IFRS, by contrast, bases effective interest rate calculations on estimated cash flows over the expected, not contractual, life of the instrument. Under IAS 39, contractual terms of debt are used only if it is not possible to otherwise estimate cash flows.

This difference, using estimated rather than contractual lives, can of course lead to material differences in calculations between IFRS and U.S. GAAP.

Fair Value Option

Both U.S. GAAP and IFRS provide for a fair value option for debt. Under IAS 39, *Financial Instruments: Recognition and Measurement*, debt may be designated as "at fair value through profit or loss" similar to the classification of investments explained in Chapter 4.

The fair value option for debt under U.S. GAAP is found in SFAS 159, *The Fair Value Option for Financial Assets and Financial Liabilities*, which was introduced in Chapter 2.

Fraud Risk No. 11.2

Improper calculation of the fair value of a debt obligation for which the fair value option has been elected.

The fair value option can create a fraud risk in the form of underreporting a debt obligation. This risk is explained in the next section.

Valuation of Debt

Contrary to the notion held by many, the fair value of a debt obligation is not necessarily equal to its par (stated) value. Although reporting a debt obligation at an amount that does not equal the face amount that will be repaid may seem counterintuitive, this is exactly what can, and often does, result when fair value accounting is applied.

One of the most important factors in determining the fair value of debt is whether or not the debt is collateralized. Uncollateralized debt will usually carry a greater risk than collateralized debt. With collateralized debt, its fair value is usually at least equal to the liquidation value of the underlying assets that have been pledged as collateral. Of course, determining the liquidation value of the underlying assets may not always be a simple task.

The primary factor that can lead to fair value of a debt obligation being different from par value is a debt instrument's yield to maturity. If the calculated yield to maturity differs from the interest rate stated in the debt instrument (e.g., the coupon rate of a bond), the fair value will differ from the face (par) value of the debt, as follows:

If Coupon rate > Yield to maturity, then Fair value > Face value
If Yield to maturity > Coupon rate, then Face value > Fair value

So, what are the primary factors that impact yield to maturity? Here is where it gets interesting. Calculating yield to maturity requires judgment regarding various risk factors. And when judgment is involved, the risk of fraud is greater.

Here are three primary risk factors to consider in developing a yield to maturity:

1. *Default risk.* This is the risk that the issuer/borrower will fail to pay some or all of a debt obligation. The primary factor impacting default risk is the financial condition of the issuer/borrower. Default risk falls under the category of nonperformance risk, one of the risk factors required to be considered under SFAS 157. Default risk may be mitigated based on the existence, nature, and liquidation value of collateral, as explained earlier.

2. *Interest rate risk.* This is the risk associated with changes in interest rates over time. If market rates of interest increase to levels in excess of the bond's rate of interest, the trading price of a bond decreases, and vice versa. When determining market rates of interest, rates should be located for debt instruments that are as similar as possible to the debt being evaluated in terms of amount and maturity dates, as well as other relevant factors.

3. *Call risk.* As explained earlier, a call feature enables the issuer to repay an obligation prior to its due date. Call risk represents the likelihood of such a call feature being exercised, which would impact the value of the debt to other participants in the market.

The fair value of a debt obligation, after assessing these and other relevant risks, is then equal to the present value of future cash flows, but using the yield to maturity as the discount rate rather than the stated rate in the debt instrument. As a result, fair value often differs from face value.

As with other fair valuations, information used to determine fair value of debt obligations may be internally generated or come from outside sources (i.e., observable versus unobservable inputs, using the SFAS 157 terminology). In some cases, a similar debt that is publicly traded may be located that can be a reliable estimate of fair value. In other cases, the discounted cash flow methodology summarized in the preceding paragraphs would be a more appropriate and reliable estimate of fair value.

But even under the discounted cash flow approach, inputs used may be a combination of internal data and external market data. For instance, the determination of a yield to maturity may best be determined by locating a similar company and utilizing information gathered from that company. This is particularly useful when assessing fair value of debt obligations of companies that are not publicly traded. Often, comparing the privately held business to a similar publicly traded company is a useful technique for determining fair value of a particular debt instrument.

The primary fair value accounting fraud risk with respect to any debt or other financial liability exists when these liabilities are designated as being carried at fair value on a recurring basis. Manipulation of fair value techniques may result in a liability being reported at a lower amount than what it should be—resulting in an overall understatement of liabilities.

An entity's estimation of its own default risk can actually have the effect of reducing the fair value of its own debt, a phenomenon that was studied carefully and criticized by many observers during the early stages of the global economic crisis in 2008. Several financial institutions in the United States and United Kingdom reported profits (or a reduced level of losses) and a stable financial condition as a result of recording gains associated with the reduction of debt obligations not for principal payments they had made, but for reductions in the fair value of the liabilities based on their assessment of default risk. To some observers, this seemed to be a devious method of financial reporting, yet it is consistent with the overall concept of fair value accounting as currently described in the standards.

CHAPTER 12

Deferred Revenue

Deferred revenue represents a liability for funds received by an entity for which it has an obligation to provide future goods or services. Most accounting issues associated with deferred revenue are fairly simple—a customer has paid for goods or services that have not yet been provided, so the amount received is reported as a liability. The amount is then reported as revenue when the goods or services have been delivered.

However, accounting for deferred revenue is not always so simple. This chapter focuses on two deferred revenue issues that can be more complicated and that also involve fair value accounting:

1. Liabilities for customer loyalty programs
2. Deferred revenue from multiple deliverables

Customer loyalty programs have become very popular with retailers and can be a major attraction for customers. Under a customer loyalty program, as a customer purchases goods or services from a business, points or other credits accumulate, providing an incentive for making additional purchases. Once a certain number of points are earned, the customer can cash in the points for additional products or services at discounted prices or even without paying anything at all to the business.

The primary fraud risk associated with customer loyalty programs is the risk of omission or underreporting of a liability for future goods or services that a business will have to provide to customers in connection with its program. This liability should generally be recorded at a fair value.

Customer loyalty programs can be considered as a subset of the broader topic of multiple deliverables, in which a customer receives multiple goods or services that could have been purchased individually for one combined price. The combined price is lower than what it would have cost to purchase each item individually.

Sources of U.S. GAAP and IFRS

IFRS for customer loyalty programs is found in IFRIC 13, *Customer Loyalty Programmes*. U.S. GAAP attempted to address the issue in EITF 00-22, *Accounting for "Points" and Certain Other Time-Based or Volume-Based Sales Incentive Offers*. However, consensus could not be reached on all of the issues in EITF 00-22. One key element initially included within the EITF 00-22 discussion, however, was addressed, and consensus was reached in EITF 01-9, *Accounting for Consideration Given by a Vendor to a Customer (Including a Reseller of a Vendor's Products)*.

As a result, there is not a true U.S. GAAP counterpart to IFRIC 13 that specifically addresses customer loyalty programs. By analogy, however, there are other sources of U.S. GAAP that can be applied. Most notably, EITF 00-21, *Revenue Arrangements with Multiple Deliverables*, can be applied to many customer loyalty programs. EITF 00-21 also applies to many revenue recognition issues beyond those associated with customer loyalty programs. Accordingly, the second part of this chapter will explain other issues associated with multiple deliverable arrangements.

Additional guidance on the deferral or revenue under IFRS is found in IAS 18, *Revenue*, which addresses some of the same circumstances as EITF 00-21.

Recognition—Customer Loyalty Programs

IFRIC 13, which was issued with an effective date of periods beginning on or after July 1, 2008, applies to certain incentives that are earned in connection with sales, not to incentives provided to initially generate a sale (e.g., free coupons provided upon entry to a store for discounts on products purchased that day, which are simply accounted for as reductions in revenue when the coupon is used). There are three types of customer loyalty programs that can result in the requirement to record a liability:

1. *Awards that entitle the holder to discounted goods and services.* Discounts could apply either in the same store or in other stores that are part of the same chain.
2. *Award credits that entitle the holder to discounted goods or services provided by another entity.* For example, renting a car may entitle the holder to earn free miles on an airline.
3. *Arrangements in which third party organizations provide a service of redeeming awards against a variety of goods or services.* Examples include credit card programs entitling a card holder to redeem points for products from specific third-party retailers.

IFRIC 13 requires that revenue be deferred when the consideration provided to a customer in connection with the loyalty program entitles the customer to a discount on a future purchase. The consideration is to be allocated among the different elements of an arrangement using fair values. A liability for deferred revenue should be recorded based on the fair value of the award credits. For example, when cash is received from a customer in exchange for goods or services plus award credits that can be used for future purchases, the following entry would be made:

Dr. Cash 1,000
Cr. Deferred revenue 50
Cr. Revenue 950

Fraud Risk No. 12.1

Failure to recognize a liability for the redemption of future award credits in connection with a customer loyalty program.

IFRIC 13 does not mandate a specific method of determining fair values of these incentives, but it does state that the amount should be based on the fair value to the holder, *not* the cost of redemption to the issuer.

Often, a reasonable estimate of fair value will be based on the discount that customers will receive when award credits are redeemed. However, IFRIC 13 also acknowledges that in many cases, not all available award credits will be redeemed by customers. Accordingly, the deferral of revenue should also be based on the proportion of incentives that are expected to be redeemed. This estimate may be very difficult or very easy to determine, based on the extent of past history that the issuer has with such incentive programs. This estimate may also be a target for fraudulent financial reporting in the form of intentional understatement of the estimated rate of redemption of award credits.

Fraud Risk No. 12.2

Underestimating the redemption rate associated with award credits of a customer loyalty program, resulting in an understated liability.

In most cases, fair value estimates will be based on the cash value of a voucher or on the value of goods or services for which a voucher can be redeemed. Four factors could impact the determination of fair value of redeemable credits under customer loyalty programs:

1. Whether the incentive is limited so that it can only be redeemed for certain products or whether it can be applied to any future purchase
2. If the incentive is limited to specific products:
   a. The relative popularity of the product
   b. The "sell by" date of the product (e.g., products with limited shelf lives)
   c. Technological obsolescence or similar indicators of the stage in a product's life cycle
   d. Subsequent price changes for the products for which a voucher can be redeemed
3. Whether the issuer also issues free vouchers entitling the customer to discounts similar to those earned in connection with sales (i.e., this reduces the fair value of the credits earned in connection with sales)
4. Expiration date of the incentive (i.e., award credits that can be redeemed over an indefinite life may be more difficult to evaluate, but usually have greater value to a customer)

In connection with the fourth factor, deferred revenue would be reduced upon the expiration of award credits that involve a "use by" date.

Fraud Risk No. 12.3

Underestimating the fair value of award credits associated with a customer loyalty program (IFRS) or underestimating the cost of honoring rebates/refunds earned (U.S. GAAP), resulting in an understated liability.

As noted earlier, U.S. GAAP for customer loyalty programs is more limited than IFRS. EITF 01-9 states that a vendor (the issuer of the incentive or the third party with responsibility under the program) should recognize a rebate or refund obligation as a reduction of revenue based on a systematic and rational allocation of the *cost* of honoring rebates or refunds earned and claimed to each of the underlying revenue transactions that result in progress by the customer toward earning the rebate or refund. Recall that IFRIC 13 requires the deferral of revenue at fair value. The recognition of a liability at cost, rather than deferring revenue at fair value, is the primary difference between U.S. GAAP and IFRS on this issue.

Measurement of the total rebate or refund obligation should be based on the estimated number of customers that will ultimately earn and claim rebates or refunds, much like IFRIC 13. But EITF 01-9 states that if the amount of future rebates or refunds cannot be reasonably estimated, a liability should be recognized for the maximum potential amount of the refund or rebate.

Fraud Risk No. 12.4

Underestimating the future purchases of a customer in connection with a rebate/refund program in connection with programs in which customers are entitled to a higher rate or rebate/refund as purchases increase, resulting in an understated liability (U.S. GAAP).

EITF 01-9 addresses one additional factor that must be considered in connection with certain customer loyalty programs. In some cases, the relative size of the rebate or refund changes based on the volume of purchases. For example, a rebate may be 5 percent of total consideration if more than 500 units are purchased but may increase to 10 percent if more than 1,000 units are purchased. If the volume of a customer's future purchases can be reasonably estimated, that estimate should be used in calculating the obligation. But if the volume of a customer's future purchases cannot be reasonably estimated, the maximum potential rebate or refund factor should be used to record a liability (10 percent in the example).

Multiple Deliverable Arrangements

EITF 00-21, *Revenue Arrangements with Multiple Deliverables*, states that revenue arrangements containing multiple deliverables should be divided into their separate units of accounting if all of the following three conditions are present:

1. The delivered item(s) has value to the customer on a stand-alone basis, as evidenced by the fact that the item is sold separately by any vendor or the customer could resell the delivered item(s) on a stand-alone basis. (The EITF notes that evidence of an observable market for the item is not necessary to meet this condition.)
2. There is objective and reliable evidence of the fair value of the undelivered item(s).
3. If the arrangement includes a general right of return relative to the delivered item(s), delivery or performance of the undelivered item(s) is considered probable and substantially in the control of the vendor.

If these three criteria are met, revenue should be allocated to each item based on its relative fair value. Then, an appropriate revenue recognition policy should be applied to each item included in the arrangement.

Fraud Risk No. 12.5

Improper allocation of revenue among multiple goods or services sold in connection with a multiple deliverable arrangement.

EITF 08-1, *Revenue Arrangements with Multiple Deliverables*, is in the process of being finalized as this book is being written. Once consensus is reached, it will replace EITF 00-21 and make several modifications, although the core concept of allocating revenue to each deliverable remains unchanged. One change made by EITF 08-1 would be to eliminate the second required condition from the previous list. Due to the issuance of SFAS 157 and its resulting change in the definition of fair value, EITF 08-1 will use the term *selling price* in place of fair value.

IFRS for multiple deliverables is covered in the broader standard IAS 18, which addresses most revenue recognition issues under IFRS. IAS 18 includes a similar, though not as detailed, provision requiring the allocation of revenue among the separately identifiable components of a single transaction based on the relative fair value of the components.

The fraud risk associated with multiple deliverable arrangements deals with the potential for manipulating the timing of revenue recognition—either recognizing revenue too early (and therefore understating the liability for deferred revenue) or, perhaps, delaying revenue recognition for a later period.

Consider the following illustration. If a company normally sells a particular piece of large equipment for $30,000 and also sells three-year service contracts on equipment for $5,000, but will sell them together for $33,000, a possibility for fair value accounting fraud exists in the allocation of the revenue. Under EITF 00-21, the total price of $33,000 should generally be allocated as follows:

Equipment sale: $33,000 × (30,000/35,000) = $28,285.71

Service agreement: $33,000 × (5,000/35,000) = $4,714.29

The $28,285.71 of revenue allocated to the sale should be recognized as income upon the completion of the sale transaction. However, the $4,714.29 of revenue allocable to the service agreement should initially be deferred and likely recognized as revenue over the three years associated with the service provided to the customer.

Recognizing $30,000 upon completion of the sale transaction (based on the fact that this is the normal sales price of the equipment) and only deferring $3,000 for the service agreement would inflate the initial year's revenue by $1,714.29.

Although the total amount of revenue to be recognized over time is not overstated in this scheme, the timing of the revenue recognition has been fraudulently stated so that certain years are overstated and others are understated. Recognizing the revenue too soon is, in effect, robbing revenue from future periods to make the current period look better.

CHAPTER 13

Asset Retirement Obligations

A sset retirement obligations represent liabilities that should be recorded presently for the costs associated with future obligations involving existing long-lived assets, such as land, buildings, and equipment. Examples of asset retirement obligations include asbestos abatement associated with a building and requirements to return land to its original condition after being used by an entity, such as with mining and other operations. These obligations may be the result of contract provisions, laws, or regulations. In some cases, an obligation exists when an asset is first acquired or constructed. In other cases, the obligation might arise after the initial acquisition, such as with the passage of new laws or regulations.

Significant use of judgment and development of estimates is involved in recording asset retirement obligations, making these liabilities a prime target for fair value accounting fraud.

Financial reporting fraud risks associated with asset retirement obligations have both direct and indirect connections to fair value accounting. Two primary financial reporting fraud risks are associated with asset retirement obligations:

1. Failing to recognize a liability for a conditional asset retirement obligation
2. Undervaluing a recognized liability associated with a conditional asset retirement obligation

There are multiple techniques that can be utilized to perpetrate each of these types of frauds. Each of these risks will be explained in this chapter.

Sources of U.S. GAAP and IFRS

U.S. GAAP for asset retirement obligations is found in SFAS 143, *Accounting for Asset Retirement Obligations*, and FIN 47, *Accounting for Conditional Asset Retirement Obligations*.

There is no separate standard under IFRS dealing exclusively with asset retirement obligations per se. But, IAS 16, *Property, Plant and Equipment*, includes a requirement to add certain asset retirement costs to the carrying value of the asset, resulting in an offsetting liability. In addition, IAS 37, *Provisions, Contingent Liabilities and Contingent Assets*, provides guidance on recording liabilities of this nature.

Recognition—U.S. GAAP

Under SFAS 143, a company is required to record a liability for any legal obligation that will result from the eventual retirement of a tangible long-lived asset. An asset retirement obligation is conditional when the timing and/or the method of settling the obligation is conditional on some future event. The event may or may not be within the control of the company.

Many companies did not record liabilities in accordance with SFAS 143 on the basis that either the timing or method of retiring an asset could not be determined or that a liability should not be recorded until the asset retirement takes place. FIN 47 was issued to clarify that neither of these reasons is a sound basis for not recording a liability. In other words, if a legal obligation exists, the liability associated with the obligation is inevitable, despite uncertainties associated with the timing or method of satisfying the obligation. Therefore, a liability should be recorded. And that liability should be recorded at its fair value.

Fraud Risk No. 13.1

Falsely claiming that an asset retirement obligation does not exist in order to omit the liability from the financial statements.

Asset retirement obligations may arise from laws, regulations, or even provisions of contracts. An example of a conditional asset retirement obligation stemming from a law or regulation could be a requirement to remove asbestos from a building prior to selling, demolishing, or making major improvements to it. One that could arise from either a contract or from a law would be a requirement to return land to its original natural condition after it has been used by a business for a specific purpose (e.g., mining, etc.).

The determination of whether a legal obligation exists can be a complicated one, requiring much use of professional judgment. This, of course, can lead to intentional misinterpretations of laws, regulations, or provisions of contracts. Here are two possible methods of fraudulently claiming that a legal obligation does not exist:

1. Suppressing information—withholding contracts or key contract provisions from auditors and others.
2. Relying on a legal or other expert opinion from someone who is not independent. An entity's internal legal counsel or other hired expert may want to see things the entity's way, which could result in a biased opinion regarding whether a legal obligation exists.

If similar entities or entities with similar assets in the same geographic region have recognized asset retirement obligations, this may be another sign that an entity has failed to recognize an asset retirement obligation.

Liabilities for conditional asset retirement obligations are to be recognized when the obligation is incurred if a reasonable estimate of its fair value can be determined. For assets acquired that have preexisting asset retirement obligations, a liability should be recognized in connection with the acquisition.

When a liability for an asset retirement obligation is recognized, the debit side of the entry is to the asset's basis. The amount capitalized should then be allocated to expense as depreciation over the asset's estimated useful life if it is a depreciable asset, such as a building (i.e., consistent with depreciating the initial cost of the asset over its useful life).

As a result, failure to record an asset retirement obligation may not have a material impact of profit or loss in any given year. The shorter the useful life or expected settlement of the liability, the shorter the time period over which depreciation may be recognized, which increases the annual impact on earnings. However, even if the impact on earnings is minimal, the balance sheet effect of recording such a liability has the potential for adversely affecting certain financial ratios. Accordingly, failure to record an asset retirement obligation should be viewed as a potentially significant fraud risk.

Recognition—IFRS

Under IAS 16, the carrying amount of property, plant, and equipment should include the initial estimate of the costs of dismantling and removing the item and restoring the site on which it is located. The obligation for these costs are incurred either when the item is initially acquired or as a consequence of having used the item during a particular period (for purposes other than to produce inventories). This additional estimated amount is then subject to depreciation, just like under U.S. GAAP, if it is associated with a depreciable asset.

Although worded quite differently (and far less extensively) than its U.S. counterparts, IAS 16 results in a similar requirement to increase the basis of an asset and record an offsetting liability for asset retirement obligations. However, in order to record this liability under IFRS, the requirements of IAS 37 must also be met. Under IAS 37, a liability should only be recognized when all three of the following characteristics are present:

1. There is a present obligation, whether legal or constructive, resulting from a past event.
2. It is probable that an outflow of resources embodying economic benefits will be required to settle the obligation.
3. A reliable estimate can be made of the amount of the obligation.

IAS 37 is explained in greater detail in Chapter 17. But the IFRS fraud risk here is similar to that under U.S. GAAP—that an entity could falsely claim that a present obligation exists.

Can a Reliable Estimate Be Determined?

A key component of the preceding SFAS 143 and FIN 47 rules, as well as the IFRS rules, is whether a reasonable estimate of the fair value of the obligation can be made. An estimate can be made only if sufficient information is available to calculate such an estimate. A company can do so when one of the following three conditions are present:

1. It is clearly evident that the acquisition price of the asset embodies the fair value of the obligation.
2. An active market exists to transfer the obligation.
3. The company has sufficient information to apply an expected present value technique.

Fraud Risk No. 13.2

Falsely claiming that it is not possible to develop a reasonable estimate of an asset retirement obligation in order to avoid recording a liability.

Under U.S. GAAP, if a company concludes that it cannot reasonably estimate the fair value of an asset retirement obligation, and therefore does not record a liability, it must make a disclosure in the footnotes to its financial statements. This disclosure must include the following:

1. A description of the obligation
2. The fact that a reasonable estimate could not be made
3. The reasons that made it impossible to estimate and record the liability

These disclosure requirements create yet another risk of fraud in connection with asset retirement obligations for which an estimate may genuinely be impossible.

Fraud Risk No. 13.3

Failing to disclose asset retirement obligations that exist but for which it is not possible to make a reliable estimate.

Measuring and Recording an Asset Retirement Obligation

Once the criteria for recognition have been met, it is time to move on to developing the estimate of the obligation's fair value. The following steps illustrate a typical approach to measuring and recording a conditional asset retirement obligation:

1. Clearly identify and gain an understanding of the full extent of the obligation (e.g., asbestos abatement, etc.).
2. Estimate the date(s) of settlement (it may be necessary to develop a weighted average of a range of possible dates).
3. Obtain estimates of the cost (measured in current rates).
4. Assign probabilities and develop a weighted average of the estimated cost of settling the obligation, if multiple estimates were obtained in the preceding step.
5. Estimate a rate of inflation and project the cost estimate out to the estimated date of settlement, resulting in a cost estimate expressed in an amount expected to be paid at that future date.
6. Determine the entity's credit-adjusted risk-free interest rate (this will usually result in a different rate than the inflation rate) using risk-free rates associated with maturity dates that coincide with the expected date(s) of cash outflows to settle the obligation (SFAS 143 requires the use of the entity's credit-adjusted risk-free rate).
7. Calculate the present value of the liability, based on the expected future cost and the credit-adjusted risk-free interest rate.

8. Record the initial obligation by debiting the asset and crediting the liability in equal amounts based on the amount determined in the preceding step.
9. Thereafter, record depreciation expense and accumulated depreciation on the asset, based on the estimated useful life of the asset, not on the expected settlement date of the obligation.
10. Thereafter, record accretion expense each year, with the offsetting credit side of the entry increasing the liability, so that at the time the expected settlement date is reached, the balance in the liability account will be the amount calculated in step 5.
11. Each year, consider whether adjustments to the estimates of the amounts or timing of future cash flows used in the calculation should be updated, and make any resulting adjustments to the calculations and entries (under SFAS 143, adjustments should not be made to the discount rate, which should remain at the rate established in step 6).

If an entity is currently recording a conditional asset retirement obligation in connection with an obligation that has existed from prior years, a cumulative effect on opening retained earnings should be calculated. In other words, the present value of the obligation should be calculated as of the date that the liability was created (some prior year), using today's cost estimates (adjusted for inflation from today to the expected settlement date) but the prior year's credit-adjusted risk-free interest rates that would be appropriate for the expected maturity of the obligation at that time.

In subsequent periods, estimates of undiscounted asset retirement obligation costs should be revised as circumstances change. As cost estimates change, the same process of calculating the present value of those costs should be performed, and both the asset and the liability should be increased or decreased for these changes.

Many of the steps outlined in the preceding process require a great deal of judgment. As a result, each step represents a potential opportunity for fraud.

Fraud Risk No. 13.4

Underestimating the costs that will be required to settle an asset retirement obligation, either through incorrect internal estimates or the use of improper external estimates.

In addition, the development of cost estimates that rely on information purportedly obtained from independent outside vendors can be subject to fraud and falsification. For example:

- Cost estimates may be "received" from sham vendors, when in fact all of the documentation was fraudulently prepared internally and made to look like it came from an outside vendor.
- Vendors that provided cost estimates exist (i.e., they are not fictitious vendors), but they are not independent from the entity (they are undisclosed affiliates).

Under IFRS, the calculation also involves cost estimating and a present value calculation. IAS 37 requires that when the three factors described earlier are present, the estimate of the future costs associated with the obligation should be discounted to present value using a discount rate that reflects current market assessments of the time value of money and any risks specific to the liability.

Summary—Comparison of U.S. GAAP and IFRS

There are two primary areas in which U.S. GAAP and IFRS differ in relation to recording liabilities associated with asset retirement obligations:

1. *The interest rate used in initially recording the liability.* U.S. GAAP requires the use of an entity's credit-adjusted risk-free rate, while IFRS uses a pretax discount rate that reflects current market assessments of the time value of money and the risks specific to the liability.
2. *Changes in the liability due to the passage of time (the unwinding of the present value calculation).* U.S. GAAP requires that the entity use the same credit-adjusted risk-free rate that existed when the liability was first measured, whereas IFRS adjusts the discount rate to reflect current conditions each period.

This results in one fraud risk under IFRS that should not be present under U.S. GAAP—the intentional use of an inappropriate discount rate in subsequent years when the liability is recalculated.

Fraud Risk No. 13.5

Miscalculating the present value of an asset retirement obligation by manipulating one or more of the factors used in the calculation, such as the discount rate, anticipated date of settlement, or rate of inflation.

Under both U.S. GAAP and IFRS, determination of the amount of a liability to be recorded involves the use of judgment and is therefore susceptible to manipulation and fraud. Here are seven key factors subject to judgment:

1. Evaluating whether the criteria for recording an asset retirement obligation have been met, which may involve legal interpretations of laws, regulations, and contracts
2. Determining whether sufficient evidence exists to make a reliable estimate of the obligation
3. Estimating at what date in the future the asset retirement obligation will be settled
4. Estimating the costs associated with the obligation
5. Determining the appropriate discount rate to be used in calculating the present value of the obligation
6. Assigning probabilities used in arriving at a weighted average amount cost estimate, if multiple present value calculations are performed based on different scenarios or multiple settlement dates or methods of settlement were considered
7. Identifying and making adjustments for subsequent changes in obligations or costs after the initial estimate has been performed

Each of these factors can be manipulated in order to either falsely omit or understate an asset retirement obligation.

CHAPTER 14

Guarantees

I n a guarantee, one party provides assurance that a performance requirement of another party is met. Here are three examples of guarantees:

1. One company has a note payable to a financial institution, and payment
   of the note is guaranteed by another company.
2. One manufacturer has a contract with a customer to provide certain
   quantity of products, and the contract is guaranteed by another manufacturer.
3. One entity leases its office space from a landlord that requires the
   guarantee of another entity.

Guarantees result in two types of liabilities:

1. A noncontingent liability
2. A contingent liability

The noncontingent liability represents the guarantor's ongoing obligation to perform under the terms and for the duration of the guarantee—a
sort of *being on standby* during the guarantee period. The contingent liability represents the guarantor's potential obligation to make payments in the
future in case events trigger such an obligation.

Guarantees create special reporting and disclosure requirements in connection with the financial statements of the guarantor.

Sources of U.S. GAAP and IFRS

U.S. GAAP for the contingent liability inherent in a guarantee is covered
in SFAS 5, *Accounting for Contingencies*. The topic of contingencies covers
potential gains and losses, not just those involving guarantees. Accordingly,

141

fair value accounting issues associated with contingencies are covered separately in Chapter 17.

The focus of this chapter will be on the noncontingent element of guarantees.

U.S. GAAP addresses the accounting for guarantees in FASB Interpretation (FIN) 45, *Guarantor's Accounting and Disclosure Requirements for Guarantees, Including Indirect Guarantees of Indebtedness of Others.* FIN 45 provides for specific footnote disclosure requirements associated with guarantees. More important for the focus of this book, however, are the requirements for guarantors to record a liability for certain types of guarantees.

IFRS for guarantees is covered in IAS 39, *Financial Instruments: Recognition and Measurement*, the same standard applied in other chapters dealing with financial assets and liabilities.

Recognition—U.S. GAAP

FIN 45 provides for disclosure requirements on many guarantees, and a requirement to record a liability for some, but not all, of those guarantees. FIN 45 applies to most, but not all, guarantees. The most common guarantees that are covered and that have important fair value considerations fall into two broad categories:

1. *Contracts that require the guarantor to make payments if another party fails to perform under an agreement.* The performance that is guaranteed can be in the form of making payments to the guaranteed party (e.g., repaying a loan to a bank), manufacturing or delivering goods to a customer, performance of services for a customer, or many other types of performance. The payment made by the guarantor can be in the form of cash, transfer of other assets, or even the provision of services.
2. *Contracts that require the guarantor to make payments based on changes in the underlying that is related to an asset, liability, or equity security.* An underlying can be an interest rate, foreign exchange rate, an index, credit rating, price of a financial instrument, or some other variable.

Commercial letters of credit and other commitments (often referred to as guarantees of funding) are excluded from the scope of FIN 45. In addition, FIN 45 provides a list of seven additional scope exceptions, such as SFAS 13 contingent rent provisions and others.

Fraud Risk No. 14.1

Failing to recognize a liability of a guarantor based on a guarantee contract.

FIN 45 requires that upon the inception of a guarantee, a liability must be recognized in the financial statements of the guarantor. Generally, this liability should be measured at fair value. However, if the contingent liability required to be reported under SFAS 5 is greater, then that larger amount should be recognized.

There are several exceptions from the requirement to record a liability by a guarantor. Among the most important exceptions are those involving affiliated entities (parent–subsidiary and brother–sister relationships) and those that are accounted for as derivatives under SFAS 133 (see Chapter 15).

Measurement

Fair value is not the same as the maximum amount that a guarantor may ultimately have to pay. Instead, it represents an assessment of the value for taking on a risk of financial or nonfinancial performance for a specified period of time, considering all market and entity-specific risks.

In many cases, the initial fair value of a guarantee is easy to determine since one party pays or promises to pay another party (the guarantor) a specified amount in exchange for the guarantee. That amount will usually represent the initial fair value of the guarantee. If the guarantee is one component of a larger transaction involving multiple components, the assessment of fair value becomes more difficult.

Fraud Risk No. 14.2

Understatement of the liability when a guarantee is initially recognized in the financial statements of a guarantor.

In addition, in some cases, consideration for entering into a guarantee contract is not to be in the form of cash. Instead, nonmonetary consideration is provided. In these cases, the fair value of the nonmonetary consideration received or receivable must be determined. See Chapter 19 for more on nonmonetary transactions.

FIN 45 does not prescribe any specific methods of measuring this liability subsequent to the initial measurement. Generally, a liability should remain for the duration of the guarantee, which may span several years. However, FIN 45 does not address how to measure the liability from year to year. Three of the most common approaches to subsequent measurement of the liability have emerged, and all three are cited as examples under FIN 45:

1. Retaining the liability at its original measurement until the guarantee has expired or is otherwise settled
2. Utilizing an amortization approach to systematically reduce the liability over the term of the guarantee
3. Assessing the fair value of the guarantee at the end of each fiscal year and making appropriate adjustments to the liability each year

As the liability is reduced, the reduction is offset by a corresponding credit to revenue of the guarantor, much like recognizing deferred revenue.

Fraud Risk No. 14.3

Improperly amortizing a liability associated with a guarantee over the life of the guarantee, resulting in reduction of the liability at an accelerated rate and an overstatement of revenue.

If it becomes apparent that the guarantor may have to perform under the guarantee arrangement, the contingent liability associated with performance may then need to be recorded as a liability. The criteria for recording a liability for this contingency are covered in Chapter 17.

Recognition—IFRS

IAS 39 defines a financial guarantee contract as "a contract that requires the issuer to make specified payments to reimburse the holder for a loss it incurs because a specified debtor fails to make payment when due in accordance with the original or modified terms of a debt instrument." Financial guarantee contracts are to be initially recognized at fair value, which usually equals the consideration received in exchange for entering into the contract.

Subsequent to the initial recognition, the liability associated with financial guarantee contracts is to be measured at the greater of two amounts:

1. The amount initially recognized, less any accumulated amortization recognized to date
2. The amount that would be recognized under IAS 37

Amortization of the liability associated with a financial guarantee contract results in the recognition of revenue. Accordingly, it falls within the scope of IAS 18, *Revenue*, for purposes of determining an appropriate revenue recognition (amortization) method. Since IAS 18 states that revenue should be measured based on fair value, the amortization—and therefore the resulting balance of the liability—should be measured at fair value under this approach.

The second approach measures the liability as it would be measured under IAS 37, *Provisions, Contingent Liabilities and Contingent Assets*. IAS 37 measures liabilities associated with provisions based on the expected expenditures necessary to settle the provision. See Chapter 17 for details on IAS 37.

Based on the preceding, a typical liability would be initially established based on the consideration received, then reduced based on an appropriate method of amortization. Measuring the liability based on the principles of IAS 37 would likely only be done in cases in which it has become likely that the guarantor will have to perform and an estimate of the expected costs of settling the obligation can be made.

Guarantees that are based on an underlying price or index are called derivatives within the scope of IAS 39. Derivatives are covered separately in Chapter 15.

PART IV

Other Fair Value Accounting Fraud Issues

In this section, we'll explore some fair value accounting issues that do not fit neatly into either the asset or the liability sections of Parts II and III. Some of the issues covered in this section could impact either assets or liabilities, such as:

- Derivatives, including hedging instruments
- Employee benefit plans that are over- or underfunded
- Contingencies (U.S. GAAP) and provisions (IFRS)
- Nonmonetary transactions

Others, such as share-based payments, could affect either liabilities or the equity section of the balance sheet. But all of these issues involve fair value accounting and could materially impact on organization's reported profit or loss if fraud is involved.

Part IV will also explain some of the most important financial statement disclosure issues relating to fair value accounting. Disclosures in the notes to the financial statements are every bit as important as the financial statements themselves. The notes explain some of the most important aspects of items reported in the financial statements—and even some important aspects of items that are not reported in the financial statements. Financial statement disclosures can provide important clues about the risk of fair value fraud in the financial statements, but these disclosures may themselves also be used to perpetrate fraud by omitting or misstating information.

Finally, this section will also cover how some specialized fair value accounting issues impact nonbusiness organizations, such as not-for-profit organizations. These organizations do not have the same financial reporting objectives as for-profit commercial businesses. But don't think that this means that these organizations are not susceptible to risks of fraudulent financial reporting that involve fair value accounting!

CHAPTER 15

Derivatives and Hedging

Derivatives are a complicated area, and one that can be difficult to understand. For those unfamiliar with derivatives, think of an insurance policy. Just as you pay an insurance premium in exchange for protection against certain specified events (e.g., fire, flood, theft, etc.), there are a wide variety of derivative instruments that provide protection in the event that certain events occur. In exchange for this protection, a payment is required.

Although this is an overly simplistic introduction to the highly complex world of derivatives, it nonetheless serves our purpose for getting started in this area. Indeed, some derivatives have virtually nothing in common with an insurance policy. But an example may further enhance an understanding of derivatives. Let's assume that the trading price for a particular stock is $100 per share. If we purchase shares at that price and the price goes up to $125, we make $25 a share. If the price goes down to $80, we lose $20. Instead of buying the shares and assuming the risk, we may be able to purchase an option to purchase the stock at $100 a share. There will be a price to purchase this option, and the option will expire after a specified period of time. But it enables us to purchase the stock at $100 even if the market price goes above $100 at any time during the option period. And we are under no obligation to purchase the stock at $100 a share if the market price declines below that level.

There are many different types of derivatives. In addition, a derivative can be either an asset or a liability. A review of several large company's financial statements and footnotes disclosed that derivatives were included in many different line items on the balance sheet, including these four:

1. Current accounts and notes receivable
2. Long-term receivables
3. Accounts payable
4. Deferred credits

The formal definitions of derivatives will be provided later. But first, here are some examples of contracts that often qualify as derivative instruments:

- Interest rate swaps
- Currency forwards/swaps
- Purchased/written options
- Commodity contracts
- Collars/caps
- Credit derivatives

Some, but not all, derivatives are considered to be hedges. As its name implies, a hedge is a derivative that is designed to offset possible future fluctuations—often future changes in interest rates, market prices, or foreign exchange rates.

Fair value accounting plays a prominent role in the accounting for derivatives under both U.S. GAAP and IFRS. In this chapter, I will explain the key fraud risks associated with derivatives and hedging. In order to do so, I will also explain several of the most important accounting principles associated with derivatives and hedging. But this explanation will fall far short of providing a complete guide to the accounting for derivatives. The goal of this chapter is to provide you with a solid understanding of the accounting concepts necessary to recognize and investigate fair value accounting fraud in the area of derivatives and hedging—not to prepare readers for all of the rules associated with derivative accounting.

Sources of U.S. GAAP and IFRS

U.S. GAAP for derivatives is found in SFAS 133, *Accounting for Derivative Instruments and Hedging Activities*. SFAS 133 has been amended several times, an acknowledgment of just how complicated this area can be.

IFRS for derivatives is located in IAS 39 *Financial Instruments: Recognition and Measurement*. IAS 39 has also been amended multiple times.

Definitions and Treatment—U.S. GAAP

There are numerous definitions and rules involved in derivative accounting. Some of the terms that are necessary to understand include *derivative, underlying, notional amount, embedded derivative, hedge, fair value hedge, cash flow hedge, foreign currency hedge*, and *effective portion of a hedge*. Each of these terms will be explained in this section, beginning with the most important—a derivative.

Derivatives Defined—U.S. GAAP

Paragraph 6 of SFAS 133 defines a derivative as a financial instrument or other contract with all three of the following characteristics:

a. It has (1) one or more underlyings and (2) one or more notional amounts or payment provisions or both. Those terms determine the amount of the settlement or settlements, and, in some cases, whether or not a settlement is required.
b. It requires no initial net investment, or an initial net investment that is smaller than would be required for other types of contracts that would be expected to have a similar response to changes in market factors.
c. Its terms require or permit net settlement; it can readily be settled net by a means outside the contract, or it provides for delivery of an asset that puts the recipient in a position not substantially different from net settlement.

An underlying is a specified interest rate, security price, commodity price, foreign exchange rate, index of prices or rates, or other variable. An underlying may be a price or rate of an asset or liability but is not the asset or liability itself. A notional amount is a quantity of currency units, shares, or other units specified in a derivative instrument. The settlement of a derivative instrument with a notional amount is determined by interaction of that notional amount with the underlying. The interaction may be simple multiplication, or it may involve a formula with leverage factors or other constants.

Some contracts may not in their entirety meet the definition of a derivative instrument. Examples include bonds, insurance policies, and leases. These contracts may, however, contain "embedded" derivative instruments—implicit or explicit terms that affect some or all of the cash flows or the value of other exchanges required by the contract in a manner similar to a derivative instrument. The effect of embedding a derivative instrument in another type of contract (called the *host contract*) is that some or all of the cash flows or other exchanges that otherwise would be required by the host contract, whether unconditional or contingent upon the occurrence of a specified event, will be modified based on one or more underlyings.

An embedded derivative instrument must be separated from the host contract and accounted for as a derivative instrument if certain criteria are met. These criteria will be explained later.

Despite these complicated definitions, the method of accounting used to recognize derivatives under SFAS 133 is straightforward, if not easy. *All derivatives must be carried at fair value on a recurring basis*—meaning, they must be revalued at the end of each reporting period and a gain or loss will be recognized for the change(s) in fair value.

However, *where* in the financial statements the change in fair value is reported (i.e., as part of earnings or, separately, as a component of other comprehensive income) differs, depending on the nature of the derivative. For all derivatives that do not qualify as hedges, gains or losses from increases or decreases in fair value are to be reported in earnings, not in other comprehensive income. But for derivatives that have been designated as and qualify as hedges, the classification can be more complicated. A summary of the treatment of changes in fair value of hedges is presented in Table 15.1.

As their name suggests, hedges are designed to provide protection against specific types of risk. A hedged item can be an individual asset or liability, groups of assets or liabilities, or certain other items, such as forecasted transactions.

The preceding classification discussion also introduces the three primary types of derivatives, explained as follows:

1. *Fair value hedge*. This is the hedge of an entity's exposure to changes in the fair value of either an asset or a liability in most cases. However,

TABLE 15.1 Treatment of Gains or Losses on Hedges

Type of Hedge	Classification of Changes in Fair Value
Fair value hedge	Earnings (profit or loss)
Cash flow hedge—effective portion	Other comprehensive income
Cash flow hedge—other portion	Earnings (profit or loss)
Foreign currency hedge:	
– **Of a foreign currency denominated firm commitment**	Earnings (profit or loss)
– **Of an available-for-sale security**	Earnings (profit or loss)
– **Effective portion of hedge of a forecasted foreign currency denominated transaction**	Other comprehensive income
– **Other portion of hedge of a forecasted foreign currency denominated transaction**	Earnings (profit or loss)
– **Effective portion of a net investment in a foreign operation**	Other comprehensive income

hedges can also address changes in fair value of portions of an asset or liability, or an unrecognized firm commitment.

2. *Cash flow hedge.* This type of hedge relates to possible variances in cash flows that could affect profit or loss and that are attributable to specific risks associated with an asset or liability or a highly probable future transaction.

3. *Foreign currency hedge.* This hedge provides protection against fluctuations in foreign currency exchange rates.

As Table 15.1 suggests, gains and losses on some hedges are included in earnings, while others are reported as a component of other comprehensive income instead. Where the gains and losses are reported depends on the type of hedge and whether the hedge is effective.

Whether a hedge is effective has a direct impact on where gains or losses are reported. For example, for cash flow hedges, the effective portion of the gain or loss is reported as a component of other comprehensive income and reclassified into earnings in the same period(s) during which the hedged forecasted transaction affects earnings. The remaining gain or loss on the derivative instrument, if any, shall be recognized currently in earnings.

Fraud Risk No. 15.1

Improperly classifying cash flow and certain foreign currency hedges as effective hedges in order to report losses as a component of other comprehensive income rather than in earnings.

A complete explanation of how to determine the effectiveness of a hedging instrument is beyond the scope of this book, and not necessary for our purposes. SFAS 133 does not require any particular method of determining a hedge's effectiveness. However, the method of determining hedge effectiveness must possess the following characteristics:

1. An entity must define a method of assessing a hedge's effectiveness at the time it designates a hedging relationship, and it must continue to apply that method throughout the hedge period (unless a better method is identified, as provided for in the next step).

2. If an entity identifies an improved method that it wishes to apply for assessing effectiveness, it must discontinue the existing hedging relationship and designate the relationship all over using the improved method.

3. An entity should assess effectiveness for similar hedges in a similar manner; use of different methods for similar hedges should be justified.

U.S. GAAP includes a shortcut method for measuring and assessing the effectiveness of certain fair value and cash flow hedges (under this shortcut method, an entity is permitted to assume no ineffectiveness in limited situations), whereas IFRS does not provide for such a shortcut approach.

Definitions and Treatment—IFRS

IFRS has its own set of definitions, most of which are very similar to those found in U.S. GAAP. However, there are a few important differences.

Derivatives Defined—IFRS

Paragraph 9 of IAS 39 defines a derivative as a financial instrument with all three of the following characteristics:

a. its value changes in response to the change in a specified interest rate, financial instrument price, commodity price, foreign exchange rate, index of prices or rates, credit rating or credit index, or other variable, provided in the case of a nonfinancial variable that the variable is not specific to a party to the contract (sometimes called the *underlying*);
b. it requires no initial net investment or an initial net investment that is smaller than would be required for other types of contracts that would be expected to have a similar response to changes in market factors; and
c. it is settled at a future date.

The most important difference between the U.S. GAAP and IFRS definitions of derivatives is found in the third characteristic. The U.S. GAAP definition requires or permits a net settlement provision, whereas the IFRS does not. As a result, more instruments generally qualify as derivatives under IFRS than under U.S. GAAP.

IFRS also recognizes a distinction between various types of hedges. These distinctions mostly mirror those described in the preceding section on U.S. GAAP. A July 2008 amendment to IAS 39 expanded the scope of instruments eligible for classification as a hedge.

Measurement

Under U.S. GAAP, derivatives are to be carried at fair value on a recurring basis, with increases and decreases in fair value reported as part of earnings, unless the derivative is accounted for as one of certain types of hedges, as explained earlier.

Fraud Risk No. 15.2

Falsely stating the fair value of a derivative, usually by overstating derivatives carried as assets and understating those carried as liabilities.

Under IFRS, derivatives are always categorized as held for trading unless they are accounted for as hedges. As such, they are carried at fair value on a recurring basis and gains or losses resulting from changes in fair value are in a company's profit or loss. The requirement to carry derivatives at fair value and to include gains or losses in profit or loss also extends to derivatives that are liabilities, with the exception of a derivative liability that is linked to and must be settled by delivery of an unquoted equity instrument whose fair value cannot be reliably measured, which must be measured at cost.

Embedded Derivatives

Under both U.S. GAAP and IFRS, embedded derivatives may need to be accounted for separately. An embedded derivative arises when a contract does not in its entirety meet the GAAP or IFRS definition of a derivative, but certain terms of the contract can affect cash flows or the value of other exchanges covered under the contract in a manner that is similar to a derivative. Insurance policies and leases sometimes contain embedded derivatives. The effect of an embedded derivative is that some or all of the cash flows or exchange that would otherwise be required by the contract will be modified based on one or more underlying, as already defined. For example, a lease containing a provision under which future rent payments change based on an inflation index would be considered to have an embedded derivative.

Fraud Risk No. 15.3

Failing to separately recognize an embedded derivative that meets the criteria for separation from a host contract, especially a derivative that would represent a liability.

When a derivative is embedded in a contract, the contract is referred to as the host contract. An embedded derivative must be segregated from the host contract and accounted for separately if the following three characteristics are present:

1. Its economics are not "closely related" to those of the host contract (see examples that follow).
2. A separate instrument with the same terms as the embedded derivative would meet the definition of a derivative.
3. The entire contract is not carried at fair value through profit or loss.

Whether the economics of the embedded derivative is or is not closely related to those of the host contract requires judgment. IAS 39 provides several examples of economics that are closely related and of those that are not closely related.

An inflation index in a lease is considered to be closely related. Therefore, following up on the earlier example, in such cases, the lease contains an embedded derivative but the embedded derivative would not be required to be separated and accounted for.

In certain cases, if a contract contains one or more embedded derivatives, an entity may designate the entire combined contract (called a *hybrid contract* when the embedded derivative is not separated from the host) as a financial asset or financial liability at fair value through profit or loss.

Accounting for derivatives and hedging is a very complicated subject filled with its own unique terminology. Entire textbooks have been written on derivatives and hedging, and those books do a far more thorough job of explaining these intricacies than I ever could here.

But, I have probably covered more than enough of the accounting concepts for our purposes—to help recognize where the risks of fair value accounting fraud exist, as well as some of the red flags associated with these fraud risks.

CHAPTER 16

Assets or Liabilities of Sponsors of Employee Benefit Plans

Some employee benefit plans are categorized as defined contribution plans, meaning that contributions to the plan are defined in the plan agreement. Often, employers contribute a stated percentage (or a range of percentages) of eligible employees' salaries or match employee contributions up to a certain percentage. Other plans are categorized as defined benefit plans, meaning the benefit that an individual receives is clearly defined in the plan and is not necessarily tied to specific contributions. Defined contribution plans are the more common of the two. The most common defined benefit plans are certain health benefit plans and retirement plans in which retired employees receive a stated or determinable payment for the remainder of their lives.

Some plans are sponsored by a single employer, while others have multiple sponsors. Employee benefit plans are normally separate legal entities, and many obtain their own audit of their financial statements. As such, the assets and liabilities of the plan normally are not also reported as assets and liabilities of the plan sponsors. However, plan sponsors are expected to make certain disclosures about their employee benefit plans.

In certain cases, however, the fair values of a plan's assets and liabilities can result in an asset or liability that must be recorded in the financial statements of the plan's sponsor, not merely a footnote disclosure. This can happen only with defined benefit plans. Those plans are the subject of this chapter.

The global financial crisis that continues in 2009 has had an impact on the financial statements of many entities. In the United States, the stock market collapse has left many retirement plans underfunded. A report from the Mercer consulting firm indicated that a $60 billion surplus in U.S. corporate pension plans had turned into a $409 billion underfunded status as of the end of 2008. Many plan sponsors that reported assets for overfunded plans in 2007 will be reporting liabilities for 2008, based on the accounting standard discussed in this chapter.

Sources of U.S. GAAP and IFRS

An important fair value liability issue was introduced into U.S. GAAP with the implementation of SFAS 158, *Employers' Accounting for Defined Benefit Pension and Other Postretirement Plans, an amendment of FASB Statement No. 87, 88, 106, and 132(R)*. As its name suggests, SFAS 158 applies only to defined benefit plans, the most common being certain retirement and health plans.

The IFRS guidance that corresponds to SFAS 158 is located in IAS 19, *Employee Benefits*, although IAS 19 has broader application than the SFAS 158 topic covered in this chapter.

Recognition and Measurement—U.S. GAAP

Under SFAS 158, a sponsor of a single-employer defined benefit plan must recognize an asset or liability for the over- or underfunded nature of the plan, defined as the difference between the fair value of the plan's assets and the benefit obligation. In the case of an employer with multiple plans, an asset would result from the aggregation of all overfunded plans, while a liability results from the aggregation of all underfunded plans.

Fraud Risk No. 16.1

Failure by a plan sponsor to recognize a liability for an underfunded defined benefit plan.

The plan itself is generally a separate entity that issues its own set of financial statements subject to audit by an independent auditor. The assets and liabilities of the plan are not also included in the financial statements of the plan sponsor. Only the potential over- or underfunded nature of the plan would be reported as an asset or liability of the sponsor.

The fraud risk here is rather simple. If the fair value of the plan's investments and other assets is overstated, then one of the following will also be present:

- The asset reported in the plan sponsor's financial statements, representing the overfunded nature of the plan, will be overstated.

- The liability reported in the plan sponsor's financial statements, representing the underfunded nature of the plan, will be understated.

Fraud Risk No. 16.2

Improperly determining the fair value of a defined benefit plan's assets, in order to make it appear overfunded or to reduce the extent of its underfunded nature.

Assessing whether a recognized asset is overstated or a recognized liability is understated is one thing. But, readers of the financial statements of the plan sponsor may not even notice the complete omission of a liability. Therefore, the first step in assessing the risk of liability omission is to read the financial statements carefully to determine whether a defined benefit plan exists.

Finally, preparing or obtaining a faulty actuarial analysis of a plan's obligation is another method of overstating an asset or understating a liability in the financial statements of a plan sponsor.

Fraud Risk No. 16.3

Preparing or obtaining a faulty actuarial analysis of a plan's benefit obligation as a method of hiding or understating the underfunded nature of a defined benefit plan, or overstating its overfunded nature.

Faulty actuarial analyses can result from any of the following:

- Incorrect assumptions and calculations used in an internally prepared analysis (e.g., incorrect determination of the present value of the defined benefit obligation at the end of the reporting period)
- Use of an external actuary who is not independent of the entity, in order to make it appear to be an independent analysis
- Making alterations to a properly prepared actuarial analysis
- Bribing an external party in order to obtain the desired actuarial analysis

Auditors and investigators can be easily convinced that fair valuations, actuarial studies, and other reports that are used in preparing the financial statements are reliable simply because they appear to have come from outside experts. But these reports and studies must be tested, regardless of whether they appear to have come from a reliable expert.

Recognition and Measurement—IFRS

The IFRS guidance that corresponds to SFAS 158 is located in IAS 19, *Employee Benefits*. Like U.S. GAAP, IAS 19 requires that an entity that sponsors a defined benefit plan recognize a liability under certain circumstances. The liability would be equal to the present value of the defined benefit obligation at the end of the reporting period minus the fair value of plan assets, plus or minus certain other adjustments.

IAS 19 encourages, but does not require, an entity to involve a qualified actuary in the measurement of all material post-employment benefit obligations.

If the difference between the fair value of plan assets and present value of the plan obligations results in an asset, IFRS permits the recognition of an asset in the financial statements of the plan sponsor, just like U.S. GAAP.

Accordingly, the fraud risks under IFRS are identical to those explained earlier under U.S. GAAP.

CHAPTER 17

Contingencies and Provisions

Contingencies represent gains or losses that may occur, but for which there is some degree of uncertainty. It is this uncertainty that distinguishes contingent assets and liabilities from other recognized assets and liabilities.

One common example of a contingency that could result in a gain or a loss is the outcome of a court case. When lawsuits are filed on behalf of, or against, an entity, the outcome of the case is often a cash settlement—either one paid by the entity or one to be received by the entity. Depending on the stage of the case at the time the financial statements are prepared, there could be a low or high degree of certainty that management of an entity feels regarding the eventual outcome of the case.

Certain elements of the accounting for contingencies involve fair value accounting. Others do not involve fair value issues per se, but require other elements of estimation and present valuing. Since significant judgment is involved in either situation, this section will cover both types of fraud risks.

Sources of U.S. GAAP and IFRS

U.S. GAAP for contingencies is found in SFAS 5, *Accounting for Contingencies*, with additional guidance in FIN 14, *Reasonable Estimates of Amount of Loss, an interpretation of FASB Statement No. 5*.

IFRS is provided in IAS 37, *Provisions, Contingent Liabilities and Contingent Assets*.

Recognition—U.S. GAAP

Under SFAS 5, a contingency is an existing uncertainty that may have financial impact, depending on future events. Contingencies can be classified as gain or loss contingencies.

Loss contingencies can result in either of the following:

1. The incurrence of a liability
2. An impairment of an asset

A liability is to be recorded in the financial statements for a contingent loss only if all three of the following conditions are present:

1. The underlying causal event occurred prior to the balance sheet date.
2. It is probable (i.e., likely) that a loss has been incurred.
3. There is a reasonable basis for estimating the loss.

When all three of the criteria are met, the balance sheet should reflect a liability. All three criteria can be subject to manipulation, especially the second and third criteria. Claiming that a loss is not likely or that there is not a reasonable basis for estimating the amount of the loss are both potential methods that could be used to avoid recognizing a liability in the financial statements.

Of course, if a liability is inevitable, it will eventually have to be recorded. But management may want to defer recognition of the liability until a future period. Many financial statement frauds are based on attempts to put off negative transactions and accelerate the positive ones—all timing differences to make the current period appear stronger.

Fraud Risk No. 17.1

Failure to recognize a liability (or to impair an asset) when the criteria for recognizing a loss contingency have been met.

One of the critical elements in determining whether a liability should be recorded is the likelihood that a loss has been incurred. If the likelihood of a loss is remote (defined as slight) or only possible (somewhere between remote and probable), a liability should not be recognized. Only if it is probable that a loss has been incurred should a liability be recognized.

Likelihood that a loss has been incurred also impacts whether disclosure in the footnotes of a loss contingency is required. Recognized liabilities for probable loss contingencies should always be explained in a footnote disclosure. In addition, loss contingencies that are possible should be disclosed, even though they are not recognized as liabilities in the balance sheet. It is only with respect to loss contingencies whose likelihood of incurrence is remote that neither recognition nor disclosure is required.

Fraud Risk No. 17.2

Omission of note disclosures regarding an unrecognized loss contingency that has a likelihood of occurrence that is more than remote.

Careful reading of footnote disclosures regarding loss contingencies is another important step in determining whether financial statements are misstated. If a loss contingency is disclosed but not recognized, it means that the entity considers the likelihood of the incurrence of a loss to be more than remote but less than probable. This is a difficult determination in many instances—and just as difficult to audit.

Gain contingencies can result in either the acquisition of an asset (e.g., cash in a settlement of a lawsuit) or a reduction of a liability (e.g., reduction in the amount recorded as payable to a vendor as a result of suing the vendor for nonperformance or substandard performance). A recovery associated with a contingent loss is included in the scope of the definition of a gain contingency. For example, if an entity has incurred a contingent liability that may be recoverable in the form of insurance, the amount that may be recovered via insurance is considered to be a gain contingency.

Fraud Risk No. 17.3

Recognition of an asset for a gain contingency prior to its meeting the criteria for recognition.

Generally, gain contingencies are not to be recorded in the financial statements until all contingencies have been resolved. However, if the gain contingency involves a recovery related to a contingent loss, it should be recorded if it is *probable* and *reasonably estimable*.

If such a gain contingency is recorded, its amount is generally limited to the amount of the contingent loss. Only when all contingencies related to the recovery have been resolved can a gain contingency in excess of the loss contingency be recorded.

Footnote disclosures should be made in connection with gain contingencies that might result in gains. However, this is another area in which care should be exercised. If misleading information regarding the likelihood or amount of a gain contingency is included in a footnote disclosure, this could lead to allegations of fraudulent reporting by investors, bankers, and others who may have placed reliance on such disclosures.

Amount of Loss to Be Recognized

If the recognition criteria explained earlier have been met, a liability should be recorded in an amount equal to the best estimate of the future amount to be paid (or the amount of the asset impairment). FIN 14 states that if there is a range of losses that could be incurred, the amount representing the best estimate should be accrued. If none of the amounts within the range of possible losses is better than the others, the liability should be recognized at the lowest amount in the range.

Clearly, a significant degree of judgment is necessary to estimate many contingent liabilities. In some cases, an entity may have a history with similar losses that can form a reliable basis for an estimate. Outside experts, including legal counsel, can also provide reliable information in formulating an estimate, as can the experience of other entities with similar losses. Estimates that are based solely on internal information in situations in which an entity has no prior experience should be viewed as the most susceptible to manipulation. These are also the most difficult to audit.

Fraud Risk No. 17.4

Underestimating a recognized liability for a loss contingency.

Though not a fair value accounting issue per se, analogies can be made to the guidance in SFAS 157. Verifiable evidence from outside the organization tends to be more reliable than estimates determined entirely by management using only internal information.

The timing of settlement of a contingent liability also raises accounting questions. If the liability is to be settled in the near term, accruing it at the best estimate of the amount due should be done. But what if the liability will likely be settled at a future date that is not near term, or if it is to be settled in installment payments over time?

U.S. GAAP does not require the use of present valuing techniques in the recording of loss contingencies. But it does not prohibit it, either. Therefore, whether or not to discount contingent liabilities to a net present value in order to reflect the time value of money is a matter of accounting policy that can be elected by management. However, discounting to present value is not an option for all loss contingencies. Present value techniques can be used only when the following conditions are met:

1. The effects of estimated future inflation must be recognized in the calculation.
2. The timing of payments is either fixed or reasonably estimable.
3. The computation of the gross liability is both objective and verifiable (meaning, the amount has been calculated by a specialist, such as an actuary, using assumptions that could be verified by another specialist).

Fraud Risk No. 17.5

Using inappropriate present value techniques to understate a contingent liability.

On the other hand, if a gain contingency meets the criteria for recognition, it must be recorded at fair value *unless* both of the following factors are present:

1. The related liability is not discounted to present value (recall from the earlier explanation that the only time that a gain contingency can be recorded is if it is a recovery related to a recognized contingent liability).
2. The timing of the recovery is dependent on the timing of the payment of the related liability.

As such, a present valuing technique would generally be required in connection with gain contingencies to be settled over time or to be settled beyond the near term, unless the preceding conditions are present.

Fraud Risk No. 17.6

Inflating the fair value estimate of a recognized gain contingency.

Recall from Chapter 2 that SFAS 157's definition of fair value is based on what market participants would assume regarding a particular asset or liability. Accordingly, in valuing contingent liabilities (or any other liability) using a present value technique, three considerations apply:

1. Discount rates should reflect assumptions that market participants would use in pricing the liability.
2. Discount rates should consider only factors attributed to the liability being measured, not other factors unique to the entity.
3. Discount rates should reflect assumptions that are consistent with those inherent in the cash flows (i.e., different rates based on whether the discount rate adjustment technique or the expected present value technique is used).

In connection with the third consideration, nominal cash flows that include the effect of inflation on future cash flows should be discounted at a rate that includes the effect of inflation. Real cash flows that exclude the effect of inflation should be discounted at a rate that excludes the effect of inflation. Similarly, after-tax cash flows should be discounted using an after-tax discount rate.

How this guidance applies to calculating present value of a contingent liability depends on the nature of the liability (e.g., is there a risk of default, is payment of the obligation deductible for income tax purposes, etc.).

Recognition—IFRS

As it relates to liabilities, what U.S. GAAP refers to as loss contingencies are classified into two categories under IAS 37—provisions and contingent liabilities—based on the likelihood of loss. Whereas U.S. GAAP requires the recognition of some contingent losses but not others, based on their likelihood, IFRS uses different terms for the different degrees of likelihood.

A provision is recognized as a liability in the financial statements only when all three of the following conditions are present:

1. An enterprise has a present obligation as a result of a past event. Such an obligation can be either a legal obligation (i.e., based on a contract or law) or a constructive obligation (one that is based on the entity's actions, established patterns of prior practices, policies, etc.).
2. It is probable (meaning, it is more likely than not) that an outflow of resources embodying economic benefits will be required to settle the obligation.
3. A reliable estimate can be made of the amount of the obligation.

If all three of these conditions are present, an entity should recognize a liability. These three conditions are substantially similar to the three conditions requiring the recognition of a loss contingency under U.S. GAAP. Measurement of the liability is explained later in this chapter.

A contingent liability, however, is not to be recognized. These are liabilities that are "possible" (rather than "probable") based on past events, but whose existence will be confirmed through the occurrence or nonoccurrence of future events that are uncertain and not within the control of the entity. Also included within the scope of contingent liabilities are present obligations resulting from past events but where the obligation either cannot be reliably estimated or will not likely require an outflow of economic resources to settle.

Contingent liabilities are not to be recognized as liabilities. But, they should be disclosed in the footnotes to the financial statements unless the possibility of an outflow of resources to settle the obligation is remote. Again, this treatment mirrors U.S. GAAP, only with a slight difference in terminology.

Contingent assets are never recognized as assets in the financial statements under IFRS. However, if the likelihood of an inflow of economic resources is probable, a contingent asset should be disclosed in the footnotes to the financial statements.

Separate from the discussion of contingent assets in IAS 37 is a section on reimbursements. This section somewhat corresponds to the U.S. GAAP discussion of contingent assets associated with recoveries connected to contingent liabilities. Only the IFRS standard for recording an asset for a reimbursement is stricter than its U.S. GAAP counterpart.

IAS 37 states that where some or all of the expenditure required to settle a provision is expected to be reimbursed by another party (such as through insurance or indemnity clauses), the reimbursement is to be recognized when, and only when, it is virtually certain that reimbursement will be received if the entity settles the obligation. The reimbursement must be treated as a separate asset. Just like under U.S. GAAP, if such an asset is recorded, the amount recognized for the reimbursement may not exceed the amount of the provision.

Due to the similarities between U.S. GAAP and IFRS in this area, the fraud risks are virtually identical. See the U.S. GAAP section for explanation of these fraud risks.

Measurement

Provisions should be recognized as liabilities based on the expected expenditures necessary to settle the obligation. Expected expenditures should be the best estimate of the expenditure required to settle the obligation.

When different levels of expenditure are possible, IFRS suggests use of the expected value method. Similar to how the expected value method is described in U.S. GAAP under SFAC 7, this method (illustrated in Table 17.1)

TABLE 17.1 Expected Value Method

Estimated Loss		Probability		Expected Value
$ 30,000,000	×	10%	=	$ 3,000,000
$ 20,000,000	×	40%	=	$ 8,000,000
$ 15,000,000	×	30%	=	$ 4,500,000
$ 10,000,000	×	20%	=	$ 2,000,000
Expected Value				$ 17,500,000

involves assigning probabilities to various possible outcomes and developing a weighted average of those outcomes based on the probabilities assigned to each.

When the effect of the time value of money is material, a provision should be recognized at the present value of the best estimate of expenditures expected to settle the obligation. This may be the case when the expected timing of settling an obligation extends beyond the near future. The discount rate(s) used in the calculation should be pretax rates that reflect current market assessments of the time value of money, as well as any risks that are specific to the liability.

Comparison of U.S. GAAP and IFRS

In comparing U.S. GAAP with IFRS in this area, the differences are subtle. For starters, U.S. GAAP for contingencies is a bit broader in scope than IFRS. U.S. GAAP defines a loss contingency as one that could result in either a liability or an impairment of an asset. Likewise, gain contingencies could result in either an asset or a reduction of a liability. IFRS, by contrast, refers to provisions only in the context of liabilities. A provision cannot involve an asset impairment.

Under U.S. GAAP, recognized loss contingencies are to be discounted to present value only under certain specific conditions. Otherwise, they should be recorded at their estimated amounts. But under IFRS, all provisions (the IFRS equivalent of recognizable loss contingencies under U.S. GAAP) should be recognized at the present value of the expected expenditures.

Under U.S. GAAP, an asset may be recorded for a recovery associated with a contingent liability if the recovery is probable and the amount is reasonably estimable. Under IFRS, the standard for recording such an asset (referred to as a reimbursement) is more difficult to meet—reimbursement must be virtually certain if the entity settles the obligation. Under either set of standards, if an asset is recorded, its amount is limited to the amount of the liability.

The amount recognized as a provision under IFRS can sometimes be larger than the amount recognized as a loss contingency under U.S. GAAP. This would happen when there is a range of possible outcomes and each point along the range has an equal chance of occurring. Under U.S. GAAP, when this happens, the low end of the range should be accrued. Under IFRS, the midpoint of the range would be accrued.

CHAPTER 18

Share-Based Transactions

S hare-based transactions are those in which an entity receives goods or services in exchange for which it provides either shares of its own stock or some other form of payment that is based on the price of its stock. Included among the possible types of share-based transactions are employee stock options, one of the more common employee benefits offered in many companies. Some share-based transactions include vesting provisions, requiring an employee to remain employed with a company for a stated amount of time in order for the employee to be entitled to the shares that have accumulated based on past service.

In some cases, an entity is required to record an increase in equity for share-based transactions, while in others, a liability is recorded. In either case, fair value accounting plays a prominent role in the recognition of share-based transactions.

Sources of U.S. GAAP and IFRS

U.S. GAAP for shared-based payments is found primarily in SFAS 123, as revised, *Shared-Based Payment*, which addresses most transactions involving an entity's employees or other suppliers. Some share-based transactions may also fall within the scope of SFAS 150, *Accounting for Certain Financial Instruments with Characteristics of Both Liabilities and Equity*. The SEC has also issued some interpretive guidance on accounting for share-based transactions.

Additional guidance can be found in EITF No. 96-18, *Accounting for Equity Instruments That Are Issued to Other Than Employees for Acquiring, or in Conjunction with Selling, Goods or Services*. EITF 96-18 addresses issues involving the measurement date for share-based payment transactions with nonemployees when the measurement of the transaction is based on the fair value of the equity instruments issued, an issue not addressed in SFAS 123.

Excluded from the scope of SFAS 123(R) is the accounting for employee stock ownership plans. Accounting guidance for these plans is provided in the AICPA's SOP 93-6, *Employers' Accounting for Employee Stock Ownership Plans.*

IFRS for share-based payments is found in IFRS 2, *Share-based Payment.* IFRS 2 provides guidance on three types of share-based payment transactions:

1. Equity-settled share-based payment transactions, in which the entity receives goods or services as consideration for equity instruments of the entity (including shares or share options).
2. Cash-settled share-based payment transactions, in which the entity acquires goods or services by incurring liabilities to the supplier of those goods or services for amounts that are based on the price (or value) of the entity's shares or other equity instruments of the entity.
3. Transactions in which the entity receives or acquires goods or services and the terms of the arrangement provide either the entity or the supplier of the goods or services with a choice of settling the transaction in cash or through the issuance of equity instruments.

All three types of transactions involve a risk of fair value accounting fraud.

Three key accounting issues must be addressed with respect to share-based transactions:

1. Should the transaction be treated as a liability or as an increase in equity?
2. At what date should the transaction be recorded (i.e., what is the measurement date)?
3. How should fair value be determined?

The classification of a transaction as liability or equity is an extremely complicated issue, and one that will be introduced but not explained in detail in this book, which focuses on the fair value accounting implications.

Recognition—U.S. GAAP

SFAS 123(R) requires that share-based transactions should initially be recognized when an entity receives goods or services. At that point, the entity is to record either a liability or an increase in equity as the offsetting credit side of the entry.

Fraud Risk No. 18.1

Misclassification of a share-based transaction as an increase in equity that should be classified as a liability.

The obvious initial fraud risk here is the misclassification of a share-based transaction as an increase in equity rather than as a liability. Doing so, regardless of whether the measurement is accurate, makes an entity's financial condition appear to be stronger than it really is, since a liability is missing from the balance sheet.

The determination of whether to record a liability or an increase in equity is based on the circumstances involved in the transaction. SFAS 123(R) provides classification guidance on six types of share-based transactions:

1. *Shares with put or call features.* These shares should be classified as a liability if either of the following conditions is met:
   a. The repurchase feature permits the employee to avoid bearing the risks and rewards normally associated with equity share ownership for a reasonable period of time (six months or more) from the date the requisite service is rendered and the share is issued.
   b. It is probable that the employer would prevent the employee from bearing those risks and rewards for a reasonable period of time (six months or more) from the date the share is issued.

   All other shares with put or call features should be classified as equity.
2. *Options or similar instruments on shares under either of the following circumstances should always be classified as liabilities:*
   a. The underlying shares are recorded as liabilities by the entity.
   b. Settlement of the options or similar instruments in cash or other assets could be required of the entity under any circumstances.
3. *Awards indexed to other factors, in addition to the entity's share price.* If the award is indexed to a factor other than market, performance, or service conditions, in addition to the entity's share price, it should be classified as a liability. If the additional factor is a market, performance, or service condition, the award should be classified as equity.
4. *Awards with substantive terms that differ from the written terms.* In these cases, the substantive terms should be considered in determining the proper classification. Generally, if the substantive terms provide for settlement in cash (or if asked to do so by the employee, the entity generally settles in cash), then a liability should be recorded, whereas

if the settlement is to be in equity (or the employee can elect equity), then equity should be recorded.

5. *Awards that include a provision permitting broker-assisted cashless exercise for part or all of an award.* These awards do not result in liability classification for instruments that otherwise would be classified as equity if both of the following criteria are satisfied:

   a. The cashless exercise requires a valid exercise of the share options.

   b. The employee is the legal owner of the shares subject to the option (even though the employee has not paid the exercise price before the sale of the shares subject to the option).

6. *Awards that include a provision specifying that amounts in excess of minimum statutory requirements* are to be withheld or give the employee the option to withhold amounts in excess of minimum statutory requirements do not automatically result in liability classification of instruments that otherwise would be classified as equity. However, if an amount in excess of the minimum statutory requirement is withheld, or may be withheld at the employee's discretion, the entire award shall be classified and accounted for as a liability.

Classification of instruments that fall outside the scope encompassed by these six categories, and that are freestanding financial instruments awarded to an employee in a share-based transaction, is covered in SFAS 150.

Measurement—U.S. GAAP

Measurement of share-based transactions is based on the nature of the party involved in the transaction with the entity. All share-based transactions with employees, regardless of whether they are classified as liabilities or equity, are to be measured at fair value as of the grant date. Fair value is based on the fair value of the equity instrument involved (e.g., the price of the company's stock) in all cases involving employees.

Fraud Risk No. 18.2

Intentional misstatement of the fair value of a company's own equity instruments in a share-based transaction, resulting in under- or overstatement of liabilities or equity.

Measuring fair value of equity instruments can be complicated and a potential target for fraud. In SAB 107, the SEC noted:

The staff understands that estimates of fair value of employee share options, while derived from expected value calculations, cannot predict actual future events. The estimate of fair value represents the measurement of the cost of the employee services to the company. The estimate of fair value should reflect the assumptions marketplace participants would use in determining how much to pay for an instrument on the date of the measurement (generally the grant date for equity awards).

If the share-based transaction is classified as a liability, it is to be remeasured at the end of each reporting period (to fair value at the end of the reporting period) until the liability is settled. Ultimately, the final measurement date for liabilities in share-based transactions is the settlement date.

This creates multiple opportunities for fair value accounting fraud—the valuation upon initial recognition, followed by revaluations at the end of each reporting period. Of course, if the intentions of management are to understate liabilities, this means that they are also undervaluing their own company's stock.

Although fraudulent financial reporting often involves understatement of liabilities, there may be times when there could be an incentive to overstate liabilities as well. The most likely instance in connection with share-based transactions is when an entity is receiving goods rather than services. In this case, the entity may have a motive to overstate both assets and liabilities, particularly if the entity's asset base is used to calculate a borrowing base with a financial institution.

Fraud Risk No. 18.3

Misstatement of the fair value of the goods or services received in connection with a share-based transaction, resulting in under- or overstatement of liabilities or equity.

Generally, the amount to be used in recognizing share-based transactions with nonemployees is also the fair value of the equity instrument involved. However, if the fair value of goods or services received in a share-based payment transaction with nonemployees is more reliably measurable than the fair value of the equity instruments issued, the fair value of the goods or services received shall be used to measure the transaction.

This is another potential area of fraud, since the determination of which basis—the value of the stock or the value of the goods or services received—is more reliable is a matter of judgment. Management may argue that the basis that produces the more desirable result is also the more reliable estimate.

If the reporting entity is a nonpublic entity, it is permitted to measure its liabilities under share-based payment arrangements at intrinsic value (a calculated value).

Recognition—IFRS

IFRS makes a similar distinction between transactions treated as liabilities and those treated as equity like under U.S. GAAP, placing them into two broad categories:

1. Equity-settled transactions
2. Cash-settled transactions

Also similar to U.S. GAAP, IFRS provides for different measurement provisions when the transaction is between an entity and its own employees rather than with other parties.

When an entity receives goods or services as consideration for equity instruments of the entity, the goods or services are to be measured at fair value, with the corresponding credit side of the entry increasing equity. Fair value should be measured as of the date an entity receives the goods or services.

Fraud risks associated with these entries could go in either direction—overstatement or understatement. If services are received, fair value may be understated, since the debit side of the entry likely goes to an expense, which reduces net income for the period. If the services received are eligible for capitalization, the risk could shift to one of overvaluation.

Likewise, if goods are received, the risk of overvaluing the goods received may increase, resulting in an overstatement of assets in the short-term. For example, if inventory is received and overvalued, assets are inflated while the inventory remains in stock, but once the items are sold, the over-valued inventory is reported as cost of goods sold and has the effect of understating profits. The effect, however, could become a long-term over-statement if the goods received are capitalized in an account that remains as an asset for multiple periods. For example, if the goods (or services) received involve construction of a building or some other long-lived asset (whether subject to depreciation or not), the overstated asset artificially inflates an entity's financial condition for several periods, perhaps for many years.

Providers of services may be third parties or an entity's own employees. IFRS 2 provides a slightly different rule with respect to services provided by employees. In these cases, rather than measuring the fair value of the goods or services received, the entity is required to measure the transaction at the fair value of the equity instruments granted. This is consistent with U.S. GAAP. This measurement should be as of the grant date, unless there is a vesting period.

Most vesting provisions are based on either length of service or performance measures. IFRS 2 states that for vesting provisions requiring a specified period of service, the entity should assume that the services to be received during the vesting period will be received. Accordingly, the services should be accounted for as they are rendered during the vesting period (rather than delaying any recognition until the vesting provision is met). For example, if an employee is granted share options upon achievement of three years of service, the entity should presume that the full three years of service will be provided, meaning that the services should be accounted for as they are provided. Again, the offsetting credit is to the entity's equity.

Likewise, an entity should assume that vesting provisions involving the achievement of performance conditions will be met and that the employee will provide the services to the entity over that period required to achieve the performance conditions. In this case, the entity should estimate the length of service required to achieve the performance condition, based on the most likely outcome, and recognize the services (and the corresponding increase in equity) over that period.

Fraud Risk No. 18.4

Utilizing a false estimate of the length of service necessary for employees to meet a performance condition required for share-based compensation to vest.

The estimation of the length of service that will be required in order for performance conditions to vest is another possible target for manipulation. Utilizing too long of a period can result in understatement of expenses, too short of a period overstates expenses.

Although it is assumed that vesting conditions will be satisfied in the future for purposes of recognizing services received from employees, vesting conditions are to be ignored for purposes of measuring the fair value of the shares or share options at the measurement date.

Recording the transaction at the fair value of equity instruments (rather than the fair value of the goods or services received) should also be done if the fair value of goods or services received from a nonemployee cannot be estimated reliably.

IFRS 2 states that determination of fair value of equity instruments should be based on market prices, if available. The various terms and conditions associated with the granting of the equity instruments should also be considered. If market prices are not available, such as with closely held companies, fair value of the equity instruments should be estimated using a valuation technique designed to determine what the price of the instruments would have been on the measurement date in an arm's length transaction between knowledgeable, willing parties.

Cash-settled share-based payment transactions, in which the entity acquires goods or services by incurring liabilities to the supplier of those goods or services for amounts that are based on the price (or value) of the entity's shares or other equity instruments of the entity, also involve a fair value accounting fraud risk. That is because the goods or services received in these transactions are to be recorded at the fair value of the liability. Further, until the liability is settled, the entity is required to remeasure the fair value of the liability at the end of each reporting period, as well as at the date of settlement. Changes in valuation from period to period should be recognized in profit or loss for the period. Once again, this treatment is consistent with U.S. GAAP.

Finally, if the entity or a supplier has the choice of settling a transaction with cash or the issuance of equity instruments, IFRS requires that the transaction be accounted for as a cash-settled transaction.

Measurement—IFRS

IFRS 2 states that for equity-settled share-based transactions with "employees and others providing similar services," fair value of the services received, and the corresponding increase in equity, should be determined based on the fair value of the equity instrument granted, since it is usually not practical to develop a reliable estimate of the fair value of the services.

For all other equity-settled share-based payment transactions (i.e., transactions for services with nonemployees who provide services dissimilar to those provided by employees and all transactions for goods), an entity should measure the goods or services received, and the corresponding increase in equity, at the fair value of the goods or services received, if fair value can be estimated reliably. If the entity cannot develop a reliable estimate of the fair value of the goods or services received, the entity fair value should be measured based on the value of the equity instruments granted.

Table 18.1 summarizes the basis for measuring goods or services received in connection with equity-settled transactions under IFRS.

TABLE 18.1 Bases for Measuring Share-Based Transactions

Transactions With	Measurement Base
Employees	Fair value of equity instrument granted
Nonemployees similar to employees	Fair value of equity instrument granted
Other nonemployees	Fair value of goods or services provided

Fair value of an entity's equity instruments should be based on market prices, if available, taking into account the terms and conditions upon which those equity instruments were granted.

If market prices are not available (such as for entities whose equity instruments are not publicly traded), the entity should estimate the fair value of the equity instruments granted using a valuation technique to estimate what the price of those equity instruments would have been on the measurement date. The valuation technique should be "consistent with generally accepted valuation methodologies" for pricing financial instruments, and should incorporate all factors and assumptions that knowledgeable, willing market participants would consider in setting the price.

Any restrictions inherent in equity instruments awarded to employees must be considered in determining fair value. The effect on fair value is based on whether they continue in effect after the requisite service period. A restriction that continues in effect after issuance to employees must be considered in estimating the fair value of the instruments. For equity share options, the effect of nontransferability should be considered by reflecting the impact of employees' expected exercise and post-vesting employment termination behavior in estimating fair value.

The term *generally accepted valuation methodologies* can be subject to a great deal of judgment. This is another area of potential fraudulent valuation, and the advice of a business valuation expert should be sought.

In some cases, an entity may not be able to reliably estimate the fair value of the equity instruments granted at the measurement date. In these cases only, the entity is required to take the following steps:

1. Measure the equity instruments at their intrinsic value, first at the date the entity obtains the goods or receives the services and subsequently at the end of each reporting period and at the date of final settlement. Changes in intrinsic value are reported in profit or loss.
2. Recognize the goods or services received based on the number of equity instruments that ultimately vest or, where applicable, are ultimately exercised. The amount recognized for goods or services received during the vesting period is to be based on the number of share options

expected to vest. That estimate should be revised if subsequent information indicates that the number of share options expected to vest differs from previous estimates. On the vesting date, the entity should revise the estimate to equal the number of equity instruments that ultimately vested. After the vesting date, the amount recognized for goods or services received must be reversed if the share options are later forfeited, or lapse at the end of the share option's life.

For cash-settled transactions, measurement of the goods or services acquired and the liability incurred should be based on the fair value of the liability. Until the liability is settled, the entity is required to remeasure the fair value of the liability at the end of each reporting period and at the date of settlement, with changes in fair value recognized in profit or loss.

CHAPTER 19

Nonmonetary Transactions

Nonmonetary transactions involve exchanges of nonmonetary assets between two parties, the provision of a nonmonetary asset by one party to satisfy a liability to another party, or the provision of services by one party in exchange for a nonmonetary asset of (or to satisfy a liability to) the second party. These transactions are also sometimes referred to as *barter transactions*. The general principle in recording such transactions involves fair value accounting, although there are exceptions to the fair value concept. For purposes of this text, the two primary categories of barter transactions with fair value accounting fraud implications are as follows:

1. Nonmonetary assets received in exchange for goods or services rendered
2. Receipt of goods or services in exchange for nonmonetary assets

Nonmonetary transactions can result in either an asset or a liability for an entity, which is why it is addressed in this section of the book.

Sources of U.S. GAAP and IFRS

U.S. GAAP for nonmonetary transactions is located in a variety of sources, most importantly:

APB Opinion No. 29, *Accounting for Nonmonetary Transactions*
SFAS 153, *Exchanges of Nonmonetary Assets, an Amendment of APB Opinion No. 29*
EITF Issue No. 01-2, *Interpretations of APB No. 29*
EITF Issue No. 99-17, *Accounting for Advertising Barter Transactions*
EITF Issue No. 04-13, *Accounting for Purchases and Sales of Inventory with the Same Counterparty*

There are also several other EITF documents that address various aspects of nonmonetary transactions. But for the purposes of this book, the three EITF documents listed here are the most relevant. In addition, SFAS 157, *Fair Value Measurements*, impacts the measurement of fair value when fair value is used to account for nonmonetary transactions.

IFRS does not include a single comprehensive standard on nonmonetary transactions. Instead, specific categories of nonmonetary transactions are addressed in several sources of IFRS:

IAS 16, *Property, Plant and Equipment*
IAS 18, *Revenue*
IAS 38, *Intangible Assets*
SIC 31, *Revenue—Barter Transactions Involving Advertising Services*

Recognition and Measurement—U.S. GAAP

U.S. GAAP and IFRS are very similar in most aspects of the accounting for nonmonetary transactions. Generally, accounting for nonmonetary transactions is based on the fair value of the assets or services involved.

APB No. 29 states that accounting for nonmonetary transactions should be based on the fair values of the assets (or services) involved which is the same basis as that used in monetary transactions. Thus, the cost of a nonmonetary asset acquired in exchange for another nonmonetary asset is the fair value of the asset surrendered to obtain it, and a gain or loss should be recognized on the exchange.

Fraud Risk No. 19.1

Inflating the fair value of an asset surrendered in a nonmonetary transaction in order to recognize a gain on the exchange.

The fair value of the asset received should be used to measure the cost if it is more clearly evident than the fair value of the asset surrendered. Similarly, a nonmonetary asset received in a nonreciprocal transfer should be recorded at the fair value of the asset received.

There are three exceptions from the general rule that nonmonetary transactions should be recorded at fair value. In each of these situations, the carrying value of the nonmonetary asset transferred from the entity (likely to be its cost less any impairment or accumulated depreciation) should be used to measure the transaction:

1. If neither the fair value of the nonmonetary asset transferred nor the fair value of the nonmonetary asset received in exchange is determinable within reasonable limits
2. If the transaction is an exchange of a product or property held for sale in the ordinary course of business for a product or property to be sold in the same line of business to facilitate sales to customers other than the parties to the exchange (EITF 04-13 provides further guidance on the circumstances under which two or more inventory purchase and sales transactions with the same counterparty should be viewed as a single transaction for purposes of this exception.)
3. If the transaction lacks commercial substance

Fraud Risk No. 19.2

Recording a nonmonetary transaction at fair value when, in fact, the transaction lacks commercial substance and is not to be measured at fair value.

Regarding the third exception, SFAS 153 states that a nonmonetary transaction has commercial substance only if the entity's future cash flows are expected to significantly change as a result of the exchange, as evidenced by meeting one of the following criteria:

1. The risk, timing, and amount (collectively referred to as the configuration) of the future cash flows of the asset received differs significantly from the risk, timing, and amount of the future cash flows of the asset transferred (a change in any one of the three elements of configuration represents a change in configuration).
2. The entity-specific value of the asset received differs from the entity-specific value of the asset transferred, and the difference is significant in relation to the fair values of the assets exchanged.

The concept of entity-specific value differs from that of fair value. Entity-specific value is explained in Statement of Financial Accounting Concepts (SFAC) 7, *Using Cash Flow Information and Present Value in Accounting Measurements* (although it is referred to as entity specific measurement in SFAC 7). Entity specific value represents the value of an asset or liability in the context of a specific entity. For instance, an entity-specific value of an asset would be based on the entity's own expectations about its use of the asset, not on what market participants would assume about the asset's use and value. Recall from Chapter 2's discussion of SFAS 157 that fair value of an asset is based on what an asset would be sold for to market participants, based on those market participants' assumptions about the asset.

If an exchange of nonmonetary assets has commercial substance, the transaction should be measured at fair value, and gains or losses may result. If the transaction lacks commercial substance, the transaction should be measured at the recorded amount of the asset(s) relinquished (less any reduction for impairment in value of the asset, if appropriate).

In certain exchanges of nonmonetary assets, there is also a transfer of monetary consideration (boot) from one party to the other. This raises the question of whether the transaction as a whole should be treated as a monetary or nonmonetary transaction. EITF 01-2 states that if the boot is at least 25 percent of the fair value of the exchange, the transaction is to be considered a monetary transaction. A monetary transaction should be recorded at fair value by both parties. If, however, boot is less than 25 percent of the total fair value of the exchange, a pro rata gain recognition should be applied by the receiver of boot, and the payer of boot should not recognize a gain.

Recognition and Measurement—IFRS

Under IFRS, IAS 18 requires revenue to be measured at the fair value of the consideration received or receivable. Accordingly, any nonmonetary transaction involving revenue, such as when an entity agrees to accept nonmonetary assets in exchange for providing goods or services, the revenue and the asset received should be recognized at the fair value of the nonmonetary asset received.

IAS 16 provides for a similar approach to the nonmonetary exchange of tangible assets. IAS 16 states that the initial carrying amount of property, plant, and equipment acquired in exchange for similar assets should be measured at fair value. This fair value measurement is contingent on the transaction having commercial substance, mirroring the treatment under U.S. GAAP.

Accordingly, nonmonetary transactions accounted for under IFRS possess the same fair value accounting fraud risks as those described earlier under U.S. GAAP.

Advertising Barter Transactions—U.S. GAAP

EITF 99-17 addresses the increasingly common transaction in which two entities engage in a nonmonetary exchange of advertising. In some cases, two Internet businesses exchange rights to place advertisements on each others' Web sites. In other cases, the more traditional print advertising is involved, or perhaps even broadcast advertising.

The accounting issue in these cases is whether revenue and expense should be recorded at the fair value of the advertising or at book value. Over time, the net effect on profit or loss of such transactions is zero, since revenue and expense are recorded in equal amounts. But, since advertising benefits may be received in different time periods than advertising benefits provided, timing differences can result (i.e., in the short term, an asset or liability may be recorded as the offset to advertising revenue or expense). Therefore, the measurement of these transactions can have important short-term implications for an organization's financial statements, perhaps overlapping fiscal years.

Complicating matters is that the recording of advertising expense can be rather complex under U.S. GAAP. Under SOP 93-7, *Reporting on Advertising Costs*, advertising can be set up as an asset or expensed in as many as three different manners, depending on the circumstances involved and elections made by management.

EITF 99-17 states that advertising barter transactions should be recognized and measured at fair value only if the fair value of the advertising surrendered in the transaction is determinable based on the entity's own historical practice of receiving cash or other consideration that is easily converted to cash for similar advertising from buyers unrelated to the counterparty in the barter transaction.

All three of these characteristics must be present. Otherwise, the transaction must be recorded based on the carrying amount of the advertising surrendered, which will likely be zero.

Fraud Risk No. 19.3

Recognizing advertising barter transactions at fair value when the criteria for fair value recognition have not been met.

In assessing the similarity of the advertising provided in exchange for cash to that being provided in the barter transaction, the following five factors should be considered:

1. Circulation, exposure, or saturation within an intended market
2. Timing (time of day, day of week, season, daily, weekly, 24 hours per day, 7 days per week)

3. Prominence (page on a Web site, location with a periodical, such as inside front cover, back cover, or elsewhere, location of the advertisement on a particular page, and size of advertisement)

4. Demographics of readers, viewers, or customers

5. Duration (length of time the advertisement will be displayed)

In making the assessment of whether a historical practice exists of receiving cash for similar advertising, an entity is limited to considering only the most recent six months prior to the date of the barter transaction.

Fraud Risk No. 19.4

Falsely claiming that the criteria for fair value recognition of an advertising barter transaction have not been met in order to avoid recording it at fair value, when the criteria have been met.

The fraud risks in these transactions could go in either direction, depending on whether an entity wishes to use fair value measurement principles or not. If revenue and expense will be recognized in the same reporting periods, it may make no difference, unless an entity wishes to simply appear to be larger than it really is.

But in cases in which the revenue and expense will not be recognized in the same period, the potential for making one period appear much better exists. For example, if the revenue to be recognized is in the current period (since the advertising benefits provided by the entity are in the current period), but the expense is in the next period (because the entity will not receive the benefits until that period), then using inflated fair values to recognize the transaction can make the current period appear more profitable than it really is.

Of course, this short-term fraud comes with a price. The next period will bear the adverse impact of recognizing an inflated expense. But fraudsters often are only concerned with making the current period look better, figuring they will take care of the next period later.

Fraud Risk No. 19.5

Inflating the fair value of advertising provided in exchange for advertising benefits received from another party in an advertising barter transaction.

Advertising Barter Transactions—IFRS

Under IFRS, SIC 31 addresses revenue recognition when two parties provide advertising services to one another. Examples of advertising provided in SIC 31 include those placed on Web sites, television or radio, as well as printed advertisements in magazines or journals, but would also include other media.

SIC 31 concludes that assessing the fair value of advertising services received (i.e., estimating the amount to be reported as advertising expense based on the benefits received) cannot be done with any level of reliability. However, a seller can reliably measure revenue at fair value of the advertising services it provides in a barter transaction. SIC 31 lists five characteristics of nonbarter transactions that can be used as a basis for determining fair value in barter transactions. The five characteristics involve nonbarter transactions that do the following:

1. Involve advertising that is similar to the advertising in the barter transaction (e.g., in a barter transaction, the entity provides a half-page color advertisement in a magazine and it ordinarily charges a standard amount for half-page color advertisements to other customers)
2. Occur frequently
3. Represent a predominant number of transactions and amount when compared to all transactions to provide advertising that is similar to the advertising in the barter transaction
4. Involve cash and/or another form of consideration (e.g., marketable securities) that has a reliably measurable fair value
5. Do *not* involve the same counterparty as in the larger transaction

If these five conditions are present, the entity would record advertising expense and advertising revenue in equal amounts using the advertising rate(s) charged in the comparable transactions.

Though worded differently than EITF 99-17, SIC 31 reaches virtually the same conclusion for IFRS as that required under U.S. GAAP. If there are any differences, it is in the fact that IFRS requires a bit more support for using fair value than U.S. GAAP, since it refers to the frequency of the comparable advertising. U.S. GAAP, however, counters with the six-month rule described earlier, which does not exist under IFRS.

But on the most important criteria, the existence of similar advertising that involves cash or other consideration, U.S. GAAP and IFRS are in agreement. As a result, fair value accounting risks associated with barter advertising under IFRS are identical to those existing with respect to U.S. GAAP.

CHAPTER 20

Special Fair Value Issues of Not-for-Profit Organizations

Introduction

In addition to many of the fair value issues described elsewhere in this book, not-for-profit organizations have some additional fair value accounting requirements that are susceptible to fraud. Unlike commercial businesses, not-for-profit organizations are rarely assessed based on their profitability, nor is profitability typically the most important goal of the organization. Financial stability is certainly important. But an organization's mission is more important. As a result, not-for-profit organizations are often measured on the degree to which and how well they are performing services in pursuit of their mission. For example, a shelter for homeless individuals and families is not measured on how much of a profit it earns for the year, but, rather, on how many people it served and how well it served those people.

Such objectives do not lend themselves to being measured in financial terms. However, some financial measures have evolved over the years that are used to benchmark not-for-profit organizations, particularly those with a charitable mission. Chief among those financial measures is an organization's program expense ratio. This ratio measures an organization's program expenses as a percentage of its total expenses. Expenses of not-for-profit organizations can be classified into two broad categories: program service expenses and supporting service expenses. Program service expenses are the direct and indirect costs associated with delivering goods or services in fulfillment of an organization's mission. Supporting service expenses represent everything else, such as the general oversight and administration of the organization and the costs of fundraising (i.e., soliciting charitable contributions).

The goal of many charitable not-for-profit organizations is to maintain a high program expense ratio. In fact, some publications and ratings agencies actually rank charities based solely or primarily on this one ratio. Although this is not fair, since it fails to account for the differences in operating characteristics from one organization to another, it is a fact of life in the nonprofit sector. Accordingly, there can be an incentive to maximize this ratio—using whatever means necessary.

As a result of the differing types of missions of not-for-profit organizations (when compared to commercial businesses) and use of different types of financial measures (such as the program expense ratio), financial reporting frauds in this sector may or may not result from attempts to make the organization look more profitable or more financially stable. Indeed, some fair value and other financial reporting frauds have a neutral effect of the net profit or loss reported in the financial statements of a not-for-profit organization.

Noncash Contributions of Assets

Many not-for-profit organizations rely heavily on charitable contributions for their support. When an organization receives gifts of cash or cash equivalents, these transactions are inherently already stated at their fair value. But when an organization receives assets other than cash or cash equivalents, such as food, clothing, equipment, or land, measurement becomes trickier.

SFAS 116, *Accounting for Contributions Received and Contributions Made*, states that when an organization receives contributions of noncash assets, these assets and the related income should be recorded at the fair value of the assets on the date of the gift. If the asset is then used or distributed in connection with a charitable program, the depreciation expense or the entire amount of the asset (if the asset is given away as part of a program) is then classified as a program service expense on the organization's financial statements.

Fraud Risk No. 20.1

Inflating the fair value of noncash assets received as contributions from donors, and the resulting expenses when the assets are used in providing services by a not-for-profit organization.

Accordingly, intentionally overstating the fair value of assets received in contribution transactions results in the following:

1. Overstating assets and income if the asset is held either in inventory or used in a charity's operations (even if the asset is depreciated, the

net carrying amount of the asset remains overstated, resulting in the net assets of the organization also being inflated)

2. Overstating both income and expense if the contributed asset is subsequently distributed in connection with a program

In the second situation, both income and expense are inflated by equal amounts. However, two benefits could nonetheless provide an incentive for this type of fair value accounting fraud:

1. Since the overstated expense is classified as a program expense, the organization's program expense ratio is artificially inflated.
2. The overall volume of activity that the organization appears to be engaged in is also overstated (i.e., even though the bottom line is not affected, the organization looks bigger than it really is, which may, in turn, have a positive influence on future donors or grant-makers).

Contributed Use of Assets

SFAS 116 requires a similar fair value accounting treatment for the contributed *use* of an asset. In these transactions, a donor has not transferred ownership of an asset to the charity, but has instead granted the charity use of the asset for a below-market rental rate (often rent-free). For example, a donor may provide rent-free use of office space to a charity.

Fraud Risk No. 20.2

Overstating or understating the fair value of rental space provided to a not-for-profit organization free of charge by a donor.

In these cases, the charity should record contribution income and rent expense in equal amounts, based on the underlying fair value of the rental. Artificially inflating the fair value of the rental has potentially the same impact as overstating the fair value of contributions of assets.

However, there may also be an incentive to understate the fair value. Recall from the earlier explanation of reporting objectives that all expenses of a not-for-profit organization are classified into two categories—program expenses and supporting service expenses. If the goal is to maximize the program expense ratio, the organization wants to increase only those expenditures classified as program expenses. Classification is based on what purpose is served with the expenditure.

If the rent-free (or below-market-rent) space is used for supporting service activities (e.g., it is a purely administrative office), the organization may wish to use as low a value as possible. Whereas, if the space is used for providing program services, the organization may wish to use the highest fair value possible.

It may be necessary to obtain third-party appraisals of rental rates in order to have reliable evidence of fair values in these cases. Some of the properties that are provided rent-free to not-for-profit organizations are unique properties whose rental value can be difficult to assess without having specialized expertise.

Promises to Give

Contributed assets and contributed use of assets may also take on one additional factor that could exacerbate the effect of a fair value accounting fraud. Under SFAS 116, unconditional promises to give future contributions are to be recorded as income currently, and if the promise extends beyond one year, the future commitment should be recorded at its present value.

Accordingly, if a donor agrees to provide office space on a rent-free basis and commits to such a gift for multiple future periods, the present value of the future rentals is to be recorded as a receivable and as contribution income on the date of the promise. Now the stakes are even higher. Inflating multiple years of future rental rates can result in an even more substantial overstatement of a not-for-profit organization's assets, income, and net assets.

In other cases, a donor has made an unconditional promise to give in the form of the future transfer of noncash assets (e.g., a promise to contribute land or a building at some future date) or the cash proceeds of assets that are currently in a noncash form (e.g., the remainder left in a charitable remainder trust after providing a benefit for a beneficiary and then liquidating the remaining assets of the trust).

Fraud Risk No. 20.3

Misstating the fair value of assets held in an irrevocable charitable remainder trust where a charitable organization has been designated as the party that will receive the remaining assets held in the trust when the trust expires.

Take the example of a charitable remainder trust, wherein a charity will receive the "remainder" (i.e., what's left in the trust) after providing a payment to the donor (the beneficiary) until the donor dies. Assuming this is an unconditional promise (often evidenced by the fact that the trust is irrevocable, among other considerations), the charity should record an asset and contribution income equal to the present value of the anticipated remainder value of the trust, after giving effect to the required payment to the beneficiary for the rest of the beneficiary's life. To record this transaction, four pieces of information must be determined:

1. The fair value of the assets currently held by the trust. In some cases this is easy, if a trust is invested very simply in certificates of deposit, publicly traded securities, and so on; but in other cases, unusual types of assets with difficult-to-determine fair values are placed into these trusts.
2. Estimate the duration of the trust (i.e., the beneficiary's life expectancy), since this will be used in the present value calculation.
3. Assign an appropriate rate of interest to be used in the present value calculation (SFAS 116 requires the use of an organization's risk-free rate of return).
4. Determination of the specific terms of the payment to the beneficiary (e.g., an annuity, a fixed interest rate, or one with more complicated terms).

Clearly, there are several opportunities for financial reporting fraud in this example. Most notably, manipulating the fair value of the trust's assets will have a potentially material effect on the not-for-profit organization's financial statements. Although much of this book focuses on opportunities for making an entity appear more financially successful than it really is, this example is a good reminder that sometimes, the opposite incentive may exist. Some not-for-profits may attempt to inflate the value of this asset. Some, however, want to omit the asset or carry it at a lower value, preferring to record the contribution income only when the organization actually receives the proceeds from the trust.

Contributed Services

SFAS 116 also provides guidance on recording contributed services (i.e., uncompensated services, or volunteer labor). Not all such labor should be recorded. But when it is, income and expense in equal amounts, based on the fair value of the contributed service, are to be recorded.

Fraud Risk No. 20.4

Recognition by a not-for-profit organization of contributed services when the criteria for recognition have not been met, or intentionally not recognizing services for which the criteria have been met.

Under SFAS 116, only two categories of contributed services are to be recorded:

1. Services that create or enhance a nonfinancial asset (such as volunteer labor associated with constructing or improving a building or other property)
2. Services that: (a) require specialized skills, (b) are provided by individuals who possess those skills, and (c) are the types of services that would typically need to be purchased if they had not been contributed to the organization

Note that a contributed service does not need to meet both of the preceding criteria. Only one of the criteria needs to be met in order for the organization to be required to record the labor at its fair value.

Under the second criterion, all three conditions must be met. Typical examples of the specialized skill category of contributed services are professional services (accounting, legal, etc.), healthcare (doctors, nurses, therapists, etc.), and trades or crafts requiring training (e.g., electricians, plumbers, etc.).

A not-for-profit may wish to record contributed services or may wish to avoid it. As with contributions explained earlier, determining which risk exists depends on the nature of the volunteer labor. If volunteers are involved in providing programmatic services, the organization generally would want to recognize this labor. If volunteers are engaged in administrative duties or fundraising, the organization often would prefer not recognizing them.

Fraud Risk No. 20.5

Improperly valuing contributed services that are recognized in the financial statements of a not-for-profit organization.

For contributed services that are recorded, they are to be recognized at fair value. When contributed services are improperly valued at artificially inflated amounts, the same types of effect on the financial statements result:

- An overstatement of the program expense ratio (assuming the contributed services were associated with programmatic activities)
- An overall exaggeration of the size and volume of activity of an organization, making it look bigger than it actually is to readers of the financial statements

Matching Requirements

One additional incentive may exist for some not-for-profit organizations to overstate the value of noncash contributions. Many government grants include a matching or cost-sharing requirement. This means the organization is eligible for the government support only if it obtains a specified level of *in-kind contributions*, the term used with respect to all forms of noncash contribution income. Some forms of in-kind that government grants permit do not meet the GAAP criteria for recognition (certain types of contributed services). However, most forms of in-kind that a government grant allows also are to be recognized for GAAP purposes (albeit, sometimes at different values). This represents another potential motive to engage in some of the fair value accounting frauds explained in this chapter.

CHAPTER 21

Fair Value Disclosure Issues

Introduction

Every bit as important as the basic financial statements themselves are the notes to the financial statements. These notes explain many of the accounting policies and treatments involved in preparing the financial statements and, in some cases, even disclose information about items that are *not* included in the basic financial statements.

From the perspective of detecting fair value accounting fraud, footnote disclosures should be reviewed for two reasons:

1. Disclosures can provide important clues that can be helpful in detecting a fair value accounting fraud risk.
2. The disclosures themselves may be intentionally misstated (or omitted), constituting a form of financial statement fraud.

Fraud Risk No. 21.1

Omission of a required disclosure in the notes to the financial statements.

Disclosure frauds can be classified as follows:

- Omitting required disclosures in their entirety
- Omitting certain required elements of a disclosure (i.e., what appears to be a note that meets a disclosure requirement is actually omitting a key piece of required information that a reader may find useful)
- Providing misleading or inaccurate information in a note

The strategy behind each of these frauds has its own special characteristics. For example, the complete omission of a disclosure seems like the most flagrant offense. However, it may be the most difficult to detect. Detection of omissions is generally more difficult than detecting misstatements of information that is included in the financial statements and notes.

When an entity intentionally omits a disclosure, it is counting on the fact that the typical reader of the financial statements wouldn't even notice the omission. Hopefully, auditors would detect such an omission, since auditors usually go through extensive disclosure checklists when they audit an entity's financial statements. Yet even with well-trained auditors, omissions can sometimes occur.

Fraud Risk No. 21.2

Omission of required information from a disclosure in the notes to the financial statements.

Including a required disclosure, but with certain elements omitted, relies on a different assumption. In this case, the perpetrator of the fraud is counting on the reader feeling comfortable that a particular issue has been addressed in the notes, without noticing that one key piece of required information is missing.

Again, a well-trained and conscientious auditor should be able to detect these types of omissions with careful attention to the disclosure checklists.

Fraud Risk No. 21.3

Inclusion of inaccurate information in the notes to the financial statements.

The third approach to disclosure fraud assumes that the reader/auditor would recognize an omission, but might not notice if certain elements of a disclosure are inaccurate. The most common types of intentional inaccuracies in notes to financial statements are those that downplay any negative information or that exaggerate positive information. All of this is done to make the entity appear more financially sound and successful than it really is.

Sources of Disclosure Requirements

Almost every one of the many accounting standards, under both U.S. GAAP and IFRS, include specialized disclosure requirements associated with the

unique accounting issue covered in that standard. In fact, a complete explanation of the many disclosure requirements is well beyond the scope of
this book.

Since the scope of this book is fair value accounting fraud, coverage
of disclosure requirements will be limited to a handful of required disclosures that are most susceptible to fraud or are most likely to be helpful in
performing a fair value accounting fraud risk assessment.

Readers should consult the specific accounting standards or a comprehensive disclosure checklist for details on these and other required
disclosures.

Financial Instruments

Both U.S. GAAP and IFRS require a variety of disclosures regarding financial
instruments, a broad category that includes many of the assets and liabilities
covered in this book. The primary sources of these disclosures are SFAS 107
for U.S. GAAP and IFRS 7 for IFRS. Additional U.S. GAAP disclosures are
found in SFAS 159, the standard that introduced the fair value option for
many financial instruments, and SFAS 157.

Under both U.S. GAAP and IFRS, perhaps the most important disclosure requirement in this area involves the methods and assumptions used in
determining fair values of each category of financial asset and financial liability that is measured at fair value. This disclosure should clearly identify the
methods used, such as the income method, present value technique, market
approach, and so on. The disclosure should indicate whether quoted market prices were used in connection with the market approach. Disclosures
of significant assumptions associated with fair value measurements should
include items such as interest and discount rates, assumed rates of inflation,
and other pertinent information.

Generally, when methods of determining fair value have been changed
from one period to the next, this should also be disclosed. As mentioned
earlier, in the economic crisis that continues in 2009, some markets that
were previously active sources of data for use with the market approach
to determining fair value have become inactive. This has and will continue to force changes in methods of determining fair value for those
securities, often resulting in the use of a completely different valuation
model.

The disclosure of methods and assumptions used represents a wealth
of information for the reader of the financial statements. Well-written and
complete disclosures should provide readers with adequate information to
be able to formulate a preliminary opinion regarding the adequacy of these

methods and assumptions. If reading the notes fails to provide this level of information, there is a chance that the disclosure is falling short of the requirements of the standards. There may be a reason for this.

Under U.S. GAAP, SFAS 159 also requires disclosure of management's reasons for electing the fair value option for each eligible item or group of items. If the fair value option was elected for some, but not all, items within a group of similar items, the reasons for this partial election should be disclosed.

Finally, SFAS 157 introduced several new disclosures to U.S. GAAP. Many of these same disclosures are being contemplated by the IASB as it develops an exposure draft that will be the IFRS counterpart to SFAS 157. This exposure draft is expected to be published by the time this book is published.

Recall that SFAS 157 introduced a hierarchy of inputs used in estimating fair value. The standard requires disclosure of the level(s) of inputs within the hierarchy that were used in developing fair value measurements. The disclosures required when Level 3 inputs are used are more extensive than those associated with Level 1 or Level 2 (recall that Level 3 inputs are the "unobservable" inputs, meaning they are developed internally by management).

SFAS 157 also provides for separate disclosures associated with fair values performed on a nonrecurring basis from those done on a recurring basis. Nonrecurring fair value measurements are typically associated with impairment issues, explained in the next section.

Required disclosures about derivatives and hedging activities vary, depending on the period covered by the financial statements. For periods beginning after November 15, 2008 (e.g., quarters ended March 31, 2009, years ending December 31, 2009, etc.), new disclosures are required by SFAS 161, *Disclosures About Derivative Instruments and Hedging Activities.* For earlier period, the disclosure requirements explained in SFAS 133 should be followed.

Readers will recall from Chapter 11 the issue of decreasing the recorded amount of a debt obligation in connection with an entity's assessment of its own likelihood of defaulting on the debt. For liabilities with fair values that have been significantly affected during the reporting period by changes in instrument-specific credit risk, U.S. GAAP requires disclosure of three factors:

1. An estimate of the gains or losses included in earnings that are attributable to changes in instrument-specific credit risk
2. Qualitative information about the reasons for those changes
3. How those gains and losses were determined

Impairment Losses

In Chapters 4, 7, 9 and 10 of this book the issue of asset impairments was covered. One of the confusing issues with impairments is the fact, especially under U.S. GAAP, that there are different standards for testing impairment of different types of assets. There isn't a single standard of impairment testing that applies to all assets.

Recall from Chapter 4 that under U.S. GAAP, one of the important issues involving impairments of debt and equity securities is whether an impairment is "other-than-temporary." When securities are in an unrealized loss position, U.S. GAAP requires the disclosure of certain information that is designed to aid the reader in understanding the information that the entity considered in reaching its conclusion that an impairment loss is not other-than-temporary:

- The nature of the investment
- The cause of the impairment
- The number of investment positions that are in an unrealized loss position
- The severity and duration of the impairment
- Other evidence considered by the entity in reaching its conclusion (such as industry analysts' reports, sector credit ratings, etc.)

SFAS 144 identifies various disclosure requirements associated with impairments of long-lived assets, including intangible assets. Three of the most important in assessing the risk of fraud are as follows:

1. A description of the impaired assets and the facts and circumstances leading to the impairment
2. The method(s) used for determining fair value (e.g., quoted market prices, present value, other valuation techniques, etc.)
3. If applicable, the business segment in which the impaired long-lived asset is reported

Similar descriptions of impairments of long-lived and intangible assets are required for IFRS under IAS 36. However, recall that IFRS permits the reversal of previously recognized impairment losses, something not allowed under U.S. GAAP. When such reversals are recorded, IFRS requires disclosure of the events or circumstances that led to this reversal.

Finally, with intangible assets being such a prime candidate for impairment, IFRS includes one potentially useful disclosure requirement not found in U.S. GAAP. For any intangible assets that are not being amortized (meaning, management considers them to have an indefinite life), the entity must disclose the reasons supporting the entity's assessment that the asset has an indefinite life.

Uncertainties

Both U.S. GAAP and IFRS include a disclosure requirement associated with measurement uncertainties. If there is an uncertainty at the balance sheet date that has a significant risk of causing a material adjustment to the carrying amounts of assets and liabilities within one year of the balance sheet date, information about the uncertainty should be disclosed. This disclosure should identify the nature of the assets and/or liabilities affected and their carrying amounts at the balance sheet date.

As a reminder, the guidance in this book should not be considered to be a complete disclosure checklist. Rather, it is intended to be useful in detecting fair value accounting fraud risks. So, the disclosures described in this chapter are limited to those disclosures most likely to aid in that effort.

PART V

Detection of Fair Value Accounting Fraud

The final section of this book is devoted to summarizing an approach to detecting fair value accounting fraud. The subject of detection may mean different things to different types of readers. Some of you are auditors—either independent auditors of an entity's financial statements or internal auditors. Other readers may be lenders, fraud investigators, investment managers, regulators, or any of a number of other readers of financial statements.

Auditor responsibilities associated with fair value accounting fraud issues can be classified into three categories:

1. Assessing the risk of material misstatements in the financial statements, including those caused by fraud
2. Gaining an understanding of the design and implementation of an entity's internal controls over fair value accounting applications in the financial statements
3. Performing audit procedures designed to gain assurance that fair value measurements are fairly stated in accordance with the applicable accounting standards, including fair value disclosures made in the footnotes to the financial statements

Other readers have different responsibilities. However, the detection of fraud is nonetheless the goal if you are reading this book, whether you are an auditor, a lender, a member of an audit committee, a stock analyst, or any of a number of other positions. Therefore, the purpose of this final section of the book is to present a framework for detecting fair value accounting fraud, regardless of your role.

The biggest difference between the process used by auditors versus the process used by others in detecting fraud lies in the second step in the preceding list. Auditors have a specific responsibility to gain an understanding of internal controls surrounding fair value measurements. Of course, management has the primary responsibility for maintaining internal controls, so managers must also actively consider internal controls. But outside parties other than auditors may limit or entirely omit any evaluation of internal controls. For example, a lender, investigator, insurer, or analyst is likely to be much more focused on the first and third steps. In fact, these parties may not even have access to the records necessary to perform any detailed analysis of internal controls. But when information regarding internal controls is available, it should be considered, as it is useful in assessing the risk of fraud.

CHAPTER 22

A Framework for Detecting Fair Value Accounting Fraud

Assessing the Risk of Fraud

Assessing the risk of whether the financial statements include fair value accounting fraud is the critical first step in the process of detecting fraud. Assessing the risk of fraud involves several key steps:

1. Understanding where the financial statements could be affected by fair value accounting
2. Considering external factors that could impact fair value accounting issues in the financial statements
3. Determining the materiality of the financial statement elements that could be affected by fair value measurements
4. If applicable, assessing the internal controls over fair value accounting issues that are in place (applicable primarily for auditors, but also in certain other instances)

The risk assessment process described here may be a very extensive and time-consuming process, such as it is for auditors preparing to audit an entity with complex international operations, or a very simple one, as it may be for an investigator looking into a specific allegation of fraud.

Once a fair value accounting fraud risk assessment is complete, attention can be turned to designing specific tests that address the risks identified in the risk assessment. These tests, or audit procedures, should target the areas of greatest risk first and expand from there.

Understanding How Fair Value Impacts the Financial Statements

To understand how fair value accounting impacts the financial statements, start by reading the statements and notes in their entirety. Then, using the summary of fraud risks in Appendix A as a guide, identify which of the accounting areas covered in the appendix are included in the financial statements (e.g., marketable equity securities, derivatives, intangible assets, etc.).

Once the fraud risk areas have been identified, read the applicable sections of each chapter in this book to gain an understanding of the specific fraud risks that apply to each broad accounting topic.

The most difficult part of determining where fair value affects the financial statements is in identifying the areas that are *not* included in the financial statements but should be. This is where the next section comes in handy. But, one more review of Appendix A is not a bad idea, either.

External Factors that Indicate Risk

After a careful review of the financial statements, an analysis of external factors is the next important step in the risk assessment process. Again, the importance of this step depends on your role. If you are responding to a whistleblower communication alleging a specific type of fraud, additional review of external information may not be as important. But if you are either auditing or relying on financial statements as an outside reader, the importance of this step cannot be overstated.

External factors can provide insight into a fraud risk assessment. For example:

- An external factor may be a direct cause of an expected fair value adjustment (e.g., a downturn in the economy would often result in an expectation that fair value adjustments would result in losses).
- An external factor may result in a motive to perpetrate a fair value accounting fraud in response (e.g., a competitor).

Here are ten examples of external factors that should be considered in assessing the risk of fair value accounting fraud:

1. *The economy in the regions in which the entity operates.* This may be global, limited to specific countries, or even local geographic regions within a country.
2. *Trends in the industry in which the entity operates.* Is this particular industry doing well or poorly, regardless of the overall economy?
3. *Market trends for the specific types of assets an entity holds.* Real estate is one example.
4. *Technological advances in the industry in which the entity operates.* Are there new products and services that could make the entity's products (and perhaps one or more of its intangible assets) obsolete sooner than anticipated?

5. *Changes in the industry in which the entity's customers operate.* For example, the entity might have a large concentration of sales to entities in a particular region or industry that is on a downward trend.
6. *New laws or regulations that affect the entity.* For example, new restrictions might affect the entity's products, perhaps resulting in the need to redesign a product, or a new law might result in an asset retirement obligation.
7. *Changes in foreign exchange rates with countries in which the entity does business.* For example, a U.S.-based company with vendors or customers in Europe.
8. *Changes in interest rates.* This would affect the entity's borrowing costs or investments.
9. *The introduction of new competitors or loss of former competitors.* This could increase or decrease pressures on a company and also impact pricing of products or services.
10. *A tightening of credit by financial institutions, making borrowing more difficult.* For example, the credit squeeze triggered by the economic crisis has increased pressures to report solid financial results.

Some external factors are common to a geographic region or a particular industry. But external factors are also entity-specific. Developing a list of entity-specific external factors requires a deeper understanding of the entity and its standing within its industry, among other factors.

Internal Risk Factors

In addition to an analysis of an entity's financial statements and consideration of the account-specific fraud risks listed in Appendix A, there are many internal factors impacting the risk of fair value accounting fraud (and many other types of financial reporting fraud, for that matter). These additional internal factors can be organized into two categories:

1. Risk factors associated with management style and the overall environment of an entity
2. Risk factors associated with the general characteristics of fair value measurements used in the financial statements

There are many internal factors associated with management style and the entity's working environment. Seventeen are listed here:

1. The *tone at the top*—management's attitudes and behavior as it pertains to ethics and integrity, especially in connection with financial and compliance matters

2. Whether the compliance and ethics function is recognized as an executive-level function of the entity, one that is respected and provided with adequate resources and authority

3. The entity's approach toward risk—is it the type of organization that freely or aggressively takes on new risks, or is it rather conservative in its risk appetite?

4. Pressures to achieve financial goals—does management apply significant amounts of pressure to achieve financial goals?

5. Whether the entity has a properly functioning hotline and whistleblower protection system, whereby employees would feel comfortable in reporting allegations of financial improprieties without fear of retaliation

6. Whether the board of directors and audit committee function properly, providing an appropriate level of oversight to the accounting and internal control function

7. Human resource policies and procedures, including hiring, background checks, orientation, training, performance evaluation, compensation, and so on

8. Systems for monitoring financial performance over time, including analysis of results compared to budget, past periods, and so on

9. The processes involved in establishing an entity's budgets

10. How an entity engages in strategic planning—for example, is the entity aggressively planning on rapid growth?

11. The entity's plans (and past practices) for acquisitions of other businesses

12. The degree to which compensation or performance evaluations are tied directly or indirectly to financial performance—it is to be expected that managers are evaluated and rewarded in part on financial performance, but if substantial portions of salaries or bonuses are tied to financial results, or promotions are excessively tied to financial performance, this can be a significant fraud risk indicator

13. The existence and functioning of a fraud risk management function at the management as well as the board level—does the board, audit committee, or other committee play an active role in its oversight responsibilities, does it require and obtain adequate levels of financial information, does it communicate effectively with management and with the auditors?

14. Whether the board of directors, especially the audit committee and finance committee, includes individuals possessing an adequate level of proficiency in accounting and financial reporting applicable to the entity

15. The extent of an internal audit function in the entity

16. Whether the entity has consistently enforced its code of ethics, including fairly investigating allegations of wrongdoing and taking disciplinary action in response to violations, regardless of the level or seniority of the offender

17. Whether mid-level managers and others with supervisory responsibilities are provided adequate training regarding their roles and responsibilities for enforcing the entity's code of ethics and awareness of fraud risk warning signals

Four additional internal factors might indicate specific risks associated with fair value measurements:

1. The degree to which unobservable inputs are used in measuring fair values (Recall that SFAS 157 assigns the inputs used in measuring fair into three categories, with the two categories of observable inputs generally being more reliable than unobservable inputs developed internally.)

2. The length of forecast periods used in fair value calculations—generally, the longer the period used, the greater the risk that is associated with the measurement

3. The degree to which fair values are determined by internal personnel versus using outside experts for such measurements

4. The level of expertise, including continuing education and training, of personnel involved in measuring fair value

The lists of internal factors could go on. But the factors listed here represent the most important to consider in evaluating the risk of fair value accounting fraud.

Materiality

Depending on your purpose in conducting a fraud risk assessment, materiality may or may not be a consideration. Auditors of financial statements always consider materiality, since to audit for every risk would be impossible. Materiality helps to prioritize which areas will be subject to additional testing and perhaps even the extent of the testing.

Materiality is usually thought of as an amount, or a few different amounts. If an auditor discovers misstatements in excess of this amount, it would be necessary to make an adjustment to the financial statements. Other, lesser, levels of materiality are often used as tools for planning certain audit procedures.

But materiality isn't solely about an amount. There are also qualitative aspects of materiality that may be important to an auditor—and therefore to an investigator, lender, or other user of the financial statements.

Qualitative elements of materiality are factors that can make a relatively small amount into a very important matter. For example, if financial statement materiality is calculated to be $10 million, but a $100,000 misstatement enables the entity to achieve a minimum current ratio required under a $20 million loan, would the $100,000 difference be considered material?

Readers need to understand that there are sometimes small amounts that, if fraudulently reported, can have a significant effect on how the entity is viewed.

Internal Controls over Fair Value Accounting

Internal control serves three purposes in an entity:

1. Reliability of financial reporting
2. Effectiveness and efficiency of operations
3. Compliance with applicable laws and regulations

In connection with controls associated with the reliability of financial reporting, internal controls can be classified and evaluated in several manners. The first classification of internal controls is preventive or detective. All internal controls over financial reporting are designed to either prevent or detect a misstatement. Misstatements can either be unintentional (mistakes) or intentional (fraud), such as a fair value accounting fraud. Preventive controls are the preferred type of internal control. However, preventive controls are not always practical, in which case strong detective controls are essential. A detective control should be designed to detect certain types of misstatements in a timely manner. Ideally, an entity has a blend of preventive and detective controls.

Internal controls can also be classified as being either entity-level or specific. Entity-level controls are those that apply equally, regardless of the nature of the financial transaction, such as the existence of a whistleblower system, performing background checks on new hires, and similar controls. Specific controls focus on particular accounting cycles or even particular accounts. Many of the most important internal considerations in the area of fair value accounting are specific to the particular fair value issue being addressed.

Formal evaluations of internal controls are primarily an area of focus for auditors, both internal and external. Investigators and other readers and users of the financial statements may not even bother to evaluate internal controls, since they are focused on one or more specific fraud risks.

An external auditor's consideration of internal control can be summarized as follows:

1. Gain an understanding of the design of all relevant internal controls (relevant for purposes of this book refers to those internal controls that impact material fair value issues in the financial statements).
2. Perform walkthroughs of internal controls in each area to make sure the auditor has a sufficient understanding of the implementation of internal controls.
3. Test the operating effectiveness of internal controls.

The third step is not necessarily done on every audit every year. Auditors may exercise professional judgment in determining the extent of reliance on tests of the operating effectiveness of internal controls. But the first two steps are required on every audit.

However, management and the board of directors should also be concerned about internal controls. Strong internal controls are essential to reliable financial reporting. The Committee of Sponsoring Organizations (COSO) identifies five interrelated components of internal control:

1. Control environment
2. Risk assessment
3. Control activities
4. Information and communication
5. Monitoring

Each of these components has application to each of the major accounting functions of an entity (as well as other functions), such as purchasing, disbursements, payroll, and so on. Fair value accounting should be thought of as another major accounting function for many entities, with appropriate consideration given to building and maintaining strong preventive and detective controls. Examples of key internal controls over fair value accounting associated with each of the five components of internal control are identified in Appendix C.

The Risk of Management Override

One factor present in many financial reporting frauds, including those involving fair value manipulations, is the override of internal controls by management. Most financial reporting frauds are perpetrated by or under the direction of senior management. Accordingly, having strong internal controls over management override is an essential ingredient to the prevention of fair value accounting fraud.

Controls over management override are often even more critical to smaller entities, where the increased level of involvement of senior management in performing controls and in the period-end financial reporting process makes these entities even more prone to financial reporting fraud. All journal entries made by senior management should be subject to a review. In some entities, the only person in a position to perform this review may be someone from the board of directors or finance committee—this is often the case with very small entities. In mid-sized entities and larger entities, an internal audit department or other persons can perform this review of management's journal entries.

Framework for Fair Value Accounting Fraud Detection

What the considerations described so far in this chapter lead up to is a comprehensive framework for detecting fair value accounting fraud. The ten steps outlined in the following box represent a recommended process for assessing the risk of fraud and developing a plan for investigating those risks.

The Ten-Step Framework for Detecting Fair Value Accounting Fraud

Step 1 Read the financial statements and notes to gain an understanding of the entity, its operations, and the financial results for the period and financial position at the end of the period.

Step 2 Identify external factors that could have an effect on the risk of fair value accounting fraud.

Step 3 Review the listing of fair value accounting fraud risks in Appendix A, marking those that apply based on the initial reading of the financial statements and notes.

Step 4 Re-read the financial statements and notes, adding to the preceding listing of the fair value accounting fraud risks most likely to apply to the entity.

Step 5 Perform ratio analysis and other analytical procedures, as explained in Chapter 23, to identify unexpected or unusual relationships or trends that could indicate a fraud risk, and add those risks to the preceding list.

Step 6 Based on the risks identified in steps 1 through 5, read the applicable sections of this book to gain a more thorough understanding of the identified fraud risks, how such frauds would be perpetrated and what additional signs of the frauds there may be to look for.

Step 7 If practical, identify and consider internal factors that could have an impact on fair value accounting.

Step 8 If practical, consider the effect of the entity's internal controls on fair value accounting—do these controls create opportunities for fraud, or do they mitigate some of the fraud risks identified?

Step 9 Design specific audit/investigative procedures aimed at the fraud risks that have been identified, prioritizing your efforts by targeting the risks that are likely to have the greatest potential for a material effect on the financial statements.

Step 10 Evaluate the results of the procedures performed in step 9, assessing whether the financial statements appear to have been prepared fraudulently.

The specific procedures applied to individual fraud risks in step 9 will be determined by the nature of the fraud risk. As stated in step 6, as fraud risks are identified, the appropriate sections of this book should be read carefully in order to understand the details of the specific risk. This reading of the applicable sections will also result in your ability to identify the appropriate follow-up procedure to be applied to determine whether a fraud has occurred.

For example, if the fraud risk identified is the use of an inappropriate discount rate to calculate a present value, you obviously need to consider all of the relevant factors and determine what you think an appropriate rate should be and compare it to the one used by the entity. This assessment may require that you identify an outside expert to provide assistance.

Four of the most commonly applied categories of detection procedures applied once specific fraud risks have been identified are as follows:

1. Evaluating whether the methods used by management are appropriate
2. Evaluating whether the inputs and assumptions applied to the valuation methods are appropriate (e.g., interest rates, growth rates, cash flow assumptions, etc.)
3. Testing management's application of the methods, using the inputs and assumptions that were verified in step 2

4. Assessing whether management has identified all fair value issues (e.g., did it omit, perhaps intentionally, a fair value loss or liability?)

The auditing standards referred to in the next section actually provide some helpful guidance that could be applied by anyone who is attempting to evaluate the fair value measurements included in an entity's financial statements. And that guidance states that there are generally three ways to audit any accounting estimate, including a fair value measurement:

1. Test the procedures used by management (i.e., do you agree with management's methods, inputs, assumptions, and calculation?).
2. Develop your own independent fair value measurement and compare it to the one reported by management in the entity's financial statements.
3. Consider the evidence that events occurring subsequent to the financial statement date may provide (e.g., an asset reported at a particular fair value as of December 31 that is sold for substantially less on January 25 may indicate a problem with the December 31 valuation).

Any user of this book will need to apply one or more of these three types of procedures in determining whether fair value accounting fraud has been committed in preparing the financial statements.

Auditing Standards

Auditors have additional responsibilities that other users of this book may not have. This book is not designed as a guide to the many auditing standards that apply when auditing financial statements that include fair value measurements. Instead, the primary standards that impact the auditing of fair value measurements will be identified. But, hopefully this book will provide auditors with practical guidance that will be useful in fulfilling these responsibilities.

In the United States, auditing standards for many years were the responsibility of the American Institute of Certified Public Accountants (AICPA). But the Sarbanes-Oxley Act of 2002 resulted in the establishment of the Public Company Accounting Oversight Board (PCAOB), which now has responsibility for auditing standards that are to be applied to audits of companies that register with the SEC and issue publicly traded securities, referred to as issuers. As a result, the AICPA's auditing standards are applicable to *nonissuers*, although the PCAOB has incorporated the AICPA standards by reference. However, the PCAOB has also issued several of its own standards.

Auditing standards of importance to detecting fair value accounting fraud can be classified as either general or specific:

1. General standards deal with the identification of the risks of misstatement in an audit (misstatements can generally be classified into two categories: those caused by fraud, which are covered in one area of the standards, and those resulting from any other reason, covered in several broad auditing standards).
2. Specific auditing standards address specific issues involving fair value or accounting estimates.

There are several U.S. auditing standards dealing with assessing the risk of material misstatement (including those caused by fair value accounting frauds), materiality, the consideration of internal control, and other broad audit issues. The primary U.S. auditing standard dealing more specifically with fair value accounting issues is SAS 101, *Auditing Fair Value Measurements and Disclosures* (as amended, and codified in AU Section 328). Other useful guidance is found in AU section 342, *Auditing Accounting Estimates*, and AU Section 332, *Auditing Derivative Instruments, Hedging Activities, and Investments in Securities*. Finally, as it relates to the detection of fraud in connection with an audit, auditors must follow the guidance of SAS 99, AU Section 316, *Consideration of Fraud in a Financial Statement Audit*.

In addition, the PCAOB, which governs the audits of companies that issue publicly traded securities in the United States, issued three useful documents:

1. Practice Alert No. 2, *Matters Related to Auditing Fair Value Measurements of Financial Instruments and the Use of Specialists* (December 2007)
2. Practice Alert No. 3, *Audit Considerations in the Current Economic Environment* (December 2008)
3. Auditing Standard No. 5, *An Audit of Internal Control Over Financial Reporting That Is Integrated with an Audit of Financial Statements*

Each of these documents provides further guidance that can aid in the auditing of fair value measurements.

Generally, most fair value estimates included in the financial statements can be audited using one of three general approaches:

1. The auditor can independently determine a fair value and compare it to the fair value reported by management in the company's financial statements.

2. The auditor can audit the processes and assumptions used by management in determining fair values included in the financial statements (i.e., similar to testing and relying on a company's internal controls).

3. The consideration of subsequent events (transactions occurring after year-end) may provide evidence supporting certain fair value estimates included in the financial statements (e.g., sales of an asset shortly after year-end may provide reliable evidence of the asset's fair value as of year-end).

Some approaches may be a hybrid of the first and second approaches. For instance, an auditor may develop an independent calculation of a particular fair value, but may base some or all of the calculation on assumptions developed by management. In such an approach, the auditor should also perform audit procedures aimed at gaining assurance that management's assumptions are reliable. In other cases, the auditor may independently develop all of the assumptions used in a particular model, or even utilize a completely different model than the one used by management.

In determining fair values, management (or outside experts hired by management) will often rely on a variety of estimates that become vital inputs in the process. If the auditor then takes the approach of auditing management's processes (the second option from the preceding list), then consideration must be given to the nature and extent of audit procedures to be utilized with respect to each of the estimates themselves (i.e., the process itself may be a sound one, but if the estimates that are used in connection with process are flawed, the outcome will also be flawed).

Internationally, auditing standards are set by the International Auditing and Assurance Standards Board (IAASB), which is an independent board of the International Federation of Accountants (IFA). From a risk assessment and response standpoint, the two most relevant of the International Standards on Auditing (ISAs) are as follows:

ISA 315, *Understanding the Entity and Its Environment and Assessing the Risks of Material Misstatement*
ISA 330, *The Auditor's Procedures in Response to Assessed Risks*

As it pertains more specifically to fair value accounting and the risk of fair value accounting fraud, the applicable ISAs are these:

ISA 240, *The Auditor's Responsibility to Consider Fraud in an Audit of Financial Statements*
ISA 540, *Auditing Accounting Estimates, Including Fair Value Accounting Estimates, and Related Disclosures* (a revised version of ISA 540

takes effect for audits of periods beginning on or after December 15, 2009)

ISA 545 (ISA 545 will be withdrawn when the revised version of ISA 540 becomes effective, since its content has been revised and rolled into the new ISA 540)

The complete set of ISAs are available for download at www.ifac.org. Additional guidance can be found in International Auditing Practice Statement (IAPS) 1012, *Auditing Derivative Financial Instruments.*

The international counterpart to PCAOB Practice Alert No. 3 came in the form of an October 2008 Staff Audit Practice Alert from the IAASB, *Challenges in Auditing Fair Value Accounting Estimates in the Current Market Environment.*

Auditor Independence

One final point regarding auditors and fair value measurements: It is a rather simple principle, but one that has surprisingly been violated many times. It is the responsibility of management to develop all fair value measurements for the financial statements. Management may develop these estimates internally or through the use of outside experts.

One of those outside experts should not be the auditor. The auditor must remain independent. If the auditor develops or assists in developing fair value estimates, the auditor has lost independence—the auditor has become a part of the accounting department of the entity. In these cases, a different auditor must be used to audit the financial statements.

Both the AICPA and the IAASB have strict rules on auditor independence. The focus of these independence rules is to make sure that auditors stick to auditing. Auditors should never be involved in preparing the financial statements or any portion of the financial statements—including the determination of fair value measurements.

CHAPTER 23

Use of Ratios and Other Analytical Procedures

Analytical Procedures as a Fraud Detection Tool

Analytical procedures can be one of the most effective methods of detecting financial reporting fraud in general, and fair value accounting fraud in particular. The process involved in using analytical procedures is as follows:

1. Develop an expectation—this could be an expected quantity, dollar amount, or ratio.
2. Compare the actual result with the expectation—is the actual result within an acceptable range of variance from the expected result?
3. Investigate the difference if it exceeds a reasonable variance.

There are many different types of analytical procedures that could be useful in detecting fraud. The most useful are:

1. Horizontal analysis
2. Vertical analysis
3. Operating ratios
4. Customized ratios

These four categories of analytical techniques are listed in order of their sophistication and ease of use. But just like many things in life, the more effort that is put into something, the more valuable it often is. This is true with analytical procedures in many cases.

Nonetheless, we'll start with the simplest of the analytical tools.

Horizontal Analysis

The most basic analytical procedure involves comparing actual results for the current period with either or both of the following:

- The budget for the current period
- Actual balances and results for the preceding period

The potentially useful extension of the second step is to compare several periods of revenue and expenses, gains and losses, over time, which can identify long-term trends. Trend analysis compares results over more than two periods, and can be a useful extension of any of the four categories of analytical techniques explained in this chapter.

Remember to also compare balances of assets and liabilities from period to period, not just revenues and expenses. Sometimes doing both types of horizontal analysis sheds an entirely different light on the trends that an entity is undergoing.

Explanations of variances between actual and budgeted amounts should be a standard element of internal control present in all entities. If this simple procedure is not being done properly, there are likely major weaknesses in internal controls elsewhere as well.

Comparing balances from one period to another is called *horizontal analysis*. Often, when a fair value fraud first takes place, an account balance takes an unusual jump or inexplicably declines from one year to the next. But keep in mind that sometimes the red flag of a fraud is that a balance that one would expect to change surprisingly remains stable from one period to the next.

Another consideration in performing horizontal analysis is to determine what, if any, level of account grouping is most likely to be useful. Horizontal analysis can be done on many different grouping levels:

- On an account-by-account basis (i.e., without grouping any accounts together)
- Rolling up similar objective categories of accounts together (e.g., instead of comparing rent expense, utilities expense, facilities maintenance, and other similar costs separately, group all occupancy-related costs together)
- Grouping revenues and expenses together by division or by functional area
- Grouping revenues and expenses together by geographic location
- Grouping revenues and expenses together by manager (particularly useful when individual managers have input into the development of accounting estimates)

In other words, look at the numbers from several different angles.

Vertical Analysis

Vertical analysis involves measuring a single account, or a group of accounts, as a percentage of some larger total. Examples of vertical analysis include the following:

- Measuring office supplies expense (or any other category of expense) as a percentage of total operating expenses
- Measuring the total expenses of one division as a percentage of total expenses of an entire company
- Measuring revenue from one type of product as a percentage of total revenue

Similar to horizontal analysis, look at vertical analysis from different angles. Perform it using different types of groupings:

- On a line item by line item basis, comparing each element of revenue to total revenue, each item of expense to total expenses
- Grouping accounts that have similar characteristics
- Grouping accounts by region, by division, by manager, or some other useful shared characteristic

Vertical analysis is useful for detecting changes in the composition of a group of accounts over time.

Operating Ratios

Use of operating ratio analysis is one of the most reliable methods of detecting financial statement fraud of any type, including fair value accounting-based frauds.

These ratios are most likely to detect fraud when the fraud impacts the numerator and denominator in a proportion that differs from the normal (properly stated) ratio. For example, if the carrying amount of current investments has been overstated as a result of recording fraudulent gains in connection with nonexistent increases in fair value, the entity's current ratio (current assets divided by current liabilities) would be artificially inflated (or an expected deterioration would not occur). Of course, there are numerous other explanations for an improved current ratio, most of which are completely honest and do not involve fraud. But, unexplained changes in key ratios, especially when this occurs with respect to multiple important ratios, should always be investigated, as these might be the first warning signs of a fair value accounting fraud.

Operating ratios that could be of use in detecting fraud can be classified in four categories:

1. Liquidity ratios
2. Activity ratios
3. Leverage ratios
4. Profitability ratios

Some of these ratios involve financial numerators and financial denominators. Others involve a combination of financial amounts and nonfinancial statistics. In assessing the risk of fair value fraud, some may be more useful than others. Their usefulness in detecting fair value fraud is dependent on the extent to which fair value issues impact either the numerator or denominator of the fraction.

Therefore, the first step is to complete the fraud risk assessment described in Chapter 22, in which the financial statements and notes are reviewed and a list of which accounts are impacted by fair values issues has been developed. After that has been conducted, begin reviewing the ratios in this section to identify those that are most likely to be of use in detecting manipulations of fair value.

Then, develop an expectation of what the ratio should be. Given all that is known about the entity and its environment, would the ratio be expected to improve, deteriorate, or remain stable from period to period? Follow this same process for each of the following ratios.

In addition to developing expectations for each pertinent ratio, it is also useful to consider the relationships that various ratios should be expected to have to one another. For example, as one ratio increases, are there other ratios that would be expected to also increase? Or would other ratios typically have an inverse relationship, declining in periods in which the first ratio increases?

Looking at ratios in this manner can further improve the ability to detect fraud.

Liquidity Measures

Liquidity ratios measure an organization's ability to meet its short-term obligations with its short-term assets. There are two most common liquidity measures—the current ratio and the quick (or acid-test) ratio.

$$Current\ ratio = \frac{Current\ assets}{Current\ liabilities}$$

The current ratio is the most commonly used liquidity measure. It assesses an entity's ability to satisfy the short-term claims of creditors with any of the current assets held at the reporting date.

Quick (acid-test) ratio

$$= \frac{Cash + Cash\ equivalents + Short\text{-}term\ investments + Accounts\ receivable}{Current\ liabilities}$$

The quick ratio takes a slightly different look at liquidity than the current ratio. Instead of measuring an entity's ability to pay its creditors using any of its current assets, the quick ratio assesses this ability using only the most liquid of current assets. For example, since prepaid expenses cannot be used to pay a creditor, such current assets are excluded from the numerator of the quick ratio.

Either of the liquidity measures can be prime suspects when assessing the risk of fraud. Short-term investments, in particular, can be subject to fluctuations in fair value and a target for fraudulent reporting. Other potential current assets and current liabilities with fair value accounting implications are receivables, certain derivatives, current portions of debt obligations, and several others described in this book.

Activity Ratios

Activity ratios, sometimes called *efficiency ratios*, indicate how effectively an entity utilizes its assets. Some of the more commonly used activity ratios are:

$$Accounts\ receivable\ turnover = \frac{Annual\ net\ sales}{Average\ accounts\ receivable}$$

$$Days\ outstanding\ in\ accounts\ receivable = \frac{365}{Average\ receivable\ turnover}$$

$$Inventory\ turnover = \frac{Cost\ of\ goods\ sold}{Average\ inventory}$$

$$Average\ age\ of\ inventory = \frac{365}{Inventory\ turnover}$$

$$Total\ asset\ turnover = \frac{Net\ sales}{Average\ total\ assets}$$

$$Fixed\ asset\ turnover = \frac{Net\ sales}{Average\ fixed\ assets}$$

$$Intangible\ asset\ turnover = \frac{Net\ sales}{Average\ intangible\ assets}$$

As with horizontal and vertical analysis, many of these activity ratios become even more valuable if they can be calculated not only on an entitywide basis, but also by region, location, product line, division, manager, and so on. The intangible asset turnover ratio can be an excellent tool for detecting overvalued intangible assets.

Leverage Ratios

Leverage ratios provide a measure of solvency of an entity. Strong leverage ratios indicate that an entity is well-prepared for surviving an economic downturn.

$$Debt\ to\ equity\ ratio = \frac{Total\ debt\ (long\text{-}term\ and\ short\text{-}term)}{Total\ equity}$$

$$Long\text{-}term\ debt\ to\ equity = \frac{Total\ long\text{-}term\ debt}{Total\ equity}$$

$$Debt\ to\ assets = \frac{Total\ debt}{Total\ assets}$$

$$Equity\ to\ assets = \frac{Total\ equity}{Average\ assets}$$

$$Times\ interest\ earned = \frac{Net\ income\ before\ interest\ and\ taxes}{Interest\ expense}$$

Leverage ratios, while they are very useful tools for analysts, are probably the least valuable of the four categories of operating ratios as a fair value fraud detection tool. Their use is limited primarily to the detection of fraudulent valuations of debt obligations.

Profitability Ratios

Profitability ratios simply measure an entity's record of producing profits for shareholders. Some of the most useful profitability ratios include:

$$Gross\ profit\ margin = \frac{Net\ sales - Cost\ of\ goods\ sold}{Net\ sales}$$

$$Operating\ profit\ margin = \frac{Net\ income\ before\ interest\ and\ taxes}{Net\ sales}$$

$$Net\ income\ ratio = \frac{Net\ income}{Net\ sales}$$

$$Return\ on\ equity = \frac{Net\ income}{Average\ stockholders'\ equity}$$

$$Return \ on \ assets = \frac{Net \ income + Interest \ expense \, (1 - Tax \ rate)}{Average \ total \ assets}$$

$$Return \ on \ investment = \frac{Net \ income + Interest \ expense \, (1 - Tax \ rate)}{Average \ stockholders' \ equity + Long\text{-}term \ debt}$$

As with many of the other ratios explained in this chapter, profitability ratios can be even more valuable as a fraud detection technique if they are calculated on the basis of product line, division, region, or other useful subcategory in addition to on a companywide basis.

Customized Ratios

The most useful analytical techniques for detecting financial statement fraud in general, and certain fair value accounting frauds in particular, involve ratios that have been customized for the specific fraud risk area. These ratios may be entirely financial (meaning that both the numerator and denominator represent account balances or groupings of balances) or they may combine financial and nonfinancial factors. In fact, some of the most valuable ratios involve financial numerators and nonfinancial denominators.

The key to successful use of this technique is to identify appropriate nonfinancial measures that should be expected to have a predictable relationship with a financial amount. What makes these ratios so valuable is that rarely does the perpetrator of a financial reporting fraud have the ability (or the awareness) to manipulate both the financial statements and the nonfinancial statistics in equal proportions.

For example, let's say we are evaluating whether a fair value accounting fraud has been perpetrated in connection with a particular intangible asset. The potential fraud involves a failure to record an impairment loss on the intangible asset. Depending on the type of intangible asset, potentially useful ratios to consider include:

- *Book value of the asset ÷ Revenue derived from the asset*
- *Book value of the asset ÷ Units of production derived from the asset*
- *Amortization expense ÷ Units of production derived from the asset*

Much like any of the ratios described in this chapter, customized ratios do not prove that a fair value accounting fraud has occurred. These ratios, when properly designed and compared over time, merely indicate that something unexpected has occurred. But that something just might be your first clue that you are on the trail of a major fraud involving the misapplication of fair value accounting. If you miss that clue, the opportunity to detect the fraud might be missed.

Summary Checklist of Fair Value Accounting Fraud Risks

The first part of each fraud risk number is a reference to the chapter in which that fraud risk is explained. The second number refers to the order in which these risks are discussed in the chapter.

Risk No.	Description
2.1	Basing fair value determinations on other known transactions, when the transactions cited are not "orderly."
2.2	Misrepresenting the highest or best use of an asset in order to inflate its estimated fair value.
3.1	Drawing inappropriate conclusions about an asset's fair value based on consideration of a range of prices or other inputs available from transactions in a market.
3.2	Misapplication of the income approach by using improper amounts for cash flows, manipulating the timing of future cash flows, or using an inappropriate discount rate, resulting in an inaccurate present value.
3.3	Using inappropriate replacement cost estimates or making inaccurate adjustments for obsolescence in determining fair value under the cost approach.
3.4	Obtaining a tainted valuation report in support of a fraudulent fair value measurement used in the financial statements, using any of five techniques.
4.1	Improper classification (or reclassification) of a security among the various categories, for example:

1. A trading security misclassified as available for sale, in order to shift the reporting of unrealized losses out of profit and loss and into other comprehensive income
2. An available for sale security misclassified as trading, in order to report unrealized gains in profit and loss rather than in other comprehensive income

(Continued)

Risk No.	Description
	3. A debt security being misclassified as held-to-maturity when in fact management no longer intends to hold the security to maturity or considers it to be available for sale in response to changes in market conditions
4.2	Failing to reclassify a debt security out of the held-to-maturity category despite selling certain other debt securities prior to maturity.
4.3	Manipulating the determination of fair value of a debt security by utilizing inappropriate discount rates in the calculation of present value.
4.4	False representations about whether a market is active or inactive, resulting in use of inappropriate values, valuation methods, or inputs to manipulate a fair value measurement.
4.5	Improperly treating a decline in fair value as a temporary impairment when it should be treated as "other-than-temporary."
5.1	Overstating the value of assets, or understating liabilities, of a joint venture accounted for using proportionate consolidation or proportionate recognition of individual assets that are jointly held by venturers, resulting in proportionately overstated assets on the financial statements of each partner in the venture.
5.2	Inflating the value of assets, or understating liabilities, of a joint venture accounted for by the equity method of accounting, resulting in an overstated asset on the financial statements of the partner in the venture.
5.3	Electing fair value accounting treatment for a noncontrolling ownership interest that might otherwise be accounted for at cost or by using the equity method, and then misapplying a valuation technique to inflate the carrying amount of the investment.
6.1	Overestimating expected future cash flows for loans and receivables, in order to avoid or minimize the recognition of bad debts or impairments.
6.2	Using inflated estimates of the fair value of collateral in order to minimize the recognition of an impairment of a loan.
7.1	Capitalizing costs incurred in developing an intangible asset internally, when the criteria for recognition of an asset have not been met.
7.2	Recording false gains from purported increases in fair values of intangible assets (IFRS risk only).
7.3	Using unrealistically long useful lives to amortize intangible assets with finite lives (including failing to shorten useful lives as new information indicates the estimate should be modified).
7.4	Inflating the estimated residual value of an intangible asset with a finite life, thereby reducing the amount charged to amortization expense each period.

7.5   Improperly claiming that an intangible asset has an indefinite life, in order to carry the asset at its basis without reduction for amortization, as would be required if the asset were classified as having a finite life.

7.6   Failing to properly test for or recognize an impairment in connection with goodwill or other intangible assets with indefinite lives.

8.1   Improperly accounting for an acquisition of assets as a business combination, resulting in a fraudulent allocation of the purchase price.

8.2   Improper allocation of the purchase price in a business combination, usually in the form of overallocation to assets not subject to depreciation or amortization, or to assets with longer useful lives.

8.3   Improper allocation of a portion of the purchase price in a business combination to intangible assets that do not qualify for separate recognition.

8.4   Improper calculation of the fair value of the prebusiness combination, noncontrolling interest in an entity that is then acquired in a step acquisition, in order to manipulate the timing or amount of gain or loss recognized in earnings.

9.1   Failing to recognize that an asset has experienced an impairment.

9.2   Recognizing an impairment loss, but understating its extent through the use of improper measurement techniques.

9.3   Improper reversal of a previously recognized impairment loss (IFRS only).

10.1   Recording phony increases in fair value of property and equipment under the revaluation option (IFRS only).

10.2   Misclassifying increases in value of property and equipment under the revaluation model by incorrectly including them in profit or loss (IFRS only).

10.3   Failure to recognize an impairment loss on property and equipment.

11.1   Improper amortization of a debt obligation based on false representations of contract terms.

11.2   Improper calculation of the fair value of a debt obligation for which the fair value option has been elected.

12.1   Failure to recognize a liability for the redemption of future award credits in connection with a customer loyalty program.

12.2   Underestimating the redemption rate associated with award credits of a customer loyalty program, resulting in an understated liability.

12.3   Underestimating the fair value of award credits associated with a customer loyalty program (IFRS), or underestimating the cost of honoring rebates/refunds earned (U.S. GAAP), resulting in an understated liability.

12.4   Underestimating the future purchases of a customer in connection with a rebate/refund program in connection with programs in which customers are entitled to a higher rate or rebate/refund as purchases increase, resulting in an understated liability (U.S. GAAP).

(Continued)

Risk No.	Description
12.5	Improper allocation of revenue among multiple goods or services sold in connection with a multiple deliverable arrangement.
13.1	Falsely claiming that an asset retirement obligation does not exist in order to omit the liability from the financial statements.
13.2	Falsely claiming that it is not possible to develop a reasonable estimate of an asset retirement obligation in order to avoid recording a liability.
13.3	Failing to disclose asset retirement obligations that exist but for which it is not possible to reliably estimate.
13.4	Underestimating the costs that will be required to settle an asset retirement obligation, either through incorrect internal estimates or the use of improper external estimates.
13.5	Miscalculating the present value of an asset retirement obligation by manipulating one or more of the factors used in the calculation, such as the discount rate, anticipated date of settlement, or rate of inflation.
14.1	Failing to recognize a liability of a guarantor based on a guarantee contract.
14.2	Understatement of the liability when a guarantee is initially recognized in the financial statements of a guarantor.
14.3	Improperly amortizing a liability associated with a guarantee over the life of the guarantee, resulting in reduction of the liability at an accelerated rate and an overstatement of revenue.
15.1	Improperly classifying cash flow and certain foreign currency hedges as effective hedges in order to report losses as a component of other comprehensive income rather than in earnings.
15.2	Falsely stating the fair value of a derivative, usually by overstating derivatives carried as assets and understating those carried as liabilities.
15.3	Failing to separately recognize an embedded derivative that meets the criteria for separation from a host contract, especially a derivative that would represent a liability.
16.1	Failure by a plan sponsor to recognize a liability for an underfunded defined benefit plan.
16.2	Improperly determining the fair value of a defined benefit plan's assets, in order to make it appear overfunded or to reduce the extent of its underfunded nature.
16.3	Preparing or obtaining a faulty actuarial analysis of a plan's benefit obligation as a method of hiding or understating the underfunded nature of a defined benefit plan, or overstating its overfunded nature.
17.1	Failure to recognize a liability (or to impair an asset) when the criteria for recognizing a loss contingency have been met.
17.2	Omission of note disclosures regarding an unrecognized loss contingency that has a likelihood of occurrence that is more than remote.

17.3	Recognition of an asset for a gain contingency prior to its meeting the criteria for recognition.
17.4	Underestimating a recognized liability for a loss contingency.
17.5	Using inappropriate present value techniques to understate a contingent liability.
17.6	Inflating the fair value estimate of a recognized gain contingency.
18.1	Misclassification of a share-based transaction as an increase in equity that should be classified as a liability.
18.2	Intentional misstatement of the fair value of a company's own equity instruments in a share-based transaction, resulting in under- or overstatement of liabilities or equity.
18.3	Misstatement of the fair value of the goods or services received in connection with a share-based transaction, resulting in under- or overstatement of liabilities or equity.
18.4	Utilizing a false estimate of the length of service necessary for employees to meet a performance condition required for share-based compensation to vest.
19.1	Inflating the fair value of an asset surrendered in a nonmonetary transaction in order to recognize a gain on the exchange.
19.2	Recording a nonmonetary transaction at fair value when, in fact, the transaction lacks commercial substance and is not to be measured at fair value.
19.3	Recognizing advertising barter transactions at fair value when the criteria for fair value recognition have not been met.
19.4	Falsely claiming that the criteria for fair value recognition of an advertising barter transaction have not been met in order to avoid recording it at fair value, when the criteria have been met.
19.5	Inflating the fair value of advertising provided in exchange for advertising benefits received from another party in an advertising barter transaction.
20.1	Inflating the fair value of noncash assets received as contributions from donors, and the resulting expenses when the assets are used in providing services by a not-for-profit organization.
20.2	Overstating or understating the fair value of rental space provided to a not-for-profit organization free of charge by a donor.
20.3	Misstating the fair value of assets held in an irrevocable charitable remainder trust where a charitable organization has been designated as the party that will receive the remaining assets held in the trust when the trust expires.
20.4	Recognition by a not-for-profit organization of contributed services when the criteria for recognition have not been met, or intentionally not recognizing services for which the criteria have been met.
20.5	Improperly valuing contributed services that are recognized in the financial statements of a not-for-profit organization.

(Continued)

Risk No.	Description
21.1	Omission of a required disclosure in the notes to the financial statements.
21.2	Omission of required information from a disclosure in the notes to the financial statements.
21.3	Inclusion of inaccurate information in the notes to the financial statements.

SEC Office of the Chief Accountant and FASB Staff Clarifications on Fair Value Accounting

In September 2008, as the global economic crisis was worsening and the fair value evidence from active markets was fluctuating wildly and, in some cases, changing in character, the U.S. Securities and Exchange Commission issued the following guidance on fair value accounting issues.

FOR IMMEDIATE RELEASE 2008-234

Washington, D.C., Sept. 30, 2008—The current environment has made questions surrounding the determination of fair value particularly challenging for preparers, auditors, and users of financial information. The SEC's Office of the Chief Accountant and the staff of the FASB have been engaged in extensive consultations with participants in the capital markets, including investors, preparers, and auditors, on the application of fair value measurements in the current market environment.

There are a number of practice issues where there is a need for immediate additional guidance. The SEC's Office of the Chief Accountant recognizes and supports the productive efforts of the FASB and the IASB on these issues, including the IASB Expert Advisory Panel's Sept. 16, 2008, draft document, the work of the FASB's Valuation Resource Group, and the IASB's upcoming meeting on the credit crisis. To provide additional guidance on these and other issues surrounding fair value measurements, the FASB is preparing to propose additional interpretative guidance on fair value measurement under U.S. GAAP later this week.

While the FASB is preparing to provide additional interpretative guidance, SEC staff and FASB staff are seeking to assist preparers and auditors by providing immediate clarifications. The clarifications SEC staff and FASB staff are jointly providing today, based on the fair value measurement guidance in FASB Statement No. 157, Fair Value Measurements (Statement 157), are intended to help preparers, auditors, and investors address fair value measurement questions that have been cited as most urgent in the current environment.

Can management's internal assumptions (e.g., expected cash flows) be used to measure fair value when relevant market evidence does not exist?

Yes. When an active market for a security does not exist, the use of management estimates that incorporate current market participant expectations of future cash flows, and include appropriate risk premiums, is acceptable. Statement 157 discusses a range of information and valuation techniques that a reasonable preparer might use to estimate fair value when relevant market data may be unavailable, which may be the case during this period of market uncertainty. This can, in appropriate circumstances, include expected cash flows from an asset. Further, in some cases using unobservable inputs (level 3) might be more appropriate than using observable inputs (level 2); for example, when significant adjustments are required to available observable inputs it may be appropriate to utilize an estimate based primarily on unobservable inputs. The determination of fair value often requires significant judgment. In some cases, multiple inputs from different sources may collectively provide the best evidence of fair value. In these cases expected cash flows would be considered alongside other relevant information. The weighting of the inputs in the fair value estimate will depend on the extent to which they provide information about the value of an asset or liability and are relevant in developing a reasonable estimate.

How should the use of "market" quotes (e.g., broker quotes or information from a pricing service) be considered when assessing the mix of information available to measure fair value?

Broker quotes may be an input when measuring fair value, but are not necessarily determinative if an active market does not exist for the security. In a liquid market, a broker quote should reflect market information from actual transactions. However, when markets are less active, brokers may rely more on models with inputs based on the information available only to the broker. In weighing a broker quote as an input to fair value, an entity should place less reliance on quotes that do not reflect the result of market transactions. Further, the nature of the quote (e.g., whether the quote is an indicative price or a binding offer) should be considered when weighing the available evidence.

Are transactions that are determined to be disorderly representative of fair value? When is a distressed (disorderly) sale indicative of fair value?

The results of disorderly transactions are not determinative when measuring fair value. The concept of a fair value measurement assumes an orderly transaction between market participants. An orderly transaction is one that involves market participants that are willing to transact and allows for adequate exposure to the market. Distressed or forced liquidation sales are not orderly transactions, and thus the fact that a transaction is distressed or forced should be considered when weighing the available evidence. Determining whether a particular transaction is forced or disorderly requires judgment.

Can transactions in an inactive market affect fair value measurements?

Yes. A quoted market price in an active market for the identical asset is most representative of fair value and thus is required to be used (generally without adjustment). Transactions in inactive markets may be inputs when measuring fair value, but would likely not be determinative. If they are orderly, transactions should be considered in management's estimate of fair value. However, if prices in an inactive market do not reflect current prices for the same or similar assets, adjustments may be necessary to arrive at fair value.

A significant increase in the spread between the amount sellers are "asking" and the price that buyers are "bidding," or the presence of a relatively small number of "bidding" parties, are indicators that should be considered in determining whether a market is inactive. The determination of whether a market is active or not requires judgment.

What factors should be considered in determining whether an investment is other-than-temporarily impaired?

In general, the greater the decline in value, the greater the period of time until anticipated recovery, and the longer the period of time that a decline has existed, the greater the level of evidence necessary to reach a conclusion that an other-than-temporary decline has not occurred.

Determining whether impairment is other-than-temporary is a matter that often requires the exercise of reasonable judgment based upon the specific facts and circumstances of each investment. This includes an assessment of the nature of the underlying investment (for example, whether the security is debt, equity or a hybrid) which may have an impact on a holder's ability to assess the probability of recovery.

Existing U.S. GAAP does not provide "bright lines" or "safe harbors" in making a judgment about other-than-temporary impairments. However, "rules of thumb" that consider the nature of the underlying investment can be useful tools for management and auditors in identifying securities that warrant a higher level of evaluation.

To assist in making this judgment, SAB Topic 5M provides a number of factors that should be considered. These factors are not all inclusive of the potential factors that may be considered individually, or in combination with other factors, when considering whether an other-than-temporary impairment exists. Factors to consider include the following:

> The length of the time and the extent to which the market value has been less than cost;
>
> The financial condition and near-term prospects of the issuer, including any specific events, which may influence the operations of the issuer such as changes in technology that impair the earnings potential of the investment or the discontinuation of a segment of the business that may affect the future earnings potential; or
>
> The intent and ability of the holder to retain its investment in the issuer for a period of time sufficient to allow for any anticipated recovery in market value.

All available information should be considered in estimating the anticipated recovery period.

Finally, because fair value measurements and the assessment of impairment may require significant judgments, clear and transparent disclosures are critical to providing investors with an understanding of the judgments made by management. In addition to the disclosures required under existing U.S. GAAP, including Statement 157, the SEC's Division of Corporation Finance recently issued letters in March and September that are available on the SEC's Web site to provide real-time guidance for issuers to consider in enhancing the transparency of fair value measurements to investors. Additionally, the SEC staff and the FASB staff will continue to consult with capital market participants on issues encountered in the application of fair value measurements.

Internal Controls over Fair Value Accounting Applications

The most commonly applied model for designing and auditing internal controls was developed by the Committee of Sponsoring Organizations (COSO). The COSO model involves five interrelated components of internal control. The components can be considered broadly, such as on an entity-wide basis. But they can also be considered in relation to specific aspects of an entity's operations, such as by function (e.g., human resources, information technology, etc.), by location, or by accounting cycle (e.g., payroll, purchasing, cash receipts, inventory, etc.).

There are several goals of internal controls. The goal addressed in this book is the reliability of financial reporting, specifically as it relates to the application of fair value accounting concepts. Examples of internal control factors relevant to fair value accounting in each of the five components of the COSO model are presented in this appendix.

Control Environment

The control environment represents the overall control consciousness of an organization. The expression *tone at the top* is sometimes used in reference to certain important elements of the control environment. The control environment establishes a structure and theme for other elements of internal control. Specific control environment factors include the following:

- The philosophy and operating style of management and the board of directors does not involve excessive risk-taking and aggressive financial reporting positions.
- A code of conduct is established that clearly includes financial statement fraud and accounting improprieties among the acts considered to be violations subject to disciplinary action.

- A trusted whistleblower system is put in place, whereby employees would feel comfortable in reporting violations of the code of conduct without fear of retaliation.
- A board of directors, audit committee, and finance committee that is independent from management, are empowered with the tools necessary to discharge their duties, and properly engaged in and committed to fulfilling their oversight roles.
- Management's commitment to ethics and integrity in the workplace is evidenced by both direct communication with employees, emphasizing the importance of ethics, as well as the setting of an example of ethical behavior.
- Management's respect for the functions of internal auditors and those charged with the responsibilities of determining fair values is clear.
- There is a clear assignment of job duties and establishment of organizational structure.
- Human resources policies and practices include proper background screening of employees involved in all key accounting and financial functions, especially those involving fair value.
- There is a commitment to ongoing training for all employees involved in fair value accounting applications to ensure a high level of technical competence.

Risk Assessment

Risk assessment is the process of identifying and assessing relevant risks to the achievement of an entity's objectives. As it relates to fair value, factors involved in risk assessment include the following:

- Responsibilities are properly assigned for the identification and assessment of risks involving fair value accounting.
- Applications of fair value accounting in the financial statements are identified and assessed.
- External factors impacting fair value measurements, such as declines in quoted prices from relevant markets, introduction of new competitors or new products of competitors, and changes in technology, are identified and assessed.
- Changes in laws, regulations, or accounting standards that could impact fair value accounting or its applications are identified and assessed.
- Risks associated with the introduction of new personnel, including outside contractors, or information systems that affect fair value accounting applications are identified and assessed.

Control Activities

Control activities are the policies and procedures applied to carry out the specific functions of an organization. This is the element of internal control that most people think of when they are asked about internal controls. Specific factors involving control activities include the following:

- There is proper segregation of duties such as the separation of functions involving the determination of fair value, the recording of fair value adjustments, and the review of financial statements.
- Controls are designed to make sure that management cannot override established controls.
- Procedures are in place to implement new laws, regulations, and accounting standards with fair value accounting implications.
- Procedures are in place to review significant new transactions (such as business acquisitions and mergers, joint ventures, and so on) for fair value accounting implications.
- Proper supporting documentation is required for all accounting entries, especially all journal entries involving adjustments to fair value accounts.
- There is periodic review of nonfinancial assets for signs of impairment.
- There is review and approval of the selections of methods used in the determination of fair value, as well as the application of those methods.
- Information technology hardware and software controls are designed to prevent unauthorized access to all systems with fair value accounting implications and leave an appropriate audit trail.
- There is due diligence in the selection and monitoring of outside consultants and vendors used to determine fair values (e.g., researching credentials, training, and relevant experience of third-party valuation specialists).
- The independence of third-party valuation specialists used by the entity is verified.

Information and Communication

Information and communication consist of the processes and records utilized to record and report transactions and to maintain accountability over assets and liabilities of an entity. Examples of elements of information and communication include the following:

- Proper supporting documentation is retained for all transactions and journal entries involving fair value accounting issues.

- Accurate and timely information is available to those who need it in making determinations regarding fair value issues (e.g., information regarding asset impairments, changes in market conditions, etc.).
- There are appropriate levels of interaction between management, staff, and outside parties in connection with fair value issues and determinations.
- Fair value accounting issues and treatment are properly disclosed and explained to the finance committee, audit committee, and/or board of directors.
- Adequate resources are provided for the thorough researching of fair value comparisons and fair value inputs to provide for a sound basis for making fair value measurements.
- Adequate channels of communication (e.g., hotlines, etc.) are provided for the reporting of allegations of accounting improprieties, such as fair value accounting fraud, by whistleblowers.
- Employees are properly informed regarding the information they are requested to provide to those in charge of fair value measurements and impairments.
- Accounting system provides for the proper collection and reporting of information needed to comply with fair value accounting standards, including all information necessary for disclosure in the notes to the financial statements.
- Proper record retention and destruction policies and practices are in place.

Monitoring

Monitoring represents the process of assessing the quality of internal controls over time. Monitoring assesses both the design and the operation of internal controls. Elements of monitoring may include the following:

- There are ongoing account reconciliations and reviews of reconciliations.
- Financial results are compared with the budget on a regular basis and variances are investigated.
- Financial performance is benchmarked against entities with similar operations.
- An internal audit function assesses the performance of internal controls over fair value accounting applications.
- There is proper ongoing communication with the entity's external auditors.

- Periodic special studies of internal controls are performed in the area of fair value accounting applications.
- Periodic special audits of procurement involve the selection of vendors used in fair value accounting applications.
- There are periodic special audits of IT security relevant to fair value accounting applications.
- Performance of third parties that are relied on for the determination of fair value is monitored.

Bibliography

Association of Certified Fraud Examiners. *2008 Report to the Nation on Occupational Fraud and Abuse.* Austin, TX: ACFE, 2008.

Epstein, Barry J., and Eva K. Jermakowicz. *Wiley IFRS 2008, Interpretation and Application of International Financial Reporting Standards.* Hoboken, NJ: John Wiley & Sons, Inc., 2008.

Hitchner, James R. *Financial Valuation, Applications and Models*, 2nd ed. Hoboken, NJ: John Wiley & Sons, Inc., 2006.

PricewaterhouseCoopers, LLP. *IFRS and U.S. GAAP, Similarities and Differences, September 2008*, www.pwc.com/ifrs.

United States Securities and Exchange Commission. *Report and Recommendations Pursuant to Section 133 of the Emergency Economic Stabilization Act of 2008: Study on Mark-to-Market Accounting.* Washington, DC: Office of the Chief Accountant, Division of Corporation Finance, 2008.

About the Author

Gerard M. Zack, CPA, CFE, MBA, has provided fraud prevention and investigation, audit, training, and internal control services since 1981. He is the president of Zack, P.C., located in Rockville, Maryland. Mr. Zack has provided fraud prevention services and antifraud training for entities throughout the United States, Canada, and Europe, working with all types of entities, from small local businesses and charities to large, multinational business and nonprofit organizations and government agencies.

Mr. Zack is frequently asked to speak on fraud-related topics at conferences and has provided customized internal training on accounting, audit, and fraud issues for more than 50 CPA firms. In addition to being a Certified Public Accountant and Certified Fraud Examiner, he is recognized as one of only nine Fellows in the 45,000-member Association of Certified Fraud Examiners (ACFE), based on his extensive antifraud experience and his contributions to the antifraud field. Mr. Zack also serves on the faculty of the ACFE.

He is the author of the book *Fraud and Abuse in Nonprofit Organizations: A Guide to Prevention and Detection* and numerous articles and presentations on fraud prevention for commercial businesses and government agencies. Mr. Zack obtained his undergraduate degree in accounting from Shippensburg University in Pennsylvania and his MBA from Loyola University in Maryland.

For more information about Mr. Zack, visit the Zack, P.C., Web site at www.zackpc.com, where you will also find a link to Gerry's blog, on which he discusses current accounting and fraud topics.

Index

Printed in the United States
By Bookmasters